PORTRAIT OF SOMERSET

ALSO BY BRYAN LITTLE

Portrait of
SOMERSET

BRYAN LITTLE

FIFTH EDITION

ROBERT HALE · LONDON

First edition, 1969
Second edition, 1971
Third edition, 1974
Fourth edition, 1976
Fifth edition, 1983

ISBN 0 7090 0915 1

Robert Hale Limited
Clerkenwell House
Clerkenwell Green
London EC1R oHT

Printed in Great Britain by
St Edmundsbury Press, Bury St Edmunds, Suffolk
Bound by Hunter & Foulis Ltd.

ACKNOWLEDGMENTS

With the exception of the photographs of the
Conestoga waggon (for which thanks are due to the
American Museum at Claverton); of Bath University (provided by the Registrar, University of
Bath); and of Royal Portbury Dock (provided by
the Port of Bristol Authority), all the illustrations in
this book were provided by Geoffrey Wright.

Since 1974, when Somerset lost about a sixth of its area and well over a sixth of its population to the new County of Avon, there have been stirrings of opinion, in some places vigorously expressed and with a renewed insistence in the last few months, for the return of all, or part, of the ancient county's lost territory. Despite much disenchantment with the practical and financial workings of Avon, whose headquarters, inevitably, are in Bristol, hardly any equivalent agitation has come from the parts of Avon which were once in Gloucestershire. The 'Back to Somerset' movement has varied in intensity. Some vocal support has come from Bath, a city whose County Borough status meant that it used to run its own planning, police, and education, with much less reliance than the rest of territorial Somerset on administration from Taunton. Close to the new boundary one can understand the pro-Somerset feelings of such villages as Bleadon or Loxton, yet not far away, at Churchill, a meeting voted to stay in the new county. More controversial, perhaps, is the position of Weston-super-Mare whose ratable value was a severe loss to Somerset, and where Woodspring, the most populous (bar Bristol) of Avon's Districts, has concentrated its administration in a large new building tacked onto the older Borough's Town Hall.

Yet it is hard to foresee any substantial changes in the arrangements inaugurated nine years ago. Loxton could return to Somerset without much dislocation, but one cannot anticipate any massive change from a Conservative government, while a Labour administration might prefer to make a Metropolitan County out of Bristol, the populous part of Avon County just north of its eponymous river, and of some of the new county's 'Somerset' section, perhaps as far as Keynsham and the disagreeably suburbanized areas along the Weston-super-Mare road and at Nailsea and Yatton. The rest of Wansdyke and Woodspring Districts, and perhaps Bath, could then revert to Somerset from which, for such purposes as county cricket and Anglican church organization, they have never been parted.

Within Somerset's boundaries as they were before 1974, and as they are still covered in this book, some changes have occurred, and there are a few architectural points on which new information has come my way. The M.5 Motorway now runs all the way through Somerset on its way to the fringe of Exeter and beyond. Most of the Minehead railway is now open again, but Trade Union objections have confined its trains, without the hoped-for mainline link at Taunton, to the section between Bishop's Lydeard and Minehead; its assortment of locomotives and carriages differs much from what it had in Great Western days. West Dock, renamed Royal Portbury Dock, has far to go before it shows a profit, and labour troubles have complicated its problems, but strenuous efforts are being made to find fuller use for the dock. Two tall gantry cranes, one serving roll-on–roll-off container traffic and the other dealing with forest products, have powerfully altered the skyline between the mouth of the Avon and Portishead, while a tall jib-crane adds to the available lifting facilities. In one corner a tank complex, for importing and distributing molasses, is nearly complete, while a quarrying company, whose main operations are conducted near Shepton Mallet, has started work on a terminal from which imported rock and aggregate will be sent from the dock, starting the journey, through the Avon gorge, along a rejuvenated railway line. Another company, whose offices are near Yeovil, has a scheme for an area, equipped close to another of the dock's corners, for bringing in imported cars. The dock's northern expanse has proved a profitable location for the laying up of large recession-bound ships.

Down-channel Hinkley Point has been chosen for a third nuclear power station to replace one of those already there; work is not, however, due to start for two more years. At Bath the main buildings of the new University are virtually complete, with the tall transverse blocks of Norwood and Wessex Houses closing the two ends of Parade, or linear campus, and with some attractive low-rise blocks of student housing out towards the edge of the breezy upland site. The concentration of the Navy's offices at Foxhill has been cancelled, while down in the city central Bath has yet to see really good modern buildings. There have, however, been some spectacular feats of reconstruction and renovation, one being the reconditioning of the Theatre Royal where a new fly tower is a bulky, somewhat graceless, but theatrically needful raising of the western end of the building's skyline. In riverside Taunton the Brewhouse Theatre, largely new work by Mr. Norman Branson, but including an earlier structure, is an important addition to the theatrical facilities available between Street and the Northcott at Exeter.

At Clevedon work has started on the reconditioning of the pier, much loved by the devotees of such Victorian iron intrusions into the briny. The more important building of Walton Castle, Jacobean in date and its design recalling some of Henry VIII's coastal forts, has largely been reconditioned as a house; Mr. Martin Sessions-Hodge, its owner, is much to be commended on the redemption of one of Somerset's (and Avon's) most unusual buildings. At Dunster another castle has entered on a new historic phase, with ownership by the National Trust and opening to the public in a 'touristic' area where many visitors sample its mixture of mediaeval, Jacobean, Baroque and Victorian attractions.

Two of my architectural discoveries concern Shepton Mallet, Street, and Wells. Preparatory studies for conducting a summer school at Norwich told me that a hospital at Shepton and several buildings at Street, including the Crispin Hall, Millfield House, and the company housing were early, comparatively restrained works by G. J. Skipper, best known for exuberant Edwardian Baroque buildings in Norwich and elsewhere in East Anglia. I have also been told that, for about a century (until it was destroyed by a fire in 1438) the central tower of Wells Cathedral had a tall spire, perhaps about a hundred feet high, made of timber sheathed with Mendip lead. The effect, very different from what one sees now, must have been like that, well known from Georgian prints, of the spire which long adorned the central tower of the Cathedral at Hereford.

B.D.G.L.
September, 1982

ACKNOWLEDGMENTS

AMONG the many kind people who have given me information needed for the writing of this book, or who have shown me round industrial plants and other features of Somerset's current economic life, I wish to thank Mr. Kenneth Hudson, of the Department of Adult Studies in the University of Bath, who suggested the names of many people who were able to instruct me on various agricultural and industrial matters. At Taunton, the county town, I had valuable assistance from Mr. R. W. Dale and Mr. L. A. D. Russell of the County Planning Office and also (as on many other occasions) from Mr. I. P. Collis, Mr. D. M. M. Shorrocks, and other members of the staff of the County Record Office. At Bristol Miss K. D. Maddever, of the National Agricultural Advisory Service of the Ministry of Agriculture, Fisheries, and Food helped me on the present state of Somerset's great dairying trade, and I also got most useful particulars, on the numbers of people making their living in the county's main occupations and industries, from the South West Regional Office of the Ministry of Labour. Out in the county I was much helped by discussions with the Managers of the Ministry of Labour's offices in Bath, Bridgwater, Frome, Taunton, and Wells.

On the vital subject of river control, land drainage, etc., and on the splendid records of the Parrett Navigation, I have had help of the greatest value from Mr. E. L. Kelting, O.B.E., of the Somerset River Authority, and from members of his staff at Bridgwater. Mr. F. N. Miller, of the Somerset Rural Community Council, gave me some useful suggestions, among other matters, on the willow-growing and basketmaking trades, and I am grateful to Mr. S. W. J. Gadsby, of Burrowbridge and Stathe, for information kindly given on the spot. I have also been glad to consult Mr. K. G. Stott, of the Department of Agriculture and Horticulture, University of Bristol, at the University's Research Station, Long Ashton.

On other Somerset industries, I had valuable help from Mr. Vernon Smart, Public Relations Officer of C. and J. Clark's of Street, and from Mr. J. Vosper of the same firm. Mr. Stephen Morland was most helpful with particulars of Morlands of Glastonbury, and at Wellington I received much information on Fox Bros., along with kind hospitality, from Mr. Lloyd Fox, J.P., and Mrs. Fox. At Crewkerne Mr. R. C. Hayward helped me on Arthur Hart and Son Ltd., and generally on the webbing and canvas trade of southern Somerset, while at Taunton I obtained information which I needed on Van Heusen's from Mr. J. A. Lord. Mr. Keith Showering, and Mr. Dan Thomas at Shepton Mallett, have provided helpful details on the origins and current activities of the Showering concern.

Mr. R. J. O. Meyer, the Headmaster of Millfield School, Street, gave me much helpful information, and arranged for me to be shown round the buildings at Street itself. Dr. F. S. Wallis, of the Wells Museum, enlightened me on the geology of Windwhistle Hill, and Mr. Leslie Alcock, M.A., F.S.A., gave me on the spot explanations of the diggings at Cadbury Camp, South Cadbury. I have to thank Mrs. Gwyneth Norman for information on various aspects of Wincanton, Rev. Mother John of the Cross, of the Congregation of Jesus Crucified, for details on St. John's Priory at Castle Cary and Mr. L. P. Wallen, Clerk to the Somerset County Council, for information on the boundaries and Districts of the future county.

Finally, for the up-to-date position at Royal Portbury Dock, I am grateful to Mr. Rodney Stone, Publicity Officer, Port of Bristol Authority. I have also had kind help from Mr. Linzee Colchester, the Archivist of Wells Cathedral.

B.D.G.L.

CHAPTER I

SCHIZZO

WHATEVER its size, any English county is so varied in its scene, and in the range of its human activity, that a full picture becomes over-detailed and laborious. Even in the small shire of Huntingdon the countryside varies widely between the flat, once marshy fenlands east of Ramsey and the gentle undulations of the farmlands round Little Gidding. Far greater and more dramatic are the variations found in the splendid county which contains East Coker and Dunkery, Bath and Sedgemoor, the hill fort claimed as Camelot and the coastal uplands near Clevedon, where the churchyard made immortal in Tennyson's *In Memoriam* looks over the Severn sea to the most southerly mountains of Wales. No record of any county can be more than a subjective impression, leaving out as much as it includes and telling as much of the portraitist as of his subject. Yet just as a human portrait must have its initial sketch so any record of so varied a territory as one of our English counties must have its preliminary plan. Such a survey can help us before we go more carefully through the county which one can enter just west of Brunel's Box Tunnel and leave (on foot!) at the bottom of the wild valley supposedly inhabited by the Doones.

Geology has decreed that most of Somerset should fall into three main zones. The northern hills culminate in the high, bleak, heather-strewn eminence of Blackdown in the Mendips. Variety, and much scenic charm, come from such outliers as Dundry which divides suburban Bristol from a smiling commuter's countryside, from the Failand hills which give Bristol so delightfully rural a neighbouring lung, from the Lulsgate massif whose rustic quiet is now disturbed by the A.38 highway and Bristol's civic airport, and from Lansdown which climbs, high above

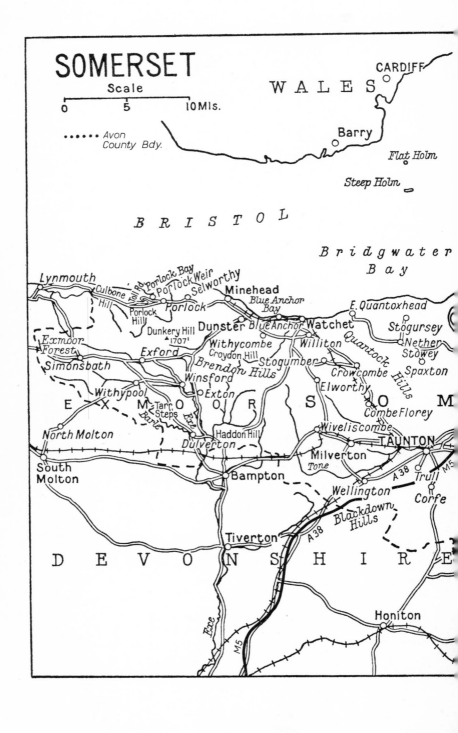

of population far above the capacities laid down by untamed geology.

An astronaut, looking down on the whole of Somerset, could see at once that in its land usage it is mainly an agricultural county, and in a very special way a grazing countryside. Only when one sees the detailed figures on the ways in which Somerset people make their living do we realize how much the county's "yokel" image has now changed. Somerset's industrial points are very real and important, yet they seldom thrust themselves harshly into a pattern which is mainly that of the Wessex countryside. Even Hinkley Point seems, from afar, as if its massive blocks could as well be the strongpoint of a feudal castle as the reactor houses of an atomic power station.

By modern standards Somerset contains no large towns. Bristol's boundary extensions, eating out into North Somerset and South Gloucestershire, have seen to it that the West of England's largest town has mostly stayed within the confines of what has, for nearly six centuries, been proud to call itself a county on its own. Somerset, unlike Leicestershire or Nottinghamshire in the once Mercian Midlands, is not dominated by its county town. For Taunton, with less than half of the people who live in Bath, is not the largest town in Somerset. Twenty thousand people make a town large for this county; it is from Bristol's overspill, and from dwellers in North Somerset who look to Bristol for many of their pleasures, that a small sliver of the county has its taste of an urban way of life. Long, narrow strips of ground, fringing highways which link London and the Midlands with the holiday delights of Devon and Cornwall, give some parts of Somerset a fleeting, profitable taste of throbbing life from afar. Yet most of the county's people, once their radios and television sets are quiet for the night and in the workaday morning, live prosperously enough. They dwell apart from the bustle of the conurbations, a little turned in on themselves, yet glad of a life which is provincial but anything but stagnant or redolent of decay.

Bath University; pool, grassy arena, campus
Claverton: Conestoga waggon at the American Museum

CHAPTER II

THE BATH CORNER

THE Bristol Avon, having curved boldly through Wiltshire from its Cotswold headwaters, first encounters Somerset as a boundary stream. The Somerset parish concerned in the confrontation is the charming one of Freshford, in which the Avon receives the larger of its two tributaries which go by the common Westcountry river name of Frome. For less than a mile the Avon parts Somerset from some flat Wiltshire meadows which soon lead to the almost Alpine steepness of Winsley's wooded slopes. Once again it becomes a Wiltshire stream, a picturesque reach of it being the base of the narrow, triangular tract of land with which Wiltshire jabs sharply, as far as Midford, into the land of its western neighbour. This Limpley Stoke salient is, for those who know their architecture, something of an irony. For, in a county reasonably rich in pre-Conquest buildings it just robs Somerset of its one chance of a palpably Saxon church. Past Limpley Stoke, and for a little way below the Dundas Aqueduct whose noble late Georgian arch takes the Kennett and Avon Canal over the river, the Avon is again a boundary river. Then at last, amid the carefully tamed scenic beauties of the valley which gently guides it down to Bathford, it belongs wholly to Somerset. For a few more miles, through Bath and to the point whence it marches with Gloucestershire and once parted Mercia and Wessex, it is a Somerset stream. But its influence on the county is wider than so short a distance would suggest. For Somerset's whole north-eastern shoulder forms part of the Avon's basin and is conditioned by its tributary brooks. In the quiet, deep-set valleys of a sweetly hilly countryside they are the making of its landscape.

Most of the Avon's tributary streams, bar the Chew which

comes in at Keynsham and another Frome which flows beneath
the centre in Bristol, join the larger river before it reaches Bath.
Their valleys, and that of the Avon itself in its most romantically
landscaped stretch, are worth lingering exploration before one
enjoys Bath's urban and architectural delights. No scenic stretch
could, indeed, be more satisfying than the Limpley Stoke valley
as a prelude to the sophistication of our most perfect Georgian
town. The river itself causes the valley's graceful curvature.
Meadows and woods, in exactly the right proportion, complete
a parkland scene, and the well ordered Regency late Gothic of
Warleigh Manor does for this valley of the Bath Avon what
Abbotsford more boldly achieves for that of the Tweed. High
above it, on the very border between Somerset and Wiltshire,
the thin, simple, Italianate tower of Brown's Folly makes a good
architectural foil, as one looks north from the hill country above
Limpley Stoke, to the no less man-made beauties of the valley
itself. One's impression is of a made and managed landscape, the
river being a mere part of the story. The nobly sweeping turnpike
road, the sadly (and one hopes temporarily) disused canal, and
the railway combine, in their closeness to each other, to make a
fine, evocative, trio of highways. Claverton, with its gateposts
and terraces, the last, formal relics of a fine Stuart mansion which
once nestled in the valley, is the one country village before one
reaches Bath's outer suburbia. High above it, on a site which
gives noble views of the valley and of the more distant Wiltshire
downs, its Grecian successor is dated 1820. It was designed by
Wyattville, an architect whose stylistic bilingualism also enabled
for him to rebuild, and in so doing to romanticize, the royal
quarters of Windsor. Here in the eastern fringe of Somerset his
somewhat frigidly correct building now houses a collection which
makes it unique, and a strange exotic in this outstanding tract of
the West of England's inland scenery.

On any reckoning the American Folk Museum at Claverton
Manor is a strange, if wholly admirable phenomenon in provincial England. Such a venture would not, perhaps, surprise us in
some country estate near London. Its actual location, in this
Regency mansion near Bath, was influenced by the frequent
residence, not far away, of one of its first sponsors. Since the
venture was started various rooms in the house have been fitted

out, with false ceilings inserted at modest yet authentic heights, with the genuine inner walling, furniture and smaller, more intimate contents of a good series of early American rooms, mainly colonial and mostly from New England or not further south than Pennsylvania. A lovably jumbled country store reminds us that American shoppers have known other selling points than drive-in stores and supermarkets, while a small, enthralling collection from the south-west drives home the point that some United States grass roots are, via Mexico, in Spain. A superb assembly of quilts, and an assortment of bandboxes out in a dainty little summerhouse, are among the most convincing exhibits, while some American dainties, and the none too pleasant gingerbread of 'Conkey's Tavern' are at hand to regale those who come to an attraction well away from other places of refreshment. Folk Museums, and reconstructed period rooms, are now reasonably common in this country. Here at Claverton one can, more unusually, savour the comforts, and some of the discomforts, which were once the lot of those who dwelt in a pre-Hollywood America. The Museum at Claverton is surely a summer-season 'must' for all who come to Somerset. Those who visit it, and who have travelled from Bath over the upland plateau behind it, will find that Claverton Manor now has as its near neighbour a new, and largely technological, University.

The numerous brooks which flow down to the Avon's left bank add much, in the varied charms of their valleys, to the attractions of North Somerset. The two leading streams converge at Midford, flowing on, past the Georgian Gothic castle of Midford itself, and past Monkton Combe with its evangelical public school, as the substantial Midford Brook which joins the Avon below Limpley Stoke. The two upper streams, rising far up in the Mendips, both encounter a wide, fascinating range of human activity and scenic charm. One goes by the name of the Cam Brook. The other, though called the River Somer in its urban stretch, is better known, from the village whose stone houses and noble early Perpendicular Church would do credit to any stretch of countryside, as the Wellow Brook.

For each one of these brooks the most scenic miles are those nearest to the junction at Midford. Both streams water a deep-set, placid countryside of quiet villages and agricultural calm. Both valleys have their antiquarian treasures. Both streams run down from what were once the busiest parts of Somerset's coalfield. Each valley is scored by the course of a railway now disused, and by that railway's forbear from the exciting late Georgian days of the transport revolution. Between the two streams, north of the Cam, and south of the Wellow Brook the high, windy ridges have their own focal points—Timsbury with its mining history and the exquisite Grecian mansion of Parrish's house, the far less attractive settlement of Peasedown St. John, the site of Turner's Tower on the high ridge which leads gently down to Norton St. Philip with its noble medieval inn-cum-wool hall, and its memories of Pepys' visit and Monmouth's sharp rearguard skirmish.

Not far up the Cam Brook there is an overgrown, quite literally dilapidated architectural relic of the Somerset Coal Canal. One has to think of these two quiet valleys, not only as streambeds draining the Mendip country, but as corridors whereby Somerset coal was once deviously taken to markets outside. The canal had two branches. When, in the 1790s, they were planned, and early in the next century when work was carried out, they were reckoned to be the key to the great strides then being made in the opening of new mines and in the production of Somerset coal. From its basin near the Dundas Aqueduct up to Midford this feeder to the Kennett and Avon (in time becoming its chief provider of traffic and revenue) ran as a single waterway. Up from Midford the scheme allowed for two channels. One was to fetch down the coal from mines (or coalworks as they were then called) near Timsbury, Paulton and High Littleton. The other canal was to tap the mineral riches round Radstock. As it happened, no canal ever ran all the way from Radstock, and a tramway helped out till in the 1870s the now defunct Somerset and Dorset Railway thrust its tough-running branch over the Mendips to Bath. But much of the canal's course was actually cut, and in the not so remote days when one could still travel on the Somerset and Dorset one could well perceive that shallow, frustrated, yet unmistakable trench as it snaked its way along the contours up the peaceful valley's southern side. For such a scheme a single-arch aqueduct, to take the canal across the Cam Brook, was a vital link. So it was built, with its channel and its towpath. Its masonry was well finished and impressive, and some twenty years back I could, by clambering and standing, dipper-like, on the stream's boulders, see a stone engraved with the date of 1803. But even then desolation, and ruin by vegetation, had gone terribly far. Here, and elsewhere along the track of the Somerset Coal Canal one sees how soon lush Nature can obliterate works abandoned by man.

A little above Midford, Combe Hay nestles deep in its tranquil valley. The village's main ornament is the beautifully placed, and stylish eighteenth-century mansion where Mr. and Mrs. Charles Robertson now live. Combe Hay manor is unusual in the disposition of its Georgian elements. For the plan of the house is rectangular, and instead of being all in the same eighteenth-century idiom it is evenly split, along its length, between an older portion which is in the early Palladian manner of Bath's more vernacular architects, and a later half whose Adam style breathes the elegant sophistication which one associates with Henry Holland, James Wyatt who sent down plans for Ammerdown near Radstock, or Bath's late Georgian master Thomas Baldwin. Elsewhere in Combe Hay, down the Cam valley from the houses and the tiny church, the seeker on foot can still discover what was once, under three successive guises, the most spectacular reach of the Somerset Coal Canal.

As Robin Atthill and Charles Hadfield have well explained the terrain of Combe Hay was the main obstacle in the canal's course between Midford and the mines. A mile and a bit made a difference in levels of over 150 feet. The first idea of the canal engineers was to overcome the obstacle not by a long sequence of locks but by a swifter, more dramatic rise. A Leicestershire engineer named Robert Weldon planned what John Billingsley, the writer on Somerset's agriculture, called a 'hydrostatic caisson lock' in which barges were to be hauled vertically up and down as they floated serenely in a wooden trunk or trough. This pioneering canal lift was built, and seems to have worked, till in a short time water from the soil seeped in through the fine masonry of its great containing lock chamber. The lift was, however, a marvel in its own time; Jane Austen, when at Bath, planned (apparently without results) to walk over and see what she phonetically called 'the cassoon'. So great an intrusion into

the ground as a lock seventy feet deep could not lastingly be
hidden so that one can still, amid the trees and deep undergrowth
of a luxuriant hillside, spot the great vertical chasm of the caisson,
and tumble among some scattered blocks left over when its
masonry lining was robbed for the locks which in time succeeded
it. What at first followed the caisson was a steeply inclined plane,
approached in a straight line by a short series of locks. This too
was a failure, so in the end the barges climbed and descended by
the normal means of a lock stairway, not directly aligned as one
sees where the Kennett and Avon canal toils up at Devizes, but
sinuously, in a sequence of twenty-two, along the sides and across
the top of a deep little combe. That valley's shape, as the Georgian
surveyors traced a course for the canal, made them give the name
of 'The Bull's Nose' to the topmost curve. There, among the
dense undergrowth of the woods, one can still find the fine
masonry of the locks which led round towards the foot of the
great excavation which once contained the caisson.

Above Dunkerton, where the road from Bath to Wells dips
down into its valley, the leading place on the Cam Brook is
Camerton, still a little gaunt with the relics of its colliery, and
with the great pyramid of spoil which blotches the hillside. The
mine closed in 1950, and Camerton was the place whence coal
trains ran down the little railway which took over from the canal.
The line once ran all the way to Hallatrow, there connecting
with the North Somerset line which once linked Radstock with
Bristol; the mines in or near the Cam valley could thus rail their
coal either to Bristol or to Bath. This railway by the Cam Brook
once carried passengers. It was unusual in that it attained greater
fame soon before, and shortly after, its closure than in its heyday.
For in the early summer of 1944, in the last, fateful spell of waiting before D-Day, the line was stacked, buffer to buffer in a long
row, with hospital trains held ready to care for a flow-back of
wounded far more than were in fact encountered. In the 1930s,
soon after its passenger traffic had ended, the line had been the
'on location' studio for the film of *The Ghost Train*. Over twenty
years later, after the last goods train had passed over its metals,
a similar use came to it, and to Freshford village, for the making of
The Titfield Thunderbolt.

Up the valley of the Wellow Brook the leading places are

the two townships (now united as a single Urban District) of
Radstock and Midsomer Norton; they were well placed to be the
social centre, in its more prolific days, of Somerset's coalfield.
They did not at first hold such a position, for about 1750 no one
believed that coal lay beneath Radstock; only in 1763 did the
sinking of the old pit lead to its discovery. But by 1791, when his
county history came out, the Reverend Richard Collinson the
parson-historian could declare, among his references to mines in
many of the county's northern parishes, that a 'coal work' had
lately been opened at Radstock, and that it was carried on with
great success. His collaborator, in this and many other matters of
topographical description and economic record, is more important than the nominal author; I shall be glad enough if this book
is in its own time as helpful as a record of Somerset at work as
the three volumes of 1791 whose descriptions were largely due to
the lately deceased Edmund Rack.

Collinson's collaborator was a Quaker, born in Norfolk but
a migrant from that county to Bath. As a tradesman in East
Anglia he became keen on the successes of such agricultural
reformers as 'Turnip' Townshend and Coke of Norfolk, and on
the improving activity of agricultural societies at work in his
own county. Shopkeeping apart, he developed literary tastes;
it was a craving for literary and intellectual society that made him
move, aged forty, to Bath. There Rack made some headway in
smart literary circles; more important were the friendships he thus
formed, and the way in which he used them to forward what
proved to be his greatest achievement—the founding of a society
whose work it became to improve the West's backward agriculture, and to bring progress to such agriculturally based industries
as the weaving of flax and woollen cloth. It was in 1777, only two
years after Rack came to Bath from Norfolk, that the Bath and
West Society was formed. Rack became its salaried secretary.
Till his death in 1787 he travelled widely, and without flagging,
as part of his work. Between 1782 and 1786, as a result of Collinson's commission, he made the descriptive, parish by parish, survey which duly got included in the parson's three-volume record.
So it is from Edmund Rack, the first secretary and the real founder
of the Bath and West Society, that we hear of such things as 'fire
engines' (i.e. steam pumping engines) in the collieries at Paulton,

of the pithead prices (3d. or 4d. a bushel) at which coal was sold, and of the distribution, in many agricultural parishes, of pasture and arable land. From this East Anglian devotee of agricultural improvement we know that in the southern parish of Stocklinch Ottersey turnips were well cultivated by Farmer Hicks who had invented a hoe for that purpose, and that in neighbouring Stocklinch Magdalen much hemp and flax were grown and that the parish had but a single pauper, "a blind old woman named Ann Symonds". At Staple Fitzpaine, in the high common land of the Blackdown Hills, all the poor of this coal-less parish had the right to cut fuel and turf. Down in the low country, at Creech St. Michael just below Taunton, the parishioners of neighbouring Ruishton could legally turn out as many as 999 sheep in the moors, while at East Lyng, further down in the moor country, the standards of cultivation were so low that Rack tartly remarked the farmer's success was that more due to nature than to skill. Somerset's countryside never had a literary observer so superb as Hardy was for his native, rustic Dorset. But here in Rack's descriptive passages are facts like those which went, in Hardy's barely fictional South Wessex, to his picture of the yokels, the farmers, and the paupers who people his novels.

Despite its setting deep amid the hills, and despite the recent building of some smart new shops, few would claim that modern Radstock is yet an attractive township. Far better is the urban scene at Midsomer Norton, where the Wellow Brook is bridged at intervals, being tamed and landscaped to fall gently in a series of tiny cataracts. Some Georgian houses of fair quality are among the buildings which line the stream, while near the town centre one finds that the Downside Benedictines have pleasingly furnished a small medieval barn as a church for Norton's Catholic parishioners. Not far away, the old parish church was most of it rebuilt in the early Revival Gothic of Charles II's time. I imagine that it reproduces, as closely as its masons could build it without detailed drawings or photographs to guide them, the tower which was there before.

Earlier this century Radstock and Midsomer Norton were the social centre of a still considerable coalfield. Over six thousand men then worked in Somerset's pits; each year they raised over a million tons of coal. Not so long ago, within the working life of some of the older miners still there, North Somerset still had about a dozen mines. Now they are down to two, and fewer than a thousand men get coal in this longest-lived, most historic of Somerset's industries. They can, however, find consolation from the assurance, even in these days of devastating shrinkage in their trade, that the surviving pair can supply industrial plants in Bristol for as long as the coal will last. But Norton and Radstock have also been forced to find new work for their inhabitants. Their success has been marked, and nearly 14,000 people still live in this Urban District. Purnell's great printing works at the much expanded, one-time mining village of Paulton, just over a hill from Midsomer Norton, plastics in the same place, and glovemaking all give work to those who dwell in Norton–Radstock. Two shoemaking factories have been set up in the area by the ubiquitous firm of C. & J. Clark of Street; we shall see how important that firm's scattered activity has become for the economy of all Somerset. Engineering and the making of paper bags both help on the prosperity of towns whose economy is now usefully varied, succeeding the long spell when farming and coal between them held sway in a coalfield where spoil heaps and the wheels of winding gear were never complete in their visual dominance.

The Wellow Brook goes back, in two branches, to make a charming feature of the old village at Chilcompton, and to serve the ornamental cascades which, in a mid-Georgian sequence of slight watery descents, give extra character to the garden of Ston Easton Park. For us it is time to return down the valley, past Midford itself and past Monkton Combe to its confluence with the Avon. The larger river soon brings us to the tributaries which charmingly water that small corner of Somerset which boasts one limb of a cromlech-like three-shire stone (the other counties being Wiltshire and Gloucestershire), and which belongs, by a strange historical accident yet now without question, to the Cotswold country.

The Somerset Cotswolds lie North of the Avon, and their three hill massifs are deeply parted by limpid brooks which flow swiftly down from the hills, past St. Catherine's with its Tudor court and small medieval church, and past isolated little Woolley and so into the eastern suburbia of Bath. The boldest, most promontorial of these bluffs is Bannerdown, well towards the Wiltshire boundary and rising slowly towards the meeting point of the three counties. Next comes the evenly proportioned, isolated height of Solsbury, commanding the fine country which encircles Bath and once crowned by an Iron Age Camp whose builders must have known, and perhaps used, Bath's springs before the Romans came. Behind it, the plateau of Charmy Down was once busy with the landings and takings off of aircraft; below it the St. Catherine's Brook curves round, and in its peaceful upper course parts Gloucestershire and our county. Last and highest of them all, with its top point nearly eight hundred feet above the Bristol Channel, the great mass of Lansdown has its memories of a battle in the Civil War, and tumbles down towards the Avon to be graced, on its ultimate slopes, by Bath's best crescents and squares. It is here, and in the ridge whose final bluff is no less attractively built over with the steeply rising houses of Bradford-on-Avon, that the famous range most linked, in its visitors' minds, with Gloucestershire hands over to another region, and to indubitable Wessex.

There was a time when this delectable complex of steep hills and deep valleys, and with it the town of Bath, could have been kept from what in the end became the county of Somerset. For in Anglo-Saxon times, when the kingdoms of heptarchic England were first carved out, the southernmost reach of Mercia touched the Avon along more of its course than did the later county of Gloucester. Where exactly the Midland Kingdom parted from Bath's river one cannot tell, but what is now Somerset's north-eastern tip seems to have been Mercian territory, and it was a Mercian magnate who founded the religious house which in time became the city's long dominant Benedictine monastery. But in Osric's time, back in the seventh century, and for a few centuries to come, the land had not been parcelled out into the counties we now know. Had the Midland shires been carved out earlier Bath, Swainswick, and Batheaston would now, I imagine, have been in Gloucestershire, not Somerset. But when in the early years of the eleventh century one first encountered the political divisions we now call Leicestershire, Worcestershire, Gloucestershire, and the rest of the Midland shires the Wessex province of England, and within it the county whose name came from the Somersaetas of its central district, had crept over the Avon and had taken in what is now the northern, more famous part of Bath. From the rural delights of the lower vale of the By Brook, and from the much loved St. Catherine's valley, we pass through the noisy street of a somewhat suburbanized Batheaston, and soon cross what is now the easternmost boundary of Somerset's largest and most renowned town.

The events of our Anglo-Saxon history could as well have put the oldest part of Bath into Gloucestershire as into Somerset. Yet the name of the county which happens to contain Bath at times seems irrelevant. For Bath's essential story has been that of a national spa. Much of its Georgian architecture has a metropolitan flavour, and its present crisis of preservation has been taken as something which concerns the nation, not merely Wessex, or Somerset, or Bath's own citizens.

In Roman times Aquae Sulis was not, like Cirencester and Wroxeter, the chief town of some Romanized tribe. It was a resort, which took visitors from all parts of Roman Britain, and some from other north-western provinces of the Empire. The story has often been the same, expressed (barring the local nature of its stone) in Bath's architecture as well as in the lists of those who have been visitors. Even the abbey, a church whose late medieval rebuilding owed nothing to Bath's national standing as a spa, is not in the late Gothic of the West Country but was designed by metropolitan master masons of the Court School who were also employed by the early Tudor kings.

It was the same, once Beau Nash, Ralph Allen the quarry owner, and the elder John Wood had got into their stride, with the architecture of early Georgian Bath. The first moves to expand the city did, indeed, leave some local traces. In Green and Broad Streets some houses of Queen Anne's time had gables of a local, outdated type which enclosed rectangular, bolection-edged windows with sashes, not mullions. But for Bath's main Georgian extensions a staid, more standardized Palladianism took over the field. Localism went out of fashion, and there were few vernacular quips of design. The stately Palladianism of Queen Square and of Allen's great mansion up at Prior Park was the fashionable, metropolitan architecture of the Whig aristocrats who ruled England from their great country houses or from the smart squares of Mayfair. Bath, unlike Bristol and unlike Somerset's clothing or market towns, became a London in the West of England, displaying the urbanity of the capital down by the Avon and on the last Cotswold slopes. So it continued as Palladianism gave way to 'Adam', and as the pattern books standardized architecture and interior design. It is thus that we must see Bath, not as a city planned, in the wholesale manner of Baroque despotism, on a tamed or equable site, but as a gracious exotic thrust down into the lovely countryside where Wiltshire, Gloucestershire, and Somerset meet. No more, on the wide pavements of its straight or curved terraces, does one sense the rural immediacy which at first confronted the Royal Crescent, and which Jane Austen's Sir Walter Elliot and his daughter Anne saw as they looked across the roadway from their Camden Crescent windows. For Bath, like most of our towns, has grown much since Georgian times. Its population has gone up fourfold; the medieval core and its Georgian extensions have become a nucleus for the enveloping suburbia of the workaday city.

Wherever they may have their homes, many of Bath's people still make their living in the city's traditional trades. The activities of the spa have lost most of the panache and social glory which they had in the days of Nash and Sheridan. But healing, more scientific than it was two centuries ago, still employs many Bath people and serves many who visit the city in search of renewed health. The baths, and the eighteenth-century infirmary which has now become the Royal National Hospital for Rheumatic Diseases, still work actively in the centre of the town, while other hospitals, and many members of the medical profession, make Bath an abnormally therapeutic town. More noticeable, and bringing more business than visiting invalids, are the thousands whose aim it is to see the Roman Baths, the Abbey, the Museum of Costume in the renovated Assembly Rooms, and some at least of Bath's urban features which have come down from the eighteenth century. These tourists throng the middle of the old city, line up to enter the Roman Baths, and crowd the none too numerous cafés which lie, and are seen to be, close at hand. Bath's shops are also the goal of chance visitors, of those who live in the city, and of thousands who come regularly from the villages and small towns of the three counties which share it as a chosen shopping haunt and as a social rendezvous. So one finds that Bath's shops, hotels, and restaurants employ some 7,000 people, and that a rather larger number work in the professions, in medical and hospital activities, and in schools and places of higher learning (Bath's new university among them) which give instruction and education to many more than the city's own young people.

Shops and schools are not unexpected in a town of Bath's traditions. Less consonant with its past, yet vital for its prosperity in the last three decades, is the city's place as a centre of Government administration, and as the working scene for some 6,000 civil servants. The local offices of various Departments of State are what any town of Bath's importance might reasonably contain. The Kingsmead area, as renovated after its devastation by the bombs of 1942, contains many of these Civil Service haunts. But the Navy, and its running even in its present shrunken post-war state, have chiefly caused Bath's present, and presumably lasting, fame as a town of many civil servants. The year 1939, and the dispersal from London of many Admiralty people in those hectic, puzzling days at the start of the Second World War, was the time when Bath's new, at the time socially unwelcome, invasion took place. All through the war the Admiralty kept its large place in the Bath scene. Buildings of every kind, including all four of the city's largest, once opulent hotels, were taken over as offices. Dispersed hutments, in brick and concrete in the manner of air raid shelters, arose to hold departments in large groups off the Warminster Road, at Ensleigh up on the Lansdown plateau, and on Combe Down at Foxhill. Naval officers paced Bath's streets in numbers that the city had not known since Nelson and *Persuasion*. Nor was the end of the war the end of Bath as a hive of naval administration. Large elements of the Admiralty stayed on, and it still seems, now that the historic name of 'Admiralty' has made way for the more prosaic title of 'Navy Department of the Ministry of Defence', that Bath's economy will lastingly be boosted by the earnings of some 5,000 men and women whose office files are concerned, in one way or another, with the running and the material needs of the Navy. There are schemes, as I write, for these civil servants to abandon many of their present buildings, among them the neo-Jacobean hideosity of what was, for some forty years from the 1890s, the Empire Hotel, and to concentrate all this activity within the one, upland, site of Foxhill.

Much older than its modern position as a place of naval administration is Bath's standing as a manufacturing town, surprising some who think of it merely as a spa full of gracious Georgian buildings. Yet industry, of various kinds, is a real part of its life. The cloth trade, no longer plied in the houses of the weavers or in mills down by the river, was there for centuries, side by side with the life of the Stuart and Georgian spa, and given literary immortality, for its late medieval days, by Chaucer's Wife of Bath. That lady, one imagines, plied her craft in the midst of the little medieval city. Geography, and in particular the course of the Avon as it flows down towards Bristol, has decreed that Bath's modern industry should be well downstream, much of it in what was still, a century ago, the mainly rural parish of Twerton. The lives, and the human problems, of those who live in the strip of ground, on each side of the Avon, below the old city are largely those of an industrial community which somehow balances the pursuits for which the 'Queen City of the West' is most famed.

Early in the Georgian period the Avon was made navigable from Bristol to Bath. Timber, glass, paving stones, coal, and many other things could thus come conveniently to the city, as far as the Old Bridge or to Ralph Allen's stone wharf a little above it. The area of Bath's main quay was much changed, and unexcitingly remasoned, when the Churchill Bridge, character-less with its one, efficient concrete span, replaced the much altered bridge which had Georgian, medieval, or even Roman origins. But lower down, behind the factories which tower above the first stretch of the Lower Bristol Road, and on the riverward side of a timber yard very close to the Midland Bridge, the masonry facings of Bath's wharves recall the thriving days of its river traffic. More important, in their unlovely, malodorous dominance over this part of the city, the gasworks have now, for a century and a half, ensured the industrial character of western Bath; the city is one of the few in England where economic geography has decreed that the west end should be the unfashion-able quarter. Such a siting for Bath's gasworks was natural enough, for it was by river that much of the coal came from the direction of Bristol, and the barges unloaded, as they came up-river, at the first convenient spot. More recently, this riverside belt of land towards Twerton has seen the rise, in the most modern style, of three new factory buildings whose forthright modernity has added much to the 'contemporary' architecture of Bath. Twerton village, with a fine Norman doorway, on one side of its church, to recall a medieval past has old traces but also much of the flavour of an industrial suburb. Between it and the main part of the city the artisan villadom of the Westmoreland district, and of Oldfield Park, grew up to succeed Bath's late Georgian terraces which had been built for humble folk, and to house an industrial population much swollen in Victorian times.

The most conspicuous of western Bath's industrial plants is that whose products, quite literally, carry the city's name all over the world. For in many countries beside Britain dockside cranes bear the maker's name plate of Stothert and Pitt. Descended from a small ironfounding concern which was active in Regency Bath, this cranemaking concern is the main unit in the city's considerable engineering industry. Not far short of 5,000 people work at Stothert's and in others among Bath's engineering firms. Close at hand, across the drab, busy highway of the Lower Bristol Road the Pitman Press is much the best known of several printing, publishing, and bookbinding firms which flourish in the city. Corsets, and footwear in a high-sited factory of C. & J. Clark's give work to some hundreds of Bath people. Some of Bath's furniture workers ply their trade in one of the three modern factory buildings lying down towards Twerton. Beyond that point, and below the straight, artificial river cut which from the 1720s eased the passage of barges with coal and timber, the westward extremity of riverside Bath contains a small trading estate. Just beyond the city's boundary the graceful arch of New Bridge, remodelled in the 1830s to designs by a Bristol architect, rises high to take what is now the main road leading out from Bath towards Bristol.

Bath: Queen Square, a Palladian terrace
Contrasting Georgian: Combe Hay Manor

CHAPTER III

THE EASTERN MARCHES

WHEN in 1668 Samuel Pepys and his party came west they crossed into Somerset, after their adventurous trip over Salisbury Plain, a little way short of the trim clothing village of Beckington, conspicuous now for fine gabled and mullioned houses, for a Georgian Nonconformist chapel, and for that rarity in the county, an excellent Norman church tower. It was there, and not at Wiltshire's eastern edge, that Mrs. Pepys and her Bristol-born serving maid Deborah Willett felt that an entry into Somerset truly brought them back to their native West Country. Pepys himself commended that country "as indeed it deserves", and it amused the little group to hear village boys talking in the Somerset dialect. They moved on, across the Frome at Shawford Bridge, and so to the fine village of Norton St. Philip; on a summer evening in another seventeen years its streets and alleys would echo sharply to the cannon fire and musketry of Monmouth's rearguard skirmish with his uncle's troops. On that warlike occasion Monmouth made his headquarters in that convincingly medieval inn 'The George', which combines, in its towering frontage, England's two great building traditions of stone and half-timber. But when Pepys was in the village he dined, one assumes at 'The George', 'very well'. Down in a pleasing little dip he had seen the church whose fine tower rises high above the houses, and which contains the curio chiefly noted by the diarist—the conjoined figures of the Fair Maids of Foscot who seem to have been a local pair of Siamese twins.

Norton St. Philip, and Hinton Charterhouse which has the vaulted chapter house, and other remains, of one of the two Carthusian priories of medieval Somerset, come as upland-outliers of that long, narrow strip of countryside which lies

Frome townscape: Gentle Street
Mells: a medieval street

against the Wiltshire border, and which is watered by the main
streams, and headwater brooks, of the Somerset Frome which
flows down to the Avon, and of the Brue whose slow, muddy
course takes it to the flat moors which stretch to the Bristol
Channel.

Somerset is not now a county to visit for medieval castles. Of
those which once flourished, Montacute for example, or the
great stronghold built at Bridgwater to guard the crossing of
the Parrett, almost nothing remains. But at Farleigh Hungerford,
as a traveller comes from Wiltshire and crosses the Frome, he at
once faces the curtain wall and wrecked towers of a guardian
stronghold well poised to dominate that placid crossing point.
The Hungerfords, heraldically distinctive with the silver circles
(or 'plates') of their arms and the intertwined sickles of their crest,
were a great family in the western counties. Here at Farleigh they
were not the first feudal owners. It was from late in Edward III's
reign, and from the time of Sir Thomas Hungerford who was the
first Speaker of the House of Commons, that they replaced an
older manor house by what amounted to a small castle, well
fortified in the manner of late medieval castellation and with its
inner stronghold boldly cornered by the rounded towers of the
type which then gave distinction to Bodiam and Cooling castles
in the south-eastern counties, and in Somerset itself to the
crenellated mansion of Nunney. The Hungerfords were clearly
a determined family. One had, in those days, to get a special
licence to crenellate before the fortification of a private country
home could officially begin. The one-time Speaker must have
felt that he had dangerous foes, for his new castellated mansion
was built before he got his licence from the crown; he found, in
1383, that he had to get a special pardon for jumping ahead of
official permission. The outer courtyard, and the fine gateway by
which a visitor now enters the ruins were the work of his son, the
first Lord Hungerford, who in 1398 took over his father's estates.
The simple little parish church had lain close by the older manor.
The new owner of the castle had no qualms over taking drastic
action. Like some Georgian landlord he took the church into
his enlarged enclosure, building a new one for the villagers and
making the older church, enlarged already by the fine chantry
chapel of Speaker Sir Thomas, the private chapel of his castle.

Here the tombs of the Hungerfords are more convincing, in their funerary perfection, than the much diminished castle ruins. The last of these monuments recalls Sir Edward Hungerford, true to family tradition a staunch upholder of Parliament, and a Parliamentarian commander in the Civil War. Those who followed him wasted the estates, and in the year after Monmouth's campaign they sold the castle. By the 1730s, when Samuel and Nathaniel Buck made it the subject of one of their many antiquarian views, and in another half century when Rack spoke of its "melancholy picture of fallen greatness", Farleigh Castle was far gone towards the decay now happily arrested by Government care.

Above Farleigh the Frome valley, now quiet in its remoteness, was once busy with the sights and sounds of the cloth trade. An early relic, a link point between East Somerset's clothing villages and the Wiltshire downs, is tucked away down a tiny lane between Woolverton and Rode. For there, half shrouded by trees, an admirable packhorse bridge is as good of its kind as one could find anywhere. Four or two centuries ago Scutt's Bridge must often have carried sturdy little horses, hard laden with their packs of wool or rolls of cloth. The animals pass no longer, but the bridge can still serve pedestrian needs.

From Freshford upwards, and all the way to Frome, the valley was once busy with its close succession of cloth mills, at first on the finishing of the cloth woven behind the broad, mullioned windows of the weavers' cottage homes, then on the mechanized production which came in with the age of steam power. Their names survive—Rockabella near the packhorse bridge, Shawford where the Bath to Frome road spans the river, Clifford's, Eden Vale, Spring Gardens just short of Frome, on a copious tributary stream and in Victorian times the largest industrial plant of them all. Of the mills themselves, less and less remains as they sink ever deeper into ivy-clad dilapidation. But twenty years ago one could still, at Eden Vale and Clifford's, mark the differences in their window planning, and see relics of their machinery dangling forlorn amid the shattered timbering of roofs and floors. Teazles, once cultivated for the mill's own use, still grow wild and scattered on the green slope above Clifford's, and a tall brick chimney rises high above the industrial desolation of Eden Vale. But at Shawford the picture is far happier. The mill, and the house close by it, survive intact. The house's back quarters have windows which prove a date some time earlier than 1700. But the front block was built on, by the Noads who then owned the property and ran it as dyeworks, about 1809; with its gracefully curved porch it is of a most accomplished Regency design. The mill seems also to have been remodelled some hundred and sixty years ago, though some of its stonework is certainly more ancient. What now pleases any visitor is to see its present condition. These mills in the Frome valley were also sited to disregard the river's meandering course. Straight channels, or leets, were cut to lead the water directly alongside, or under, the mill buildings; from a large-scale map, or from a bird's-eye view, one can still see how the system worked. Here at Shawford the grey-green water from the straight-cut leet still glides, in two channels, beneath the mill, driving modern machinery which generates electric light and power. The mill itself has now found a use which would certainly have surprised its earlier builders. In the middle years of last century the Noads parted with the place. It was run, thereafter, by the Kemps who long used the mill as a dyeing establishment, tinting wool which they sent on to the still numerous cloth mills of the district. Ninety years ago, so the directories tell us, some sixty men found work at Shawford. More recently the mill, the house, and the other buildings have become the property of a family whose members care much for the arts, and for music in a special degree. They have turned the upper storey of the mill into a concert hall where private recitals, most notably of opera, take place from time to time, with the strains of Mozart and other masters competing with the smooth swish of the Frome's waters below.

Despite early Church associations and the founding, by St. Aldhelm, of a religious community at Frome the town's history has mainly lain in handicrafts and in more modern industry. Its churchyard does, however, contain the grave of that saintly non-juror Bishop Thomas Ken, deprived of the Wells bishopric under William III and in his last years a resident guest, just over the Wiltshire border, of the like-minded Lord Weymouth at Longleat. When in 1711 he died he asked for burial in the nearest parish of his old Somerset diocese. Frome was that place, so there within his erstwhile pastorate the best known of Somerset's Anglican bishops lies at rest. His grave is east of the church; near the building's other end the Victorian High Churchmanship for which Frome became well known made the steep climb to the church more remarkable by adorning it with the boldly sculptured panels of a Way of the Cross. But the church itself, long and much remodelled by the Victorians, fails to match the architectural quality of Frome's temples of Protestant Nonconformity.

For some centuries the heart and essence of Frome's being lay in the making of cloth. The river, curving through the lower parts of the town, gave it the water it needed for dye-houses and finishing mills. Above the level of its central market place steep streets lead toilsomely to the upper plateau which became the useful site for weavers' houses and the coal-fired mills of a later age of mechanized production. These are the streets which help to give Frome a townscape uniquely attractive in all Somerset.

Frome's market place, with its mainly Victorian frontages, is not to be despised as an element in the local scene. Its best feature is the plain Georgian frontage of the George Hotel; to one side of this façade the excellent corner building, with Ionic Grecian embellishment, was in part the hotel's Assembly Room but also houses Frome's branch of the Westminster Bank. The Somerset branches of this particular concern are often lavishly accommodated in specially constructed buildings of some pretension, though here in Frome this is not the reason for the bank's palatial housing. Yet in many cases what is now the Westminster Bank is in the building which was at first that of the more local, legendary Stuckley's Bank, with its origins, round Langport in the central meadowlands, among farmers and river traders. Stuckey's Bank, like the Bristol and Exeter Railway which also served Victorian Somerset, was lavish with its buildings—Venetian Gothic at Wells, proud late Georgian at Bath, an Italianate *palazzo* at Weston-super-Mare, and at Highbridge ornate Gothic of the more normal Victorian type. It was merged, eventually, with Parr's Bank, and then when the Westminster took over Parr's the one-time Stuckey buildings came in with the transfer; in any Somerset town they are apt to be worth noticing.

At one end of Frome's market place the river, a serious flood risk when it had five arches in Rack and Collinson's time, can still cause trouble when wintry weather swells its waters. The present bridge, gracefully Regency with its single, shallow-headed arch to span the main channel, long anticipated what has more lately been done in towns like Bath. For it was built in 1820–21; its designer was G. A. Underwood, the County Surveyor, an inhabitant of Cheltenham who combined much work in that fast-growing spa town with his 'county' bridges for the magistrates of Somerset in the stage-coach age. Close by the bridge a newly renovated building is among the best glories of Frome.

The Blue House, succeeding a much older almshouse for the care of poor old women, was built in the 1720s, as a combined charity school and old women's almshouse. Its plan, linear and rejecting the courtyard arrangement, has a kinship with that of the Wardenry at Farley in Wiltshire. The schoolboys were to use the central block, an admirable work of vernacular Baroque, with its clock tower, its large Georgian windows, its main door-way with a 'broken' pediment, and its statues of a liveried school-boy and of a grim old almswoman. The wings, with their simply edged windows still in the mullioned tradition, were to house the old women. The school, after a chequered history, was given up when in 1921 its boys migrated to the newly founded grammar school. Almspeople stayed on, but in forty years the buildings sadly needed renovation, and changes to make them comfortable by today's exacting standards. Demolition, despite the high standing of the Blue House on the Government's list of historic buildings, seemed possible. But a fine rally of public opinion, and of financial aid from various sources, saved the day. The Blue House was well restored and refitted, and is now used again as a central, companionably placed set of old people's flatlets. Its rescue is all the better because Frome has, in the meantime, lost its second outstanding building of a similar type. This other alms-house-cum-charity school stood at Keyford on Frome's southern fringe. It was dated 1803, and its inscription mentioned Bishop Beadon who had just come to Wells from Gloucester and recorded the hospital's establishment, not for boys and old women, but by an exact reversal for girls and "poor old men past their labour". It was almost as fine a building as the hospital down by the river; it is represented, in a sculptured relief in Frome parish church, on the mural monument of its founder, Richard Stevens, who died in 1796.

For an ascent towards Frome's upper plateau one has a good

choice of picturesque routes. The most gentle slope, curving round from the market place, is that of King Street, giving its choice, for those who admire old buildings, between a fine, solid house of the early eighteenth century and the more ancient Old Church House whose main window, designed to let light pour generously on to a broad loom behind it, is transomed and is vertically split into as many as six lights. The market itself, at its upper end, curves round into the wide, sweeping ascent of Bath Street whose buildings are, as it were, a local parody of some of the later hillside terraces in Bath itself. Between these two high-ways one finds a street whose scenic merit would, in most towns, suffice to make the place a tourist's haunt.

Early last century, when cobbling survived on each side of its central runnel, and when its gabled houses kept more of their projecting windows and late Georgian shop fronts, Cheap Street was even more quaintly attractive than it is today. Even still, with some changes in its buildings, with its neat paving, and with its rivulet running deeper and more concealed than in its days as an open drain, it makes a steeply descending, unvehicular shop-ping street whose charm is hard to rival even in Stonegate at York or in Canterbury's Mercery Lane. Gentle Street, climbing stiffly towards the Portway from close by the piazza which spreads out west of the parish church, is hardly less attractive in its unaltered charm. Unlike Cheap Street, it keeps its cobbled surface, and though it lacks a central rivulet it is a quieter, more unsullied backwater, more peacefully inviting the visitor with its mixture of gabled Tudor or Stuart houses and two solid, excellent residences of Frome's Georgian townsmen. The town is indeed lucky which nowadays contains two such hillside walkways as Cheap and Gentle Streets in Frome. Nor are they the end of the town's steep ascents towards its once open plateau country. Catherine Street, leading on to Badcox Lane, has much of the same scenic quality, and of 'group value' in its buildings. In the upper of the two roads, one passes, or can enter if it is open in its present capacity as a branch of the County Library, what was once the Badcox Lane Baptist Chapel, rebuilt in 1814 and in later years, and distinguished for the goodness of its Greek Doric, four-columned portico. It forms but one unit in Frome's excellent ensemble of Nonconformist architecture.

Nonconformity, as befitted a town of largely Puritan outlook whose weavers and dyers sent many recruits to Monmouth's scratch army, soon became, and has remained, a powerful local force. Defoe, himself a Dissenter and always observant in such matters, mentions "several large meeting houses" in his *Tour of England* which gives a valuable account of the town. The Methodist chapels, among them the severely fronted one at Keyford whose building date was 1811, came later than Defoe's travels up and down England in the reign of Queene Anne. But Rook Lane Congregational Church, set back from the road near the top of Bath Street, was new when Defoe saw it; the date in its broad pediment, 1707, is that of the Parliamentary Union with Scotland. The chapel may claim, with some reason, to have England's finest Nonconformist façade, in its character like a sober clothier's house with its two tiers of windows and its central doorway capped by the broken, triangular pediment then favoured by the masons of Frome. The interior, thanks to a fierce Victorian re-pewing, disappoints, though the pulpit, the gallery, and two massive Tuscan pillars to uphold its ceiling, are those of the original building date. This chapel is now disused as a place of worship, and its members go to services elsewhere. As the future of so outstanding a building is of national concern plans are actively afoot for its conversion into an arts and cultural centre.

Churches and meeting houses were not, however, the only things in Frome to attract the tradesman and economic expert who later gained immortality as the writer of *Robinson Crusoe*. Daniel Defoe had much to say on the thriving cloth trade, the London market outlet, and the exports of this Wiltshire–Somerset border country. He also speaks of the "many new streets of houses" of what was then, surpassing Birmingham, Manchester, or Sheffield, one of England's wealthiest inland towns. What he found was a pioneer example of an industrial housing area. Some of the streets and houses which were new in Defoe's time have now yielded to clearance and trim modern blocks of flats. But many survive, worth visiting before more are inevitably swept away.

Frome's new, or upper, town was laid out on the flat ground between the older settlement downhill and the high road known, from its objective, as Vallis Way. It is a district, now somewhat decayed, of straight streets and rectangular intersections, more so than in much of Bath and as much of a new settlement as Salisbury had been in the Middle Ages or as Devonport was at about the same time. In Bell Lane and elsewhere some gables, and some mullioned windows, suggest a date before 1700 which could still have made these houses 'new' when Defoe came to Frome. Many others among the houses in this part of the town are more evidently of the eighteenth century; the main point about the district is that here, before the great onset of mechanized industrialism, one had a West of England counterpart to the great expanses of workers' houses which arose, in later decades, in towns which had once been smaller than Frome, but where the roaring pace of the Industrial Revolution made them far surpass the population which Frome claimed before that great social upheaval got fully under way. This housing for hand-loom weavers created its own community, but no new church was started till in 1836 work began on Holy Trinity, pre-Victorian Early English by Goodridge of Bath; its well composed façade makes a fine ending as one looks along Trinity Street, lined with earlier houses but taking a new name from the church itself. Many of the inhabitants of the new town of Frome could by now have worked in the cloth mills lately built in the Vallis Way district and elsewhere in the town. Only when Frome's cloth trade showed signs of a second decline did a large factory arise, in Selwood Road, amid these streets and houses. Butler and Tanner's first printing works are just a century old, for the buildings span a date range of 1866 to 1870. They are of stone and brick, and their style is an industrial version of Italian Romanesque; here in the middle years of Victoria's reign one had what in time became Frome's chief source of work for a somewhat diminished population.

With a figure of 12,411, Frome's population reached its peak at the Census of 1821. Since then, the town has never had so many people, and it is still some hundreds short of that maximum of George IV's first year on the throne. But a large population did not, on its own, mean prosperity, and the years of transition from hand-loom weaving to mechanized production were painfully pinching, in Frome and elsewhere, for those who strove to continue in their own ways of work and life. But changes did come, and albeit with fewer people, and with much organized emigration to the United States. Frome prospered continually, as a clothing town and in other ways, till late last century. Though it never got its intended canal, coal for the machinery in its mills came in carts from the Radstock pits and later still, by rail, from nearby Vobster and more distant sources. About 1880 a really serious blow came when Sheppard's of Spring Gardens, with nearly a thousand workers in their three late Georgian mill blocks, were forced to close. They had never modernized as they should have done, and their buildings were found to be crammed with what was described as 'antiquated machinery'. Some smaller firms worked gallantly on, but by about 1914 Frome's clothmaking had decisively declined. But not till the middle of the 1960s did the last of its cloth mills cease production. Beyond the station and down by the river Tucker's Wallbridge mill went on with its output of high quality cloth. Tucker's was part of a concern whose other activities were carried on at Laverton's two mills at Westbury, a few miles away in Wiltshire and close under the steep edge of Salisbury Plain. After Wallbridge closed all the company's work was for a time done at Westbury; the Wallbridge buildings are now used, for carpet-making, by one of the firms which have brought new types of production to vary Frome's industrial scene.

Like Radstock in recent years Frome had had to face the need for other, more varied work to replace a single, declining staple industry. It was a great blessing that its printing trade came to it so long ago, and that several hundred people now take money home from the local printing works. But engineering, in the works of several firms and with products ranging from earth-moving equipment, through fuses and aircraft parts, to small brass pressings is now Frome's main industrial pursuit. Plastics have also become important, and in Vallis Way, where a few years back this work was done in what was once Houston and Brittain's Georgian mill the firm of Wallington Weston have put up new production buildings, using a mixture of reconstituted stone and of dark red tiling betokening the Marley Group to which they belong. Where Frome has greater trouble is in its lack of industrial work for women, such as C. & J. Clark's of Street have so usefully provided in other Somerset towns. All in all one feels that although there is prosperity, and a measure of slow growth, it is a somewhat static town. The same problem more acutely besets the whole belt of eastern Somerset which runs down, through profound countryside little known even to many inside the county, for several miles to the south of Frome.

West of Frome one has the lower courses of the streams, coming down from the Mendips, which converge to form the Mells river, and which water the attractive spots of Vallis, Mells, and Nunney.

Vallis Vale, running down to the ruins of Hapsford Mill, is Frome's most local beauty spot, deep set and wooded to meet all the requirements of romance. The Victorians, and Victorian lovers in particular, much favoured it, and local rhymesters penned verses to celebrate the charms of "sweet Vallis". The vale's charms are enhanced by one's discovery of good relics of the stirring, though in Frome's case somewhat frustrating days of the industrial and transport revolutions. Hapsford Mill has its melancholy industrial remains. First a grist mill, it was enlarged about 1824 when it turned over to the scribbling and carding of wool. Later still it turned out box and livery cloths for the Frome clothing firm of Sinkins and Wood; the wreckage of their machinery remained a few years back. Higher up, crushed down beneath the branches of trees growing near it, and through some of its excellent masonry, the Murtry aqueduct, of three shallow arches, was built about 1800 to carry the Nettlebridge branch of the frustrated Dorset and Somerset Canal. On this, as many other aspects of trade, transport, and industry in the Mendip country, Robin Atthill is the unchallenged expert and has had much to say. For me, as for some others, this work of Georgian civil engineering has come as a happy discovery on a walk into the unexpected.

Mells' industrial past has been well described by Robin Atthill; there remain its present aspect, and its modern fame as the home of a small, yet prominent Catholic community.

Mells is noted, in Christopher Hollis's autobiographical book of 1958, as being "Along the road to Frome". That is, of course, if one comes from Vobster and its derelict coal mines, or more likely, in this context, from the great Catholic stronghold of Downside Abbey. Earlier still, in pre-Reformation times Mells' Benedictine links were with Glastonbury, the village being an eastern outpost of that abbey's great holding of Somerset estates.

The monks kept, and improved, their Mells property from Anglo-Saxon times to those of Henry VIII. In 1535, four years before the abbey's end, Glastonbury's agent, or bailiff, at Mells was a yeoman of Cloford, John Horner; Thomas Horner became the buyer, after the abbey's fall, of the middling rich Mells property. This family's rise in local society lay behind Jack Horner of the nursery rhyme. Thomas Horner's descendants have remained at Mells to this day. Their forbear, as it happened, had obtained an 'improved' estate; the trim village still bears witness to the forward policy of estate management carried out by Glastonbury's later abbots.

It was Abbot John Selwood, a native of this Selwood Forest country of Frome and East Somerset, who included Mells in his late fifteenth-century development plan. He proposed to rebuild Mells, systematically and with small houses of the late medieval type, in the manner of a Roman town whose four streets met at a central crossroads. He finished no more than the northern limb of his cruciform plan; his one street runs neatly, without the irregularities one associates with 'picturesque' medievalism, to the churchyard with its noble late Gothic church which speaks more of prosperous clothiers and weavers than of their monastic landlord. More remarkable than the body of the church and its graceful porch, and of note not only for Mells and an adjacent village but in a wider context of architectural authorship, is the western tower. Probably of about 1500, it has a splendid array of buttresses, blank and fretted windows, and tall or short pinnacles. In England's supreme county for church towers, the beauties of Somerset's towers are evident, while Professor Pevsner and others have well analysed their variations of detail and design. But we still know nothing of the names of their designers; no accounts, or other papers, survive to tell us who planned such masterpieces as the towers of Evercreech, Huish Episcopi, or Bishop's Lydeard. Yet one can be sure, from their resemblances, that some pairs of these towers were designed by the same men; they must have been built when parishes deliberately rivalled each other in their efforts to glorify both God and their own copious generosity. Nowhere does a common authorship seem more certain than at Mells, and at Leigh on Mendip three miles away. Leigh, when its tower was built, was part of the manor and parish of Mells.

Glastonbury Abbey was the landowner in both places, and John Horner's fee as bailiff covered work in each village. One tower almost exactly copies the other in this duo of superbly worked stone and dainty pinnacles.

The Horners became prominent in county affairs; they were well known beyond Somerset's borders as staunch supporters of the Liberal Party. They moved in the highest Liberal circles, so much so that they became allied, by their daughter's marriage to Raymond, the eldest son of Henry Herbert Asquith, to a famous Liberal family in the high days of their power. But the First World War dealt savagely with the hopes of that time. Raymond Asquith, and Edward, who was the last Horner in the male line, both died in action. The gabled and mullioned manor house passed to Mrs. Raymond Asquith. Thanks to Mrs. Raymond Asquith's conversion to Catholicism Mells now contains cultivated manor house Catholicism not unlike that which existed, here and there in southern England, in penal times. But the group which has given Mells its modern Catholic fame is of convert, not of immemorial faith; one has, very specially, the memory of Ronald Knox, living at Mells in his last years, saying Mass in the manor chapel, and there dying a few years back. For Catholic purposes the chapel at Mells is a second church in the parish of Frome. So there, in a side chapel in a hexagonal church only opened in 1967, that brilliant Oxford convert is specially commemorated.

Nunney is cut through by another of the brooks which contribute to the Mells river. It is a charming village, remarkable for the number of its dated houses; their range runs from 1693 to 1744. But where Nunney stands out beyond most Somerset villages is in its dominance by a castle. As at Farleigh, the fortified work at Nunney dates from the late medieval period of military building. Sir John de la Mare, replacing an older manor house, got his licence to crenellate in 1373. Like Sir Thomas Hungerford at Farleigh he generously interpreted what he was allowed to do, but his inner fortification was closer knit and more compact than that which the first Speaker of the Commons built to dominate the Avon crossing. Sir John's outer curtain wall has gone, but his tall and sturdy central tower, with its early Perpendicular detail, is most imposing as it rises above the limpid moat, with its great corner towers boldly rounded and each of them comprising more than half a circle. Between them, good lengths of walling were built to form the long sides of this rectangular home-cum-fortress. But on the eastern and western sides the corner towers almost converge, and the walling between them runs to no more than a couple of feet. As Leland put it when he saw Nunney Castle about 1540, they were "gatheryd by cumpace to joyne in to one". Its four rounded towers certainly give much character to this most intimately accessible of Somerset's castles.

From Frome upwards, and on to the farming countryside of East Somerset, one can follow the winding course of the town's namesake river. A straighter route is that of the railway by which, after the loop through Frome station has rejoined the main line, the fast trains to and from Plymouth run, more effortlessly than they did under steam, to the summit of the line between Paddington and Taunton. That summit occurs near Witham 'Friary', misnamed because its medieval religious house was not one of friars but of that most austere and devoted order of monks the Carthusians. Dr. Reid of Wells has uncovered traces of their buildings in the fields of Witham Hall Farm, while the severe, simply rectangular early Gothic parish church probably served the lay brothers. More important than its physical remains is Witham Priory's place in history. Its founding, by Henry II, was part of his penance for Becket's death. It was the first of pre-Reformation England's nine Charterhouses. It started badly, but the man who effectively set it on its way was the greatest churchmen who lived in medieval Somerset. Hugh of Avalon was Prior of Witham for only six years. He became a friend, an adviser, and at times an admonisher of Henry II and Richard I; his was a strong, attractive personality so that however much he may have wished it he could not stay lastingly within the confines of a Carthusian cell. He spent his last fourteen years as the most renowned and saintly of Lincoln's bishops, coming back when he could to spells of retreat and recollection at Witham. It was as St. Hugh of Lincoln that he was canonized, his remains being moved, in 1280, to his cathedral's splendid new Geometrical Gothic extension known as the Angel Choir.

West of Witham a quiet landscape of farms and woods rises gently to the seclusion of the Cranmores, and to the easy slopes of the last important Mendip hill, crowned by the decaying landmark of the mid-Victorian, Italianate Cranmore tower which takes its place among Somerset's fairly numerous 'follies'. Down by the main railway one is still in the Selwood Forest country, now enclosed and given to cultivation, but still remote and seldom visited. Times without number, in Great Western trains, I have traversed this stretch of East Somerset, but I have never got to know it as I should have liked. Soon after Witham station one crosses the watershed between the Avon's basin and the streams of the county's central lowlands. Farms and woods stretch away, past Brewham and the Brue's headwaters, to the high wooded escarpment where the county boundary parts Somerset from the Wiltshire domains of Maiden Bradley and Stourhead. Alfred's Tower, just inside the neighbour county and awaiting speedy restoration, looks down towards Avalon and the flatlands of the great Saxon monarch's deciding crisis.

Bruton, lying quietly astride its infant river and along its sleepy street, is among traditional Somerset's best gems. Few country towns of its size can boast so splendid a parish church, so perfect a survivalist Gothic, college-like almshouse, or so daringly flung and narrow a pack horse bridge. Add the relics of an Augustinian abbey, a public school whose origins go back to the last years before the Reformation, and out at Wyke Champflower a perfect Jacobean Gothic, early Laudian chapel of ease, and Bruton's historic cup brims over. Yet over Bruton, as elsewhere in this south-eastern corner of Somerset, there lies an air of stagnation; there is no concealing the district's standing as a 'problem area'. By our latest standards Bruton's streets (among them one with the odd name of Quaperlake) are strangely quiet, with a traffic density recalling that of forty years ago. The town gets little of the through tourist traffic which makes life noisy, but profitable, for those who live on the county's main through highways. Nor does Bruton have the industry to give much work to those who live there. The dispensing of education, at the King's School and not far away at Sunnyhill, is among its main pursuits.

Less attractive than Bruton, Wincanton is a busier place. It has its racecourse, its shops, much through traffic, and down by its small river the unlovely, yet work-providing Unigate plant; its motor transport section is scarcely less important, as a factor in the town's economy, than the departments where dried milk products and cheese are made. Before one reaches it from Bruton, the quiet countryside out towards Wiltshire demands a visit to another of Somerset's monastic sites, more notable than Witham for the extent of what remains of its priory. The Augustinian house at Stavordale was small, lightly endowed, and never of much note. It was one of the many readily expendable units in the sum total of England's medieval monasticism. Like the little priory at Longleat it collapsed, of inanition, before the great enforced closures under Henry VIII. For in 1533, only three years before the compulsory fall of the poorer monasteries, it became a property of the far larger Augustinian proiry at Taunton. The Zouches, by then, had become the priory's patrons. John, the seventh Lord Zouche, who lived there as a lay resident in his disgraced, declining years, had died there in 1526, having founded the exquisitely wrought, fan-vaulted chantry which projects from the sanctuary's northern side, and which now runs out from the living room of a private house. For at Stavordale it was the church, somewhat remarkably, which eventually became the main part of the present residence. It was almost rebuilt about 1440; as befitted so modest a priory it had a simple, unaisled nave, and beyond it a choir limb which was also a plain rectangle. The church long served as the barn and the house of a remote farm. In this century it has, with a modern wing, become a more ambitious country house. What were once the nave and choir are divided, horizontally and by party walls, into the present rooms. So while such important monasteries as Bruton, Keynsham, and Montacute have disappeared almost wholly without trace, here by the headwaters of the Cale we have something substantial of a much less important foundation.

Wincanton itself is not a vastly appealing town. It has lost the 'respectable brick structure' of its Georgian town hall; worse still, Victorian rebuilders destroyed the church's chancel. This was built in 1748, with a rounded east end and what was clearly a good classical altarpiece. It may, perhaps, have been almost as good as the fine, slightly older chancel still surviving at Bruton. But its designer is known, and is not unremembered in Somerset. Nathaniel Ireson of Wincanton was among the 'local' architects who in the Georgian period so pleasantly adorned provincial

Beckington: Norman church tower
Nunney: the castle

England. His much worn statue still stands in the churchyard at Wincanton; its inscription as Rack or Collinson noted, called him a "master builder". He was a Midlander who migrated to Wessex; born in 1686 he was old enough to form his taste in the pre-Palladian decades. His idiom, as one sees from his buildings and church monuments, was the vernacular Baroque also used by that Dorset building dynasty, the Bastards. In Wincanton it appears in some of the Georgian façades which give character to the town centre, particularly in Ireson's much altered house, and in the oddly composed front of The White Horse Inn, built in 1733 for the Deanes who combined innkeeping with a far-flung carrier's business.

Below Wincanton, and towards the Dorset border, the wide, pastoral valley leads on in the direction of the Blackmore Vale— the Tess country of Hardy's best known novel. The Cale is one of the few rivers rising in Somerset whose waters flow to the English, not to the Bristol Channel.

A little past Wincanton a traveller comes to one of the county's saddest places. The names of the conjoined villages of Abbas and Temple Combe recall ancient monastic and knightly ownership; more recently they housed the community whose heart was the junction station of Templecombe, much damaged by war-time bombing but revived, for some years, as the meeting place of the Southern and the Somerset and Dorset lines. It was always entertaining to see the swiftly passing, green-liveried Waterloo expresses, and the humbler trains from Bath or Bournemouth with their unmistakably Midland engines—mechanical exotics in these Wessex pasturelands so far from Derby.

A more cheerful place, with a modest bustle of shops and through traffic, is Milborne Post, close to the Dorset border before Sherborne. Despite its present good appearance it was long more important than it is now. Under the Norman kings, and from before their time, it was a royal manor. It was long a borough, and sent its members to Parliament. Yet its palmy days seem to have been just before, and soon after, the Norman Conquest; as evidence for its high standing one has, in its church, imposing work of the 'overlap' between Saxon and Norman Romanesque. More striking still, outside the village by the meadowlands of the Ivel's headwaters, the brick and stone mansion of Ven House is among

Palladian balance: Newton Park
Keynsham: in the Civic Centre

the best country houses in Somerset. James Medlycott, a migrant
from London but of Shropshire origins, built it in the reign of
William III; the first drawings for its layout showed the parterres,
and the water garden in the Dutch manner which had become the
vogue in the reign of this monarch from the Netherlands. With
its 'giant' Corinthian pilasters and its heavy attic storey, Ven
belongs to the severe Baroque af Wren and Talman; it was an
innovation when, in this countryside of building in stone, the
house was mainly erected in brick. Another novelty lay in its
furnishing, from the start, with the sash windows in use in the
Netherlands and now introduced, by Court influence, to the
builders and joiners of England. We now turn, in this south-
eastern nook of Somerset, to the county's northernmost reaches
where the dominant tone is not that of London or the Court, but
that of the great provincial city of Bristol.

CHAPTER IV

THE BRISTOL FRINGE

BELOW Bath the Avon valley, as one saw it from the Lansdown crescents or from such an elevated vantage point as the first stretch of the Bristol road via Kelston and Bitton, was once renowned for its beauty. The less appealing parts of Bath have now engulfed some of it. Much of the rest, as one draws closer to Bristol, has been smirched by ribbon development and by the great city's outer suburbs. Only for a short distance by road, and along the river's actual course where its flow is broken by the early Georgian locks of the Avon's historic 'improvement' does one now find unsullied natural beauty. The grassy Lansdown slopes, as they run up towards the high-perched village of North Stoke, towards Bath's racecourse, and towards the Civil War battlefield on the Gloucestershire border, loom high above the valley country between the two famous cities of the lower Avon. More prominent still, with a planted clump of trees to define and heighten its summit, Kelston Round Hill juts gracefully from the main massif; clearly seen from all places along the valley, and from high vantage points both in Bath and Bristol, it is a fine marker between the two towns. It stands, as it were, for the combined territory of Bristol and Bath, striking a unifying note between two much differing towns.

Above and below the graceful arch of New Bridge the Avon, like other waterways in Somerset, has of late had its course trimmed, deepened, and even altered in the cause of flood prevention. It soon opens out into what was, in Collinson and Rack's time, a single riverside meadow of most unusual size. It is now cut through, before the Bristol road reaches the busy, stop-lit crossroads at Newton St. Loe, by the two railway lines which were once those of the Great Western and the Midland Companies.

Above this busy scene, hidden away behind the crest of its low hill, the village of Newton St. Loe is in itself delightful, has a church with excellent monuments, and stands on the threshold of one of the county's finest estates. A quarter of a century ago, the mansion of Newton Park lay empty and its future was hard to foretell. It stands now, with far older buildings beyond it and new ones around it, as a fine example of an old country house put to new use and cherished as the pearl of its own countryside.

Like Wardour Castle in southern Wiltshire Newton Park contains a medieval castle and a Georgian mansion; the second of the two lies on a wholly separate site, newly exploited some distance from the more feudal headquarters of the older landlords. The main buildings to survive from the times of the Botreaux and Hungerfords, who succeeded the St. Loes, are the fine castle tower, and the inner gateway with its vaulted passage. Both date from soon after 1400, and the tower's battlements are decked out, in relief, with family coats of arms. Close at hand, an outer gateway and what were once stable blocks are later Tudor or Jacobean.

Even without its Georgian splendours Newton Park would be among the showplaces of ancient Somerset. But the artificial lake, contrived to tune in with Regency ideas of the picturesque, and the mansion, neatly flanked, in Palladian architectural geometry, with domestic wings, redouble the estate's beauty. By the time that George III ascended the throne the Langtons had for nearly a century been the owners of the Newton property. They were a prosperous merchant family from Bristol. Not for the first time, it was now an infusion of Bristol money which transformed a portion of northern Somerset. The mansion at Newton Park, probably by a Bristol architect and with some ornate interior plasterwork to compensate for the plain, unpillared simplicity of its interior, was being built in 1762; at the back a two-storeyed bow-window projection thrusts out to command a good view of the valley below. The owner in the 1760s was Joseph Langton whose second marriage must have given him the urge to replace an outdated castle by a stylish mansion in the manner then approved. His daughter and heiress, Bridget Langton, married William Gore who added the Langton name to his own. Last century, a Gore-Langton marriage with the second Duke of Buckingham's daughter allied this Whig family to the peerage. When the third duke died childless his family's Temple of Stowe earldom passed to this lady's son. But in 1940 the next earl died childless. The Duchy of Cornwall stepped in, buying the estate, in the main, as a valuable agricultural property. For a time the mansion lay forlorn and potentially derelict. Its resurrection, like that of many other country houses, came from post-war England's great educational needs. For the City of Bath, as the Ministry of Education's chosen agent, leased Newton Park as a training college for women teachers. New buildings have been added to allow for expansion and to meet new needs. The Georgian mansion was well reconditioned, the castle tower became an excellent library, and the buildings near it accommodate some of the numerous girls under training. Some 'stately homes' have been given new, yet deeply changed, life by being open as show places. Here at Newton St. Loe that new life has come in a different, yet no less preserving a way.

Down river from Newton St. Loe the Avon valley soon passes into a zone where modern houses for Bath and Bristol commuters, concentrated along the main road yet not confined to its course, have destroyed most of its one-time scenic charm. Saltford village has lost much of its ancient character, though one must never overlook the astonishing, extremely rare merits of the late Norman domestic work in what seems, from afar, to be a somewhat barnlike manor house. But it is down by the actual river that one finds the most placid conditions, notably by Saltford lock, and in its Georgian inn 'The Jolly Sailor' whose first patrons were not the crews of slavers or direct-running West Indiamen, but the trowmen and bargees of the river navigation which made a port of Bath. A little lower down, the Avon again ceases to be Somerset's exclusive possession, becoming the boundary with Gloucestershire before it dives, for a few vital miles, into the keeping of the much expanded city and county of Bristol.

Below Saltford, where the fair-sized stream of the Chew flows down to join the Avon, one finds the most transformed of Somerset's urban communities. Thirty years back one could still think of Keynsham as a country town, clearly distinct both from Bath and Bristol. In its High Street, and near its fine church with its noble seventeenth-century Gothic tower, one was unaware of Fry's red-brick chocolate factory down by its loop in the Avon. The Somerdale estate, built like a minor Bournville to house some of the workers in what was, by then, part of the Cadbury empire was unobtrusive till one had crossed the railway. Only the increasing traffic in its High Street reminded Keynsham's inhabitants and visitors that the town was vulnerable, in such a position, to great expansion and a swamping overspill. Now, however, the commuter tide, most of it from Bristol, has more than trebled Keynsham's size as thousands who work in Bristol have made their homes in what one may now call the semi-countryside. South Gloucestershire, in such places as Winterbourne, Patchway, and Frampton Cotterell, has borne the brunt of an architecturally unlovely permeation. In Somerset, Keynsham is among the places most altered by this social surge of the last twenty years. Its modern by-pass has, indeed, restored some ease and peace to a high street which was, five years ago, clogged and devastated by the traffic which it had to contain.

Bar its church and the Brydges Almshouses on the Bristol road, Keynsham lacks old buildings of real distinction. Yet it is a place of some historic note. Its Augustinian Abbey, founded about eight centuries ago by one of the earls of Gloucester, was a religious house of middling importance; excavation has proved that here, as in the neighbouring house of Victorine Canons in Bristol, the fourteenth-century builders achieved work of distinction. The Brydges family, with a large mansion on the site of some of the Canons' buildings, were the successors to the Augustinians as Keynsham's chief landlords; their tombs in the church prove a certain opulence and taste. Keynsham, and the meadows just across the Avon in Gloucestershire, had their place in Monmouth's campaign of 1685. For here was the northerly limit of the claimant duke's ill-fated promenade from Lyme Regis to Sedgemoor. His purpose, at this point in a somewhat vacillating campaign, was an attack on Bristol. A night skirmish in Keynsham itself, successful for the royalist cavalry patrol which had come into the town, played its part in shaking Monmouth's already wavering resolution, and in deflecting him from his second choice among the main cities of Stuart England. Later on, and till well within living memory, the brass industry of the Bristol region lingered on, at Keynsham and Saltford, much longer than in the larger city where the small river of the Bristol Frome no longer furnished its great wheels with enough water power.

But present-day Keynsham, the township of some thousands of commuters into Bristol, is what now attracts attention. Its people number little fewer than the official target of twenty thousand. The town's growth, on both sides of the Chew, has mostly been on its southern side. At one end of the High Street, a modern shopping centre, with a tower block of modest height to contain the council offices, is better laid out than some of its kind. Across the road a park has a riverside stretch, with the lower portions of mill buildings where brass was once made, which has been more intelligently planned, and adorned with better buildings, than such public places normally are in towns of Keynsham's size and standing. Yet one cannot claim, amid its current activities and its modern housing sprawl, that this near neighbour to Bristol is among Somerset's more attractive settlements. Few places in the county can, in the last two decades, have seen so great an onrush of change.

Once it is clear of Keynsham the Chew Valley is a haven of rural peace, only temporarily broken by the dramatic flood of July, 1968. Compton Dando and Publow, each village with an excellent church, come at intervals before one reaches the busier scene of Pensford, where the Bristol to Wells road crosses the little river; a little above the village the whole valley is dramatically spanned by the great arches of Somerset's noblest viaduct, built to carry the North Somerset railway line which until recently took the coal from near Radstock to industrial users in Bristol. Pensford village has gained, twice over, from the road diversions of modern times. Its ancient bridge was spared when a new one, giving a straighter course to the main road, was built a few yards downstream.* Then on the Wells side of the river the picturesque, precipitous village street, with its old houses and stone-capped lock up, was by-passed by the easier, more sweeping gradient of the new road laid out for the horse-drawn stage coaches of the first transport revolution. Not far above Pensford

---

* The medieval bridge survived the flood of 1968; the more modern one did not.

the Chew again flows through a scene whose rural calm, so near
to an urban community of half a million people, comes from this
Chew Valley's country's position as Bristol's southern green
belt. The old village of Whitchurch has, indeed, been somewhat
smothered by suburbia. But the Chew Valley, shielded from the
houses of southern Bristol by the great saddleback massif of
Dundry Hill, remains unsullied as a choice living area for well-
placed Bristol commuters. The hill itself, with its splendidly
pinnacled church tower of 1482, and with its contrasting downward glances on to council-house suburbia and a pastoral countryside, is a delectable northern rampart for Somerset.

Dundry Hill stands so clear above its setting and a walker
can, on its high ridge between the prehistoric fort of Maesknoll
and the medieval quarries, feel so skied and remote from the
land on either side, that the hill seems higher than its greatest
elevation of a little over 760 feet. The steepest ascents, up from
Bristol, are on the northern side. The city itself has encroached
on those slopes; here and there the new city boundary of the
1950s crept a little above the contour of 500 feet. But the housing
areas of Highridge, Withywood, and Hartcliffe do not, as a rule,
come higher than the three-hundred-foot mark. Yet with massive
point blocks interspersed, in a second wave of development, amid
the far lower houses of the groups first built in Bristol's southern-
most expanses, these newly populated areas are obtrusive enough.
Above them all, seen from the city centre on the Dundry skyline,
but like Sham Castle above Bath in that it is not on its hill's
summit, is Dundry Village's admirable church tower. It is akin,
in its coronal of traceried pinnacles, to those of Gloucester
Cathedral, and of St. Stephen's in Bristol which was the parish
church of many of the merchants who put up the tower as a
landmark. The church itself is small and unworthy of its great
tower. It was once a mere chapel in the large parish of Chew
Magna, and the Bishop of Bath and Wells, who was lord of that
wealthy manor, drew good money from the great quarries to
whose revenues he was entitled. For Dundry, unlike its Mednip
neighbours, is a ridge of splendid, creamy oolitic limestone. From
its quarries, now disused but still evident as they pit and scar the
higher end of the ridge, stone was cut for the finer work of
builders in Bristol. They used it at least as early as 1260 and then,

more notably, it was carted or sledded down to give high quality to the architecture and carving of the abbey church which is now Bristol Cathedral, and to the great parish church of St. Mary Redcliffe.

Below Dundry Hill the lush countryside of the Chew Valley contains, as its rarest curiosity, the late Neolithic circles and standing stones of Stanton Drew. The stones rank, in their pattern of circles, avenues, and more isolated features, as the third finest Stone Age monument in Wessex; such a complex must have been no mean centre of cult and devotion. The stones, whether fallen or standing, are in the meadowlands not far from the river; one circle, and a more individual composition, are close to Stanton Drew church. One assumes that when the stones were set up the district was far less tamed and cultivated than the present rich dairy country of the Chew Valley. What now seems surprising, when one thinks of Stonehenge or the barrows in the Cotswolds and on the Wiltshire chalk downs, is that such a monument should arise not on open down or moor, but low down in what is now the rich pastureland of a sophisticated countryside.

Chew Magna, with its spacious high-towered church, its late medieval church house, some pleasant Georgian houses, and its neat shops, has much of the air of what it actually is, a village as much the home of commuters as of those who make their living within the parish. It was not always so, for Rack tells how in the 1780s a few edge tools and stockings were made at Chew Magna, and how ruddle, for the marking of sheep, was produced in the parish. A little higher up the valley, Chew Stoke was famous, all through the eighteenth century and till the year of Waterloo, for its clockmaking and bell-founding family of the Bilbies. Hundreds of bells, in the church towers of Georgian Somerset and elsewhere in the western counties, came from the bell pits in the village, tucked away and remote from any means of transport more convenient than waggons lumbering along muddy or rutty roads. Cold weather, could, however, sometimes lessen the Bilbies' transport problem. For when in 1739 Thomas Bilbie recast six bells for the church of Weston near Bath the Weston parishioners waited till the following February, and a hard frost, before a team of men and boys went over to Chew Stoke, in two waggons, to fetch home the rejuvenated peal. The Bilbies, as one gathers from the rhymes on some of their bells, must have been picturesque, aggressive, self-advertising men. For they were not averse to boasting of their achievements, on their actual handiwork, not without bantering denigration of their rivals in the trade. So at Milborne Port, on bells cast in 1736, they said

> Come Here Friend Knight and Cockey too
> Such Work as This You Cannot Do

Of 'Knight' I am ignorant, but 'Cockey' was a well-known bell-founder in Frome. Nine years earlier, at Mark in the flatlands of the lower Brue, Thomas Bilbie had marked the opening of his career in these words:

> Come Here, Brother Founders and Here You May See
> What Sort of a Workman Young Bilbie may be
> He'll Challenge all England for casting a bell
> Who will be the workman can be but dun well
> Sing Prais unto God

Chew Stoke, and the country between it and the steep northern slopes of the Mendips, are now best known for the most modern, most dramatic alteration in Somerset's landscape. The Chew Valley lake, impounding the waters of the Chew and of some other streams, came as a vast addition to the resources of the Bristol Waterworks Company. Its beauty, and the quality of its fishing, soon made it as famous as the older reservoir of Blagdon. As one looks down from Dundry, or from the Mendips where the old road from Bristol to Wells toils steeply above the Harptrees and Compton Martin, the quiet, shallow expanse of Somerset's largest lake spreads out among its girdle of hills. Some roads were submerged as the new reservoir first filled, but the loss of farms and houses, in so great an area, was strangely small. This lake in the Chew Valley improves, as a popular attraction, on that at Blagdon. For though it is a reservoir, and not a natural lake, with its brink fenced off from indiscriminate access, stretches of road run close to it at several places, making its close-range admiration an easy matter as Bristolians drive out to view this great new means of quenching their thirst at home.

Chew Stoke and Blagdon are but two of the places in northern

Somerset whence the hard water of the Mendips is piped to
Bristol, and to other places now served by the Bristol Waterworks. Two of the oldest reservoirs, blatantly artificial and
unscenic as they lie, one above and one below the main Bristol
to Bridgwater road, are close above the charming village, and
the hospital, of Barrow Gurney. They are on the lower slopes of
Dundry, and of the geologically different hills which one may
call the Lulsgate massif.

For the open space of their upper plateau, and for the scenic
beauties of their northern fringe, the Lulsgate hills are much
valued in Bristol. The busy highway of A.38, still important to
Somerset despite prospects of a motorway to de-congest at least
a part of its length, carries a dense, roaring volume of motor
traffic across the plateau as far as Redhill. The road sweeps past
Bristol's smart modern airport, opened in the 1950s to replace
one, near Whitchurch, which lay closer to the city's suburbs.
Past Lulsgate the hills give northward shelter to the rich, romantically beautiful vale of Wrington. They shield Barley Wood,
with its memories of Hannah More and a dress circle view, across
the Yeo valley and the Misses More's earlier home at Cowslip
Green, of the steeply towering, highest massif of the Mendips.
Below them lies Wrington, like Chew Magna in its being another
commuters' village where professional people and business
executives from Bristol are more in evidence than those whose
living comes from arable fields and pasturelands. Here too, as we
move deeper into Somerset from its eastern borders, we have
another of the superb late Perpendicular church towers which
are the specific, supreme glory of the county's medieval building.

The Lulsgate massif's northern escarpment starts badly where
the Backwell quarries have slashed and gouged, as hideously as
any in the West of England, into the very substance of the hills.
Below them, in its own way, the scene is little more pleasing,
being much marred by the ribbon development which has crept
far along the much used road from Bristol to Weston-super-Mare.
But near Brockley and Cleeve there is a less blemished countryside
of woods and rocky hills. Brockley and Goblin Combes are
both, like the great gorge at Cheddar, dry valleys which emerge
into open plateau country. Each on of them, at its lower end, is
beautifully shrouded by tall trees. Both of them, particularly

Brockley Combe with its road all the way to the top, are much loved by Bristolians out for an easily gained breath of country air. The Weston road, after a steep drop down Rhodyate Hill which divides one end of the Lulsgate hills from one of Somerset's three Cadbury camps, comes to Congresbury and so to the fringe of the great flatland of the North Moor. Excavation has now shown that the camp itself was notably resettled in the 'Dark Age', or 'Arthurian' phase of Britain's history. Congresbury, with its old village cross and the Ship and Castle Inn whose signboard sports Bristol's well-known arms, has yet greater distinction in the high quality of its church hall. For this building is no ordinary parish meeting place, but is the medieval portion of what was once an unmanageably large vicarage. A large late Georgian block is still the vicar's home. The older portion, repaired and well adapted to its new purpose, is a fifteenth-century priest's house, built in Bishop Bekynton's time for the incumbent of this well financed living. With its two storeys it now survives as one of the finest of England's medieval parsonages.

The low-lying, watery country of the North Moor runs in, like a narrowing estuary, between the Lulsgate hills and the slim ridge which contains Somerset's most northerly Cadbury Camp and reaches almost to Clevedon. Here, in the drained pasturage whose usefulness was increased by many late Georgian Enclosure Acts, we have our first introduction to the flat, once fenlike levels which mean so much for the topography and livelihood of Somerset. The North Moor is not the largest of these expanses in the county. But in our particular East to West progress it can serve to introduce what is, for most Somerset people, the idea of a 'moor'.

In much of Somerset a moor is not a rolling, upland, heather-clad expanse, the haunt of grouse or red deer. It is low-lying and flat, and was once impassably swampy and clogged with fenny vegetation. The one thing it shares with moors of the more generally accepted type is peat, so that peat-cutting, more for gardening or agriculture than for fuel, is still prominent and conspicuous in the Somerset moor country, mainly north of the Polden Hills. Nowadays, and since the Enclosure Acts of the age of agricultural improvement, the moors are better drained,

applied to the landscape itself. Wraxall and the great Victorian mansion of Tyntesfield lie on the hill's southern side, while between them and the coastal heights near Portishead the flat, triangular inlet of the Gordano valley is the most northerly, and the most shut in, of Somerset's moors; it was once traversed, from end to end, by the somewhat ramshackle 'light' railway which linked Portishead and Clevedon, and so across the wider moor country to the larger resort of Weston-super-Mare.

From the direction of Bristol one can approach Clevedon by two widely differing ways. One of them, as it skirts the drained moor, leads to the manorial centre and the old village. It runs past Clevedon Court, avoiding the seaboard till in the end it brings those who use it to the rocky little promontory whose ancient church overlooks the tidal pill of the Land Yeo and the harbour quarter of the parish. The other approach is more dramatic, consciously 'scenic', and in tune with Clevedon's growth as a 'romantic' resort and as a place of residence. It continues, as a high-perched footpath with superb cross-channel views, to connect the Portishead road with the golf course and with the Victorian gentility of Walton Park. It passes Walton 'Castle', a Gothic mock ruin, Jacobean in date and of note among such buildings as being one of England's oldest examples of a 'romantic folly'. Both entries to Clevedon are in their differing ways exciting; both lead to a coastal town of varied interest, rapid modern growth, and no small charm.

Manorial Clevedon, though remote and until well into the last century poorly furnished with roads, was long a larger and more important place than Weston-super-Mare. In 1801, at the first census, its recorded population of three hundred and thirty four was more than that of the rival resort which now so much surpasses it. For so old a settlement, its medieval manor and church are unusually far apart. Clevedon Court, now on the road built to give Bristolians good coaching access to the growing town, was long so much of a fastness that Locke, the agricultural 'improver' who added extra matter to Rack and Collinson's account, and who wrote in 1806, spoke of it as "a residence fitting for the Prince of Hermits". It is now outstanding among Somerset's ancient manor houses. Most of these buildings, as at Cothay and Lytes Cary, are mainly of the last, or Perpendicular

Medieval manor: Clevedon Court
Medieval parsonage, Congresbury

phase of England's secular Gothic. But at Clevedon the essential fabric, despite earlier portions and later changes, is of the fourteenth century. The main structure of the great hall, and of the porch, are of that period, with some simple, chamfered arches supporting a date not long after 1320. The projection which contains an upper chapel was probably added a little later. Its windows are important, not only in their own country but in all England, in that they are not pointed but rectangular, and that their whole area, not merely their lower portions, is filled with the flowing reticulated tracery which was a special glory of Decorated Gothic.

The Court's ownership changed several times before one of the Eltons, a family which had prospered in the business life of Bristol, bought it in the reign of Queen Anne. They were responsible for some alterations, and for many activities and associations which make Clevedon more interesting than most places of its kind. Sir Abraham Elton, the buyer of the house and the first Elton baronet, put in a floor which reduced the hall's inner height, and made an upper set of rooms. In Georgian days the Elton baronets split their time and money between their country holding and their Bristol business pursuits. It was in the next century that the baronets' cultural tastes gave Clevedon its strong literary links. The association of the place with the men of letters had, indeed, started before 1800 when Coleridge lived in a cottage there, just after his marriage and for a few weeks before he fled back to the library resources of Bristol.

The early Victorian Eltons were a family of strong literary tastes and somewhat varied achievements; among the things which made them stand out from the generality of such families was the ceramic oddity of Sir Edmund's Elton ware. Sir Charles, who came into the baronetcy in 1842, was himself a prolific writer who knew many leading men of letters. Thackeray came often to Clevedon Court, and as the Eltons and Hallams had intermarried Arthur Hallam, Tennyson's close Cambridge friend, was a nephew of this sixth Elton baronet. When Arthur Hallam died in Vienna his body was brought back and buried in the Elton vault. It is thus that the romantically sited, headland churchyard at Clevedon got its mention, after Tennyson's pilgrimage visit, in his long poem *In Memoriam*. The Danube having given to the

Severn "the darkened heart that beat no more", Arthur Hallam was laid, here on the Somerset coast, "by the pleasant shore, and in the hearing of the wave". Walter Bagehot, whose home was for some years at Clevedon, gave the town yet another link with writing, this time in tune with the strong political interests of the seventh baronet, Sir Arthur Hallam Elton who also did much towards the resort's Victorian development.

Clevedon's blossoming as a resort started early last century; like other Somerset seaside towns it had a spell of demure Regency elegance before the more smothering growth of the Victorian years. By 1829, as the topographer Rutter said, it had "acquired comparative importance as a bathing place", and though it had no sandy beach its "advantage of more varied and picturesque scenery" gave it a pull over Weston-super-Mare. Two years later, when Clevedon's people numbered 1,147, those of Weston were less than two hundred more; for another decade the two resorts ran almost neck and neck. As in the other two resorts high up in the Bristol Channel Clevedon's attraction lay less along the foreshore than in the shelter given by its dominant hill to rows of villas looking westward, down Channel, and not straight over to Wales. Below the sheltering height of Dial Hill Regency villas are still set back behind what is now Clevedon's select shopping centre of Hill Street; other villas of the same period lie along the coast; with their backs towards the Walton Road and their main rooms so placed as to view the ships and look over to Newport and Cardiff. Such was the state of Clevedon when its new church, by Rickman and Hussey of Birmingham, was built, and when the fifth Elton baronet's widow put up the pseudo-Jacobean villa which she called 'Mount Elton', not far from the same church. From then onwards Clevedon's growth was one of Victorian villadom. Many houses and other buildings are palpably the work of contemporary Bristol contractors. Prominent Bristol men had houses in the growing town. From their endeavours Clevedon became what it is today, a happy hunting ground for lovers of Victorian villas and places of worship.

Modern Clevedon, with its short but varied sea front, and with its undoubted scenic charm, is more geared to day visitors, to commuting residents, and retired people than to large droves of holidaymakers coming to stay a week or more. Nor does it largely encourage the more 'popular' amusements which give character to Weston-super-Mare. Though it has well over 12,000 people they number much less than a third of those in Clevedon's far larger neighbour down the coast. As in many resorts the needs of residents and visitors are not Clevedon's only concern. For out on the Bristol road Hale's bakery, now turning out cakes for a national, and no longer a local market, gives work and wages to many people; it makes a large, conspicuous industrial addition to the town's eastern fringe. Here in this low-lying, un-rocky part of Clevedon one has reminders of a long rural history before the place caught the fancy of Bristolians in search of the seaside blended with the picturesque.

Many of Clevedon's past problems have been concerned with the warding off of undue rushes of water—fresh water from the moors and the streams which helped to flood them, salt water from the dramatic tides and the storms of the Bristol Channel. Clevedon's Enclosures, at the very end of the eighteenth century, provided for the draining of the local moor, for the cutting of new rhines, and for the parcelling out, among the Eltons, the Hollymans, and other owners, of the long, narrow, water-girt rectangles of newly useful pasture. Closer to the sea the sea wall, piled up as a barrier between the flats and the level farmland, was of old a constant anxiety. In 1607, when all the flatlands of Severnside were drowned by a great inundation, the wall, at Clevedon and elsewhere in the estuary, was overwhelmed; the disaster was a terrible warning for the future. So one finds, from papers of the next two centuries, many details of what the occupiers of the land did to make the wall's Clevedon sector more secure. Loads of stone, shipped down in trows which were the barges peculiar to the waters of the lower Severn basin, came down from near Bristol to fortify these coastal pastures of northern Somerset. The need for such a barrier is no less now than it was two centuries ago. Past the pill of Clevedon, and down the coast towards the mouths of the sluggish Kenn and Yeo, the modern wall is constantly repaired and improved. Its sloping outer face, reached and battered at high tide by the turgid sea water, is carefully faced with massive masonry. Along the top, the breezy path leads on towards the main area of the North Moor, a prelude to the far greater flat expanses of central Somerset.

CHAPTER V

NORTHERN SEABOARD

FROM Clevedon southwards to Highbridge and the Parrett's estuary the Somerset foreshore is backed by a variety of drained moors, rocky steeps, sand dunes, and tidal flats. But though the coast varies much in the twenty or so miles between the Land Yeo and the Parrett one constant, unpleasing scenic element is the brownish colour of the actual sea. One cannot conceal this turgid product of the Bristol Channel's narrowing outline, of its dramatically high or low tides, and of the downpouring of the Severn's silt. For the resorts along Somerset's coast the hue of their water is an unquestioned drawback, gallantly fought with such devices as swimming pools but denying their bathing visitors the boon of clean water. Those nurtured, as I have been myself, on the limpid iridescence of South Devon or Cornish sea find it hard to relish what they find, not far away, between Glamorgan and Somerset. The strength and purity of the Atlantic air, whistling straight up-Channel and felt, with all its beneficence, as far up as Weston or Clevedon, comes as some compensation to those who walk on or above the weed-caked rocks, and the grey-brown sand, of Clevedon, Burnham, and Weston-super-Mare.

From Clevedon's southern extremity the sea wall continues, up against the high tides or not far inland from the outer coastline, past the flat fields of Kingston Seymour, beyond the Yeo's deeply scoured mouth, and so past Wick St. Lawrence to another coastal stretch where rocky steeps, and not alluvial flats, fringe the broadening sea of the Bristol Channel. The low ridge of Middle Hope is of no great height; at its most elevated spot, not far from Sand Point, it only slightly tops 160 feet. For a little over two miles the coast's configuration is more like that of Pembrokeshire than it is to Cornwall, or even to North Somerset's coastal ridge between Clevedon and Portishead. But for unspoilt beauty, surprising at such great nearness to a large seaside resort, and lying close to historic buildings of great note, the National Trust's Woodspring Priory estate is unchallenged along the Bristol Channel's southern side.

Where Woodspring scores, in sharp contrast to the bungaloid ugliness one finds close behind the dunes of the adjacent Sand Bay, is in its emptiness of building along a primeval stretch of rocky, indented coast. Ploughed fields and pastures lie close behind the cliffland, as indeed they do behind many famous coastal stretches, confronting a bluer sea, in Devon and Cornwall. What matters is that Nature, untouched or pleasingly tamed, still has a free hand at Middle Hope; it is no surprise to know that the territory has long been known as a nature reserve. Added to the estate's natural beauties one has the admirable bonus of medieval monastic remains. A headland on the estate is called St. Thomas' Head. For before the Reformation the little Priory at Woodspring was the West Country's chief shrine in honour of St. Thomas of Canterbury. King Henry II had, indeed, made his act of reparation elsewhere in Somerset. For the Carthusian priory at Witham was part of his penance for the crime he had hastily countenanced. Here at Woodspring the link with Becket's death and canonization was equally direct. For Reginald Fitzurse, the First Knight of T. S. Eliot's play, was the maternal grandfather of William de Courtenay who soon after 1200 founded this remote little priory; its inmates, like those of Stavordale, were Victorine canons who followed the Augustinian rule. Relatives of one of the other murderers were among the priory's benefactors, while its greatest treasure, preserved for veneration in the church's north chapel, was said to be a little of the murdered archbishop's blood. The priory's history was uneventful and, one gathers, edifying. It was never richly endowed and its inmates were always few. When in the last decades before the Reformation its modest church was almost all rebuilt the destroyed choir was left ruined so that the new, attractive upper stage of what was once a central tower rose pleasingly above what was now the church's eastern end. Then in the centuries after the Dissolution it was the church, as at Stavordale, which became a dwelling house. So the delicate little tower, with its fan-vaulted lower space, rose jauntily above what was, till lately, a farmer's home. For many years the public have had no access to the priory remains, or except at its Sand Point end to the unsullied beauty of the Woodspring estate. Now, however, the coastline of Middle Hope has become a choice possession of the National Trust. The Landmark Trust has bought the Priory, its restoration has been started, and on 29th December, 1970, the eight hundredth anniversary of Beckett's death, the Bishop of Bath and Wells rehallowed the church. Some choir stalls from the priory are in the parish church at Worle, and it was at Kewstoke, nestling prettily in the shadow of Worlebury Hill which shelters Weston, that the reliquary which held the saint's blood long lay hidden in the walling of the church in whose parish Woodspring lies.

Sand Bay, between Sand Point and Worlebury's wooden northern side, is a sad scenic contrast to the untouched beauty of Middle Hope. Somerset's most northerly dunes divide its first sandy beach from a narrow road, and from houses whose number increases till at the bay's southern end they cluster, unattractively, behind a simple esplanade. The sand itself, fine and clean at first, slopes slowly down, below high water mark, to a muddier mixture and to a chocolate-coloured sea whose invitation to the bathers is of the slimmest. More attractive, and with its islet outliers the secret of Weston's being, is the high mass of Worlebury Hill, scarred by quarries and once noted for the mining of calamine which was an ingredient of brass and zinc. Near its centre, and close by the picturesque Monks' (or canons') steps which climb stiffly between Kewstoke and part of Worle, it is crowned by the observatory tower, once the stack of a windmill, which commands the best of Somerset's views up-Channel towards the mouth of the Usk and across to Cardiff and its guardian bluff of Penarth. Then among the woods at its western end the tip of Worlebury is cut off from the rest of the hill, and additionally fortified along its southern side, by the ramparts of an excellent Iron Age hill fort; its many storage pits are among this country's best evidences for the food-preserving aspect of its prehistoric economy. Below the ramparts and the trees one soon comes, amid a welter of high Victorian terrace and villa development, to the more elevated, and more residential area of the Bristol Channel's largest seaside resort.

Weston-super-Mare has two distinctions within Somerset. It is, after Bath, the county's largest and most populous town. It is also, of all Somerset's urban communities, the most completely, though not entirely, Victorian; for lovers of Victorian buildings it is as happy a hunting ground as Bath is for Georgian enthusiasts. It has, however, its reminders of a late Georgian start to its career as a seaside haunt. Nor did it, like Blackpool or Bournemouth, begin the new, transforming phase of its history from nothing, or on a totally unoccupied shore. For where the beach curved northwards from its broadest, most exposed part the rocky islet of Knightstone gave shelter, and a navigable approach whereby, at high water, small fishing craft could come conveniently near the shore. Hence, from an early date, a tiny coastal village, still proving its ancient existence by the Norman font in the old parish church, and by the late medieval base of that church's tower.

For centuries Weston stayed much as it had been in the Middle Ages; fishing, and the pasturage of the parish moors, were long its mainstay. Not surprisingly, it was a late starter among our seaside resorts. For Bath and Bristol, with Ralph Allen a pioneer in the last years of his life, went first for the early development of Weymouth. For those who visited Georgian seaside towns were expected to drink the water as well as plunge into it, and Weston's chocolaty, often distant surge, was inviting neither for one purpose nor the other. Two things, however, Weston had abundantly—good air and striking views. It was for the scenery, and for his serene contemplation of its views towards the Quantocks and the setting sun, that the Rev. William Leaves, the vicar of Wrington, and a man of literary tastes, chose Weston for the thatched cottage which he built as a 'romantic' summer retreat. This was in 1791; within another twenty years Weston's more systematic growth had begun. Mr. Cox and a doctor named Parsley bought land and houses from the Pigotts of Brockley who were Weston's manorial lords. A hotel and some villas went up, and some Bristol money was now laid out on the improvement of a resort within so reasonable a distance of the city. The Jacobs family, best known as the makers of much of Bristol's ornamental coloured glass, laid out some of the southern, low-lying beachside district which came to be known as Jacob's town. At Knightstone, another prominent Bristolian was the presiding genius. He was Dr. Edward Long Fox, the Quaker physician who was famous for his advanced, humane private asylum at Brislington. He bought the property, which may already have had some salt water baths, and built the present, mansion-like bath house, with its pediment, a handsome portico, and other details which reveal a late Regency date. He built other houses at Weston, and it was to the salty baths and sea breezes of the new resort that he brought some of his less afflicted patients for the good of their health.

So one still sees, in such roads as Park Parade with its neat row of Regency villas built, like those off Hill Street at Clevedon, to look down-Channel to the beginnings of Exmoor, that Weston's resort development was well under way before Victoria's accession. Admittedly it had not gone far when in August of 1819 Mrs. Hester Piozzi, Dr. Johnson's old friend and now aged nearly eighty, escaped to Weston, as well she might, from the "stewpot and gridiron" conditions of Bath in late summer. Though the breezes, contrasting with those of her home at such a time, were "most salubrious" she found the little resort "neither gay nor fashionable". Nor had things gone much further in another three years. For when in 1822 Weston's first guide book came out its author noted that, as "health and not dissipation" was Weston's lure, its public amusements, in sharp contrast with what now greets Weston's myriad visitors, were remarkably few.

The 1820s saw such forward moves as the building of a new nave for the church and of the resort's first assembly rooms. But progress remained modest, and in 1841 the little town's people still numbered no more than 2,103. But in a few more years the great change came; as at Brighton what enabled Weston to become a large, 'popular' resort, for Bristol day trippers as well as those wishing to stay longer, was the coming of the railway. The Bristol and Exeter at first had a terminus at Weston branching off from its through line. It lay far deeper towards the seafront than the present station or the excursionists' platforms still known as Locking Road. The battlemented Bristol and Exeter Inn, and the townscape nearly as far as the lower end of High Street still betoken this decisive revolution in Weston's means of access. The arrival of the first Bristol and Exeter trains signalled the way for Weston's great flood of seaside urbanism. Yet at about the same time one more range of buildings went up which belonged, in spirit, to an older tradition. The Royal Crescent was being built in 1847; in some respects it is most distinctive among England's crescents so named. Despite Weston's views down and across the Bristol Channel it looks partly inland, and northwards, towards Worlebury's slopes. Its centre, like that of the Royal Crescent at Cheltenham, is unmarked by any special feature and it is, with its series of giant recessed arches, its continuous, bracketed cornice, and its pierced balconies in an Italianate idiom also seen in Bristol, among the most originally articulated urban features of its own type and shape.

The Royal Crescent gives Weston a dying echo of things Georgian; thereafter the resort grew as an overwhelmingly Victorian, mainly Italianate town. Oriel Terrace, close by the old church, was, indeed surprising both for its lack of oriel windows and for its use, gables, strapwork, mullioned windows and all, of the Elizabethan style for a terrace; the same pheno-menon occurs in parts of Bristol. The churches, inevitably at their time were for the most part Gothic, with Manners and Gill of Bath, Charles Hansom and H. Lloyd of Bristol all represented, and finally Bodley in his exquisite All Saints'. But in the crescent at the upper end of Ellenborough Park, in the massive terrace blocks round and beyond the sheltered retreat of Madeira Cove, and up above the 100-foot contour in the villadom and terraced ponderosities of Weston's more secluded residential zone, stylistic degeneration and mock-Italian detail held full sway. Weston, like most of England's seaside towns, is a paradise for sleuths after whimsy and Victoriana. By 1859 development had gone far enough for the writer of a Bristol Directory to say that its hillsides were "studded with temples of health and mansions of the rich, and its ocean-bounded valley is thickly covered with handsome habitations".

Modern Weston's outskirts, as befits a town of well over 40,000 people, have spread far inland. But the part of the resort which its visitors know and appreciate is most of it cradled between the villa-studded bluff of Worlebury and the longer, beckoning, somewhat inaccessible promontory of Brean Down. Near the esplanade the firm sands are, as they have long been, a fine resort for walkers, the exercisers of dogs, sunbathers, and children riding donkeys or in quaintly designed little pony carts. Away in the distance towards South Wales, and beyond the scarce perceptible lowtide shoreline of a sea whose colour differs little from that of the sand on which it spreads its burden of Severn silt, the mid-channel islets of Steep Holm and Flat Holm add much to the scene. Flatholm, beyond the deepwater channel and a part of Glamorgan, lies outside my scope. But Steep Holm, chunky, compact, and precipitous, belongs to Somerset and is much prized as a nature reserve. The Bristol Channel's less lofty version of the Bass Rock or Ailsa Craig, it stands as a picturesque sentinel for the narrow reach of the Bristol Channel whose final stages include Newport and Avonmouth, the Severn Bridge, and the lonely estuary above it, with its sparser traffic toiling up to Sharpness and the ship canal to Gloucester.

Weston-super-Mare, like Blackpool or Brighton though on a smaller scale, is essentially a resort of 'popular' attractions; as such it successfully gives pleasure to many thousands who come for the day or to stay for longer spells. Its position makes it an inevitable, and obvious favourite among people in Bristol or Bath, while the Great Western Railway long ago made it a resort easily reached by its many employees in Swindon. At longer range, it is much favoured by holidaymakers from near Birmingham, and Weston is an easy goal for day visitors, from the great Midland conurbation, whose motor coaches have stopped, on the way, at the Clifton Zoo. So the districts along, and just behind its long, curving beach, are gaily crowded with strollers, with those who go, perforce, to bathe in Weston's large swimming pool, or who shop and eat in the town's great variety of shops and restaurants. Tourism, and catering for its visitors, are thus, overwhelmingly, Weston's economic mainstay. But hotels, cafés, and shops are not the whole of Weston's modern story, for it also has its industrial side. Inland, at Locking, near the R.A.F. station, the various concerns installed in a trading estate give a range of work to people who live in or near the resort town. Some of them, like thousands of visitors, came down to Weston from the Birmingham district. Far more of Somerset, and typical of a policy whereby work is taken to the home areas of workers, is out on the main Bristol road where C. and J.

Clark's of Street now have a considerable, well spread factory for the making of shoes.

Though Brean Down comes as the most dramatic southern terminal of the bay at Weston a lesser hill is also prominent as one looks down the esplanade. The low ridge is picturesquely capped by the gaunt, roofless nave, the central tower, and the chancel of a Norman church. This is at Uphill, where the little hill rises boldly above the River Axe, and above the village's own pill which long served as a local harbour. The little inlet may have been a port under the Roman Empire; it was certainly used in the Middle Ages and in more recent times. The church may have been built so that its Norman tower could serve seaward watchers. Another story, like that which applies to other hilltop churches such as that of Brentor near Dartmoor, is that a church was started down in the village, but that the Devil repeatedly moved the stones uphill, thus hoping to make it harder than it should have been for Uphill's inhabitants to perform their religious duties. It certainly proved inconvenient to have a church so placed, the more so when the growth of Weston caused a sympathetic increase in Uphill's parishioners. So in the 1840s a new church, by James Wilson of Bath and a smaller, cheaper version of his church of St. Stephen up Lansdown, was built near the houses of the village, on a lower site near the copse now glorious every spring with its astonishing carpet of bluebells. Up at the old church the chancel and the tower were kept roofed to serve as a cemetery chapel. But in more recent years it has also been used for ordinary services, continuing its career both as an attractive Weston landmark and as a well loved place of worship.

The knoll at Uphill, like Brean Down, is an outlier of the Mendips, that ridge of hills whose continuous range ends above Axbridge but which seems reluctant to die away before reaching the Bristol Channel. Another, and much larger detached massif of the Mendips is Bleadon Hill; one end of it is by now a favoured residential lung of Weston itself, enough suburbanized for the hill to be reckoned not as part of the Mendips but of the Somerset seaboard. Bleadon Hill is itself a beautiful feature of the local landscape. No less attractive, in their more artificial way, are villages nestling round it. Bleadon has its slender church tower and its church nave is graced by one of the late medieval stone pulpits which are specially numerous in this north-western zone of the county. Hutton has its ancient Court, and in the church a Payne brass of 1496 which is better than the Somerset average. Most surprising, in so busy a district, is Christon in its calm, unaltered rusticity; one hardly expects to find a village so little changed, and less populous than it was a century ago before Weston sprawled out.

From Weston's Esplanade Brean Down seems very much a part of the Weston scene, enclosing the bay on its southern side as an essential, protective arm of rock and undulating skyline. Yet its integration with Weston is far from complete. Between it and the beach at Blackrock the muddy, swirling estuary of the Axe severs the down from Weston and Uphill. Easy access to the down is only from the south, across the river by way of Brean whence the narrow promontory takes its name. But that access, once circuitously gained, is infinitely worth the toil. For Brean Down, stabbing out towards Steep Holm and the open water of the Bristol Channel, is like another—and far grander—Sand Point. In its bold projection it surpasses all other stretches of the Somerset coast; it was no wonder that prehistoric man made its readily enclosed tip the site of a hill fort. One element excepted, it recalls many a headland in Devon or Cornwall, and a walker along its ridge, where furze and springy turf ride high above the tidal flats on each side, can forget that below him, at high tide, there is none of the clear water and blue-green iridescence of the more westerly coastline. The muddy sand of Weston Bay and the Berrow Flats is far exposed when the water is out; only at its tip is this most dramatic of Somerset's headlands lastingly washed by the sea. Its views, in every direction, are superb and of an escapist, almost island quality. The down is, as it were, a maritime Dundry in the extreme contrast between its landward views. For to the north one has busy Weston and the suburbs which have sprawled inland towards the railway. Southwards one has a long prospect of dunes and moor country, only in recent years made populous by the bungalows, shacks, and holiday-camps of the Brean and Berrow country.

I cannot pretend that sand dunes are my favourite scenery, least of all when they lead down to sand on which one can play, but off which one cannot enjoyably bathe, and when they are backed, as along the Belgian coast and here at Brean and Berrow, by extremely unattractive buildings. In the years of its solitude, with little behind it but its two old churches and the cottages of its 'unimproved' villages, the Somerset coast between Brean Down and the northern boundary of Burnham must have had a certain lonely charm. Such as it was, that beauty has now largely disappeared. Yet holidays on this unpromising coast are enjoyed by thousands who seek its bungalows and holiday camps, while the dunes themselves do Somerset vital service in the protection which they give to the lush cow pastures of Brent Marsh and of the low country far inland. Those meadows are themselves overtopped, to a height of over 450 feet above the nearby sea, by one of Somerset's most far seen, and noblest, scenic features.

Though Glastonbury Tor, with its tower and its memory of martyrdom, is better known and loved in Somerset, the slightly lower, no less graceful hill of Brent Knoll is known, as a scenic relief in a flat stretch of driving, to millions who pass through the county; it is also more visible than is Glastonbury Tor from across the Channel in South Wales. Below it the busy, too often congested main road of A.38 and the M.5 motorway run close to the hill on its way between the Midlands and the more distant South-West, reminding many Somerset people that here, and in some of the county's more southerly districts theirs is a corridor county between workaday England and its favoured holiday haunts in West Somerset, Devon and Cornwall. For motorists conditions along this road can be intensely trying, most of all during holiday weekends. But for those who live close enough it can prove a goldmine, so that bed and breakfast, the sale of such dainties as Cheddar strawberries and free-range eggs, and the dispensing of food, cool drinks, and tea can be as profitable as the admittedly good farming of England's premier dairy county; the shortness of the intervals between one place of refreshment and another proves how much its through traffic means to Somerset's economy.

Brent Knoll, unsurprisingly crowned by the fine relics of an Iron Age hill fort, is a noble hill, commanding views across to South Wales and back into the depths of Somerset. The two villages at its foot are Brent Knoll (or South Brent), and East Brent where the main road from Weston forms a triangle with that from Bristol and the North. Both villages, along with their

neighbour Lympsham, were once westward outliers of the great
belt of Glastonbury Abbey's estates which almost joined the great
monastery to the sea. Both, as one finds from the valuation of
abbey property made in 1535, were valuable holdings. In both
of their excellent churches one finds references, one complimen-
tary, one satirical, to a monastic past. For at Brent Knoll the
splendid bench-ends of the early sixteenth century display,
among many other subjects, a version of the old fable of the fox
and the geese. Sly Renard is shown preaching to the geese,
dressed not as himself but in the choir vestments of a mitred abbot;
later in the same sequence he is shown shackled in the stocks, and
then being hanged by his erstwhile congregation. At East Brent,
beneath its splendid plaster ceiling dated 1637, the nave has bench-
ends of a similar type. Religious subjects, among them the symbols
of the Evangelists, are here much to the fore, but one also finds
the arms of the abbey, and the initials of Abbot Selwood whose
building venture we have seen at Mells.

Though Burnham has its attractions, especially on a fine
summer evening at high tide, it cannot rank as one of England's
most beautiful seaside towns. Yet its past, and many aspects of its
present, are full of interest; its history ranges from an important
place in agricultural 'improvement', through the story of its
early spa and resort development, to a striking place in Somerset's
railway and shipping history. Added to these, its church has some
sculptural relics hard to equal in their rarity value.

Primeval Burnham must have been as remote and desolate
as the villages just up the coast. Its church is its one medieval relic.
The west tower, simple by Somerset standards but a fine, sturdy
structure, leans over to one side, one assumes from the shifting
of its foundations so close to the sandy dunes. Inside it, the
Jacobean pulpit, and the Georgian brass chandelier by Bayley the
brass founder of Bridgwater are worth noticing; still more so are
the sculptures which now rest at Burnham because a parson of the
parish became Bishop of Rochester.

In the Middle Ages, and in the Georgian period, the Rochester
bishopric was so poorly endowed that its holders often combined
it with some other post. All the Georgian bishops also held the
rich deanery of Westminster. Dr. Walter King, the rector of
Burnham in the last years of the eighteenth century, became

Bishop of Rochester, and therefore also Dean of Westminster, in 1809. His tenure of the deanery was marked by the first of the abbey's nineteenth-century refurnishings. The chosen idiom was early Revival Gothic; the process proved fatal to the great Baroque altarpiece which had, since Queen Anne's time, adorned the choir. So this reredos was dismantled and dispersed. I do not know where most of it went, but Dr. King saw to it that some charming fragments were sent to decorate the chancel at Burnham. Their origin, before their erection at Westminster, is no less interesting than their ultimate story. For they were part of the altarpiece first set up, to Wren's design and under the short régime of James II, in the splendid Catholic chapel which the king built in Whitehall Palace. Grinling Gibbons, and the younger Artus Quellinus of Antwerp, were the carvers. When James lost his throne William and Mary had the reredos moved; its pieces were stored, for a time, at Hampton Court. Then Anne ordered their removal to Westminster. At Burnham the pieces which were once parts of a single composition are now dispersed about the church. But the large angel figures below the tower, the *gloria* of cherub's heads close by them, the group of cherubs surrounding an open Bible, and the exquisite reliefs of censing and acolyte cherubs assisting at High Mass, are all lovely remains from what must once have been the most splendid altar backing put up in post-Reformation England. It is a nice irony that these Catholic carvings now rest but a few miles from the battlefield where his forces' victory gave James II the spell of political security during which he built and fitted out so sumptuous a chapel in his palace in the capital.

With its parish reaching far inland, Burnham long remained poor and primitive. Collinson, or more probably Rack, found the main village bleak and cold, exposed to the winds, and full of "multitudes of rabbits" burrowing among the dunes. A more vivid human picture comes from Burnham's leading eighteenth-century personality. Richard Locke, the compiler of a survey of the whole county not long before his death in 1806, ranks with Rack and John Billingsley as one of those who in his time did most of his county's backward farming. His special achievements were in the five thousand acres of Burnham, where he owned and farmed a considerable holding. His grandfather, so he tells us,

Royal Portbury Dock; cranes and ships
Off Weston: Brean Down and Steepholm

was "the first classical scholar this dreary place was ever known to furnish to Society". His own picture of Burnham as it was about 1750 is one of a primitive, starveacre place. For, as he puts it in his own words, it was still "an inconsiderable parish of poor renters and cottagers, who existed without hot dinners, silk clothing, carriages of pleasure, mahogany furniture, clocks, watches, or even tea kettles, notwithstanding the profusion of these at present". He adds that "the farmers carried their dinners to the markets in their pockets" in the same way that labourers did to the fields in another half century, and that the coats the farmers wore, and their blankets as well, were made of their own wool spun by their wives and daughters. In 1754 the place had been worth 10s. an acre. But after the "planting and agriculture" which Locke, a land surveyor as well as a farmer, gradually introduced into Burnham its value, per acre, was quadrupled. Such was the improved state of pastorally prosperous Burnham on the eve of great changes in its sandy, rabbit-haunted seaward belt.

The man who hastened the next advance in Burnham's prosperity was the curate of its church, neatly combining his sacred duties with the closely joined functions of a lighthouse keeper and of a spa pioneer. For the Rev. David Davies, presumably from the other side of the Bristol Channel, compared the geological strata of Burnham with those of Cheltenham, deducing from his studies that mineral water might exist beneath this village on the Parrett's estuary. He decided to dig wells, hoping to turn the place into a seaside spa; the financing of his researches was unique in the history of spa development. A lighthouse of some kind had long existed at Burnham, guiding ships past the treacherous shoals at the river's mouth. Davies built a new one, and got an Act of Parliament under which he could levy tolls on the ships passing it. He used the money, a good sum in those days of Bridgwater as a much thronged coasting port, to sink his wells. They lay close together, within a hundred yards of the high water mark. One was sulphurous. The other, said to resemble some of Cheltenham's waters, was saline chalybeate. Opinions on their virtues differed widely. One writer mentioned the "active medicinal properties" of one of the springs. But another, presumably referring to the sulphur well, compared its smell to that

Weston-super-Mare: Royal Crescent
Church into house: Woodspring Priory

of a cess-pool blended with bad horseradish. Here, however, were Burnham's beginnings as a resort, and a group of villas built near the church came to be known as Daviesville. The villas, and Steart House which served as a bath house, survive, along with some simple Regency terraces of Burnham's more predictable growth as a seaside resort. But Burnham's chief expansion, as one sees from many of its buildings, was a Victorian affair, and the town still gives the pleasures of sea air and fine views to many who come both for the day and to stay longer.

At each end of Burnham one can still recall its maritime importance.

In 1815 the Rev. David Davies leased out his lighthouse. Trinity House was now interested in it, and at its instance some improvements were made. Later on they took over the lighting of Bridgwater's sea approach. A survey was made, and in 1832 a new lighthouse, tall and graceful, was built out to the north of what was now a growing resort. This lighthouse, and another on wooden piers at the water's edge close below the dunes, do duty today. The slender white tower, with a charming pair of flanking cottages built to house its keepers, is a nice piece of essentially Georgian design.

A slipway, at the southern end of Burnham's esplanade and aligned to the course of the railway which came in 1858, is the last relic of what was once an important maritime venture. The railway was the Somerset Central, the first element in what soon became the blue-engined Somerset and Dorset. Plans for a tidal harbour and commercial docks at Burnham came to nothing, though this aspect of the line's business long flourished, not far away, at Highbridge. But a passenger service, in a series of paddle steamers ending in a two-funnelled ship, was kept up, between the Parrett and South Wales, for some thirty years. It connected directly with Burnham's railway terminus; here and there in the slipway embedded lengths of railway line show how trucks were hauled up and down between the station and the waiting boats.

Highbridge must rank as one of the least attractive places in Somerset; for thousands it is but a bottleneck incident in their toilsome crawl along A.38. It is, however, an interesting though repulsive town. It once played a key part in the county's water and rail communications. Its industry, divided between timber yards, its well-known brick and tile works, and the new factory used, by Morlands of Glastonbury, for the making of sheepskin slippers and pram covers, still makes it a busy place. More interesting, once a visitor finds them, are the relics of Highbridge's activity as a port, and of its canal and railway links with the great tract of low land between the Mendips and the Poldens.

What made Highbridge was its site at the mouth of the Brue, whose channel long split it between the parishes of Burnham and of Huntspill. The bridge was really a dam which gave the hamlet its name; at high tide the water on its seaward side was far higher, when the sluices were shut, than the Brue's fresh water just inland. Seagoing coasters, such as had long come to the place by Locke's time, caused travellers much astonishment when their keels, under such conditions, lay almost level with the road. Ships of 80 tons came regularly; as the nineteenth century progressed the scope of their usefulness was greatly enlarged by the easier distribution of the coal and other heavy goods which they brought in from Bristol or South Wales.

The first move was the cutting, through the peaty levels, of the Glastonbury Canal which came out, through the old channel of the Brue, to a new and larger wharf at Highbridge. Opened in 1833, and greeted with joyous ceremonies at Glastonbury, it was a late-comer to the canal system and its time of prosperity was short. Coal, manufactured goods, iron, and salt went inland, while from central Somerset came the expected products of elm timber for floors, corn, cider, and cheese, particularly 'Caerphilly' which came to be much liked by Welsh miners for sandwiches eaten down in the pits. But the Bristol and Exeter Railway soon bought the canal, transferring its interest, when new railway developments were afoot, to the newly projected inland line of the Somerset Central. The new railway, superseding the canal and linking the Avalon country both to the Bristol and Exeter Railway and to the Bristol Channel, opened in 1854. The Clarks of Street, anxious for a better transport outlet for their growing business, were prominent among its backers. Highbridge became an important place on the line, keeping much of its position after the Somerset Central became part of the far larger system of the Somerset and Dorset. It was there, till well within living memory, that the Somerset and Dorset repaired its blue engines.

The coasting port near the mouth of the Brue also became a centre of the railway's maritime ambitions. The old mouth of the river was widened out in a long, narrow harbour, a shipping point for such firms as Ritson's the timber merchants, Burnett's the importers of wines and spirits, and John Prior Estlin who was, in 1875, a coal merchant and a maker of bricks, tiles, and drain-pipes. The Estlins were related to the Bagehots, the family involved in the well-known trading concern of Stuckey and Bagehot, based on Langport and deeply concerned with the whole of central Somerset's system of waterborne trade. High-bridge was a natural focus of their interest; it was no accident that Stuckey's was, in 1875, the only bank with a branch in the town. Their building, Gothic, ornate for such a place, and tacti-cally placed at the harbour end of the main street, continues as the Westminster Bank.

The ships which visited Highbridge carried cargoes, like those once freighted along the canal. In the 1930s the railway gave up its shipping interests. But for a few more years, through the Second World War and until 1948, Highbridge remained a coasting port. Its harbour, long and narrow with its wharf on what was once the railway side, lies mud-clogged, forlorn, and overgrown, a sad reminder of past maritime activity. The railway station, with a few stopping trains in what was once its Great Western part, is little less forlorn. For the Somerset and Dorset works function no more, and that railway's portion of the station lies smashed and derelict.

Past Highbridge, on A.38 or along the verge of the Parrett Huntspill and Pawlett are the last places before the seaward end of the Polden range. Near Huntspill the main road and the railway cross what is, bar the Chew Valley lake, the most striking sheet of water added, in the last few years, to Somerset's land-scape. The broad, straight channel of the Huntspill River, run-ning straight into the lowland distance with Glastonbury Tor rising away at its end, is the most ambitious, and among the most useful, achievements of an organization which is vital to the prosperity of central Somerset—the Somerset River Authority. Along with the far older King's Sedgemoor Drain, it is Somerset's equivalent of the old and new Bedford Rivers which combine below Earith, to divert the Ouse's waters straight across the Fens.

A little way to the south Pawlett, with one of Somerset's best Norman doorways in the church which lies not quite on the top of its low hillock, looks far over the meanderings of the tidal Parrett and the riverine flats of Pawlett Hams. The river, the main road, and the railway soon converge at Dunball, whose modern wharf is an outlier of the port of Bridgwater and the place where much of its trade, notably in timber shipped in trim Dutch or Scandinavian motor coasters, is done. Here one has the outlet of yet another of the great drainage channels which take water from what were once the most drowned of the moors. Above the last reach of the King's Sedgemoor Drain the steep, pleasingly wooded slope is that of the last stretch of the Polden Hills, calling us inland, from the roar of modern traffic pounding along A.38, to Somerset's quieter heartland.

CHAPTER VI

THE MENDIPS

AN orographical map shows that the main ridge of the Mendips runs, without any pronounced dip in its height, from Cranmore Tower to a point well west of Blackdown. The same continuous elevation is clear from such a distant vantage point as the roof level of Bath's hilltop University. Yet eastern and western Mendip differ widely, both in the nature of their summit country-side and in the slopes by which their top ridge is climbed. In eastern Mendip the countryside is altogether more gentle, more restrained in its mien and less fiercely precipitous in its approach, than in the high plateau which is best reached up the dramatic, rocky valleys of Cheddar Gorge and Burrington Combe.

South from Cranmore tower some streams flow down, in a delectable set of quiet little valleys, to form the Alham River which itself goes on to swell the Brue. Batcombe is the best village in this placid, little known countryside. It lies tucked away among the hills north of Bruton, with a splendid church tower which is unusual among those in the county of any similar quality. For its parapet, though pierced and traceried, is plainly squared off, lacking the crown of pinnacles which, in a county so supremely rich in such splendours, normally comes as the cul-minating glory of a tower with its niches, 'engaged' pinnacles, and windows delicately fretted to let out the sound of bells. Dairy and arable farming both flourish among these kindly, southward-looking slopes and valleys of eastern Mendip, and as the soil is lighter, and less alluvially rich, than in the drained moors and lush pastures in the middle of Somerset, the county's best cheese farms are here in the rolling countryside between Wells and Wincanton.

One village in this eastern Mendip country is more famed for quarries than for cheese. Doulting lies, noisily enough, on the main highway from Shepton Mallet to Frome. The Victorians heavily restored, and indeed largely rebuilt its church. But it remains of much architectural importance, not only for its exquisite porch whose gable outline resembles that at Mells, but for a feature not uncommon in Somerset, an octagonal central tower with a spire above it. Close at hand, a noble medieval barn stands witness to the manorial owners of Doulting for over eight hundred years. From the fields not far beyond it a view runs clear, between the Mendip slopes and the quiet hill country of Ditcheat and the Pennards, to Glastonbury on whose abbey Doulting long depended.

As far back as the eighth century King Ine of Wessex gave Doulting to the monastery of Glastonbury; the gift came as a memorial to St. Aldhelm the king's nephew, who had died at Doulting. From then onwards, and till Henry VIII's great dispersal of monastic estates, the manor of Doulting remained among the many Somerset possessions of the county's greatest abbey. But Doulting, like Dundry among the estates of the Bishop of Bath and Wells, was in one respect unusual. Many of its assets lay in the great quarries north of the village centre. Collinson speaks of them; he refers to their "fine white freestone like that of Bath, but harder". From Doulting's deposits the creamy white stone, surely among the loveliest ever cut in England, was taken down to build Wells Cathedral where one still sees it, and for work (as late as the very eve of its dissolution) on the abbey at Glastonbury and in many parish churches of the district. The barn, now Doulting's main relic of a long Benedictine mastery, was built to store the crops of a reasonably wealthy farmland.

Shepton Mallet, nestling close beneath its hills and cut through, in its lower parts, by the Doulting Water (sometimes misnamed the Sheppey) which once turned the wheels of numerous fulling mills, is among the chief settlements of the Mendip foothills; despite various endeavours, new building activity, and schemes for central redevelopment, it has something of a fight to keep its present prosperity equal to that of a now distant past. Bar the parish church, with its superb wagon roof and the adornment of a western tower which is, most probably, the earliest of Somerset's great Perpendicular towers, and the early Tudor Market Cross with its arcading late Georgian in its refashioning* Shepton's central area has no really outstanding buildings. Yet there is no questioning its great character, or its attraction as a stone-built country town.

Historical records, and architectural details in its church's nave, prove that Shepton was of some note well back in the Middle Ages. Its certain origins are Anglo-Saxon, and it has its place in Domesday. But what made the town, and what must have helped its people to get ahead of their neighbours in the building of a truly splendid late medieval church tower, was the cloth trade. The early weavers worked, of course, in cottages almost anywhere in the town; the finishing mills had to be placed, at intervals in the town itself and down as far as Bowlish, along the clear, swift-flowing Doulting Water running down on its way from the Mendips to the moors.

Like Frome and other places on their Mendip streams, Shepton had a long, full career as a clothmaking town. Its clothiers were the men who finished the church and built fine Georgian houses in the town and, better still, down at Bowlish. Many of Shepton's weavers and tuckers turned out for Monmouth; the town was one of the two in Somerset to be twice occupied, briefly on each occasion, by the scratch force of the claimant duke. Shepton prospered in the Georgian period, and its store of buildings was enriched by some good Nonconformist chapels and by the charming church, with 'churchwarden' Gothic windows in the priest's house which was more easily perceived from the road than the actual chapel, of a Catholic mission which had got started in the 1760s; till its recent replacement by an unattractive successor it was the county's oldest place of Catholic worship.

But Shepton's road access, like that of many other English towns better conditioned to animal transport than to that plied in vehicles, remained steep and primitive. Then in 1826, in the turnpike heyday when the convenience of stage coaches was well served by the buildings of hundreds of miles of easily graded roads, Shepton's townscape was much changed when the viaduct known as Town Bridge was built, to bring in a new stretch of road from Cheltenham and Bath, and to span the town's valley

---

* The work was actually done as late as 1841.

at a level much higher than that of the stream and the picturesque old streets below its arches. Clothmaking by now was in its last agonies in Shepton. Pigot's Directory of 1830 speaks, indeed, of some "respectable clothing establishments" still at work in the town. But the depression of the local cloth trade, and "severe injury" from Yorkshire were also admitted, while Pigot's pages also mention the crêpe trade, and silk throwing, which were to give some further boost to local prosperity. In another dozen years Shepton's cloth trade was dead. But there, and at Croscombe a few miles down the valley, crêpe, silk, and finely knitted hosiery became the substitutes for woollen cloth. Yet these were never so strikingly successful as cloth had been in its best days; one gets the impression of Victorian Shepton as a struggling, somewhat stagnant place. The prison, first built in the town under the early Stuarts but imposingly enlarged after the closure of the noisome, riverside gaol at Ilchester, brought an element of new work and activity to one steeply sloping part of Shepton. After a spell when it housed Army prisoners it is now used again for civil offenders. In the 1860s the lumpy, incongruous pile of the brewery which duly became the 'Anglo-Bavarian' added notably to the varied brewing facilities of the little town whose first railway had reached it a few years before. As it happens, the local brewing trade has continued to give work to the people of Shepton Mallet.

Modern Shepton, with some 5,600 people, is a busier place than it must have been late last century or in the 1930s. Most of the motor traffic running down from the Midlands, or from the Bristol area, towards the South Coast avoids the town centre, cutting through Shepton's eastern fringe on its way to the well-known crossroads of Cannard's Grave. Downstream from the town centre, some slopes in the Hillmead area have lately been filled, in the worthy interest of better housing and hygiene, with some blocks of flats, of white brick and with a boldly 'contemporary' skyline, which would be in keeping with some totally modern districts but which are severely unsympathetic to their sub-Mendip setting. In the very middle of the town demolition has emptied a considerable space, and some sort of rebuilding is needed both to house the local authority and to make Shepton a better shopping centre both for its own people and for those who come in from many villages round. But sharp controversy has raged over the precise details of the new buildings proposed, and the Government has rejected one plan of renovation put forward. Yet whatever happens one must assume, and demand, that such striking features as the church, the market cross, and the small relic of the wooden shambles still surviving, somewhat mournfully, in the market place will be preserved, with their pleasing effects enhanced.

Shepton people, joined in their places of work by many others from villages not far away, make their living in ways very different from those which were the town's mainstay two centuries ago. Though the town is busy it has been a struggle to keep its prosperity steady. Closures of some trades have made way for new activities in the same buildings—egg-processing instead of bacon-curing for instance, and a variety of occupations (including book storage) in the small trading estate now housed in what was at one time the lager-brewing Anglo-Bavarian brewery. C. and J. Clark's, in a spread-out factory on the town's southern fringe, are the largest local employers, and Shepton has gained greatly from the beneficent process whereby their manufacturing work has been spread all over Somerset. But the best known concern in Shepton, for some years the headquarters of a large commercial empire now being merged into a yet larger grouping, is the factory given over to the preparation of the widely popular drink known as Babycham.

Five years after Queen Victoria had come to the throne Pigot's Directory, in a section dealing with Shepton Mallet, listed Francis Showering as a beer-seller in Garston Street, that long highway of weavers' houses leading out towards the town's eastern fringe; in this street, by a happy chance, the firm developed by his descendants has bought and restored many ancient properties. Samuel, the father of Francis Showering, combined shoemaking and innkeeping; for the second purpose his place of business was the 'Sun' in the Market Place. By 1848 Francis Showering, as the licensee of another inn facing the market, had moved closer to his father. But he soon moved out, to the 'Ship' in Kilver Street, to the eastern area of Shepton which became the scene of his family's wider, yet long modest activities. There, in a few more years and on a site facing the road running out to Cannard's Grave, he built the small brewery whence Showerings, for another eighty years, supplied a few inns and some private customers. An arch of last century still led, in 1967, to the old brewing premises, the inscription "KILVER STREET BREWERY" still faced the road, and on the adjoining house a plaque dated 1860, and with the initials FMS, suggest the time when the Showering family added brewing to innkeeping.

Till after the Second World War the Kilver Street brewery remained a very small concern. Cider had by then joined beer among the firm's products, and their service direct to customers had caused the addition, to the Showerings' assets, of a small fleet of motor lorries. Only in the 1950s did the business embark on the expansion which led to nationwide fame, and to a great visual transformation of the Garston Street and Kilver Street area of Shepton Mallet.

Showerings' massive buildings, unattractive but essential if over three million bottles of Babycham are to be made each week, run far back on each side of Garston Street. Above the road one finds the logical sequence whereby the perry pears are delivered and pulped, with their juice kept in two tiers of stupendous storage vats, each one of enough bulk to hold 12,500 gallons. The fermented juice is then ready to be piped under the road to the lower buildings where the equally streamlined sequence of dilution, filtering, agitation, bottling, and sealing is carried out before the myriads of little bottles go out to the drinkers of Babycham. The lighter side is seen in the section of the premises lying north of Garston Street. For there, in a paddock, the factory's visitors can see a herd of dainty little chamois frisking about in the un-Alpine surroundings of the Mendip slopes.

Though Showerings output at Shepton is vast, and though the scale of the buildings, and of the machinery, is appropriately imposing the production of Babycham needs astonishingly few workers. Those who work in the factory at Shepton only slightly exceed 200, so that Showerings are a much smaller local employer than C. and J. Clark's. Of those who do produce Babycham, or who are based on Shepton and drive the firm's numerous lorries, many more come in (as people do to Clark's shoe factory) from such nearby villages as Ditcheat and Evercreech, while Showerings, like Clark's, provide motor buses for those who do not journey in their own cars. Across the road from the factory are the oldest of the buildings whence Showerings administer a commercial empire far wider than what they have in Shepton Mallet itself. In Somerset the cider works at Nailsea, the making of British wines in what was once a small cider factory at Marston Magna, and the growing of their own perry pears in six orchards dispersed in the southern reaches of the county are controlled from buildings whose condition, and whose surroundings, are a great credit to the firm, and to the way in which it has used ample funds for the preservation, and enhancement, of what Shepton has kept from its vanished transport routes and its industrial past.

Showerings' offices and works are not far from where the Doulting Water flows into the town. Any mill on such a site would have had an advantage over those lower down that valuable stream. So a fine late Georgian mill, with a cupola atop, straddles the stream a little above the main road. The mill may have been that of the clothiers Esau and John Chamberlain, listed in the Directory of 1830 as carrying on their trade in Kilver Street; up at one side a fine house, with mullioned back and side windows but with a Georgian façade, could have been the mill-owner's home. Like others in Shepton this Kilver Street mill turned over to crêpe when the town's clothing trade collapsed. More recently Showerings bought it, and put it admirably in order to serve as their offices. More attractive still, and well showing how modern commercial buildings can scenically be linked to the relics of older transport and industry, is their handling of the site above the mill. For the two millponds, with a boat-house on the brink of the upper one, have been treated, as in Georgian industrial estates like those at Warmley and Longfords in Gloucestershire, as 'ornamental water'. Lawns, shrubs, and rockeries attractively surrounded them, and an old circular dove-house survives in the ensemble. More strikingly, the upper lawns are diversified by some of the sturdy piers and arches of the Charlton Viaduct, widened to allow for double track, which till recent years dramatically carried the Bath extension of the Somer-set and Dorset Railway as it curved round Shepton on its great climb up to Masbury on the main Mendip ridge.

Downstream towards Wells the charming village of Cros-combe looks towards Shepton rather than to the little cathedral city. It gets its place, along with Shepton, in the early Victorian directories giving details on such tradesmen as hosemakers and silk throwsters; from its days of prosperity as a clothing village its fortunes were intertwined with those of Bowlish and Shepton. Nowadays, with its clear stream and several ancient, stone-built houses, it is a more appealing place than Shepton. But its real glory lies not in its old houses, or even in the good medieval architecture, and the stone spire, of its church. For Croscombe is one of several places in Somerset where the church's early Stuart embellishment is rarer, and of more note, than what survives from before the Reformation. Some of the pews are Jacobean, and the heavily canopied pulpit is dated 1616—the year when Shakespeare died. The screen, with crudely Baroque elements like those also found in a screen at Bridgwater, towers up in an imposing fret of arches, obelisks, and strapwork; the royal arms, gaily tinctured, shine down from the honoured place which would, in a medieval screen, have gone to the Rood.

North of Doulting's quarries, and below the long, straight road which runs along the Mendip ridge, there lies a tangled, broken countryside of steep valleys whose streams go to feed the Frome. Here are the sad Nettlebridge valley, with its long abandoned coal mines, and the many civil engineering relics, well tracked and recorded by Robin Atthill, of the frustrated canal which should have carried the coal of these parts to customers in Frome and Dorset. It is a countryside well studded with villages once populous with miners. Its greatest charm lies in a delectable spot well away from the main, more modern population centre of its own parish. Holcombe's old church is still, as in Collinson and Rack's time, "romantically situated in a circular hollow, on the brow of a very deep valley". Though lonely, set apart, and not very often used it is in good order. As at Cameley near the source of the Cam Brook its supersession, in the modern village, by a much later building has spared it the horrors of a Victorian outscouring, so that George I's arms, a gallery, some box pews with a row of hatpegs, and the Commandments, Creed, and Lord's prayer well painted, in 1817, by James Emery of Wells, all survive from its sober Hanoverian ordering. Holcombe old church lies deep in a very peaceful scene; as one walks over from the line of the Fosse Way the quiet air resounds, at the times of Sanctus, consecration, and

Angelus, with deep booms from the high tower of the Mendip country's greatest modern wonder.

Despite the stream which rises there, and rattles down towards Snail's Bottom and Radstock, the somewhat unattractive upland village of Stratton-on-the-Fosse is the last place where medieval monks, with their need for fishponds, millstreams, and the disposal of effluents, would have located a monastery. But for reasons other than those which determined the sites of our ancient abbeys, Stratton has, since the Regency, been the site of what has now become the most imposing monastic grouping in England. Though Glastonbury lies wrecked and empty of the black monks who once built and adorned it, here at Downside that great Somerset abbey is, in a manner, revived by the present-day Benedictines of their Order's English Congregation.

The community now worshipping and working at Downside goes back to St. Gregory's Priory, at Douai in northern France. This was among the monasteries and friaries set up, on the Continent, in penal times. The French Revolution, driving these 'refugee' groups of monks, friars and nuns from the Continent, gave them the chance to resume their religious life in late Georgian England where the Catholics had now gained a wide measure of tolerance. At first, and in some cases for a long time, these English monks and nuns from abroad had to settle in properties made available by families among the Catholic gentry. This was first true of the Benedictines of St. Gregory's, and of the pupils of the school which they kept for the sons of such families. For some years they were in Shropshire, in a mansion put at their disposal by Mrs. Fitzherbert's relatives, the Smythes of Acton Burnell; hence the name Smythe for one of the present houses of Downside School. But in 1814 they came, by purchase, to their present territory, buying the seventeenth-century mansion of Mount Pleasant at Stratton-on-the-Fosse, in a countryside where there was no nearer Catholic congregation than the one at Shepton Mallet. From that single house, and from the important, Early English conventual additions soon made to the designs of Goodridge of Bath, the large sprawling buildings of the monastery and of the school have gradually accumulated.

Like the site of the abbey, the ground plan of the buildings at Downside is quite unmedieval. Not only did the monastic buildings grow piecemeal, in a situation far removed from that which went with the building of such genuinely medieval monasteries as Bath, Muchelney, and Glastonbury, but there was a factor, most relevant at Downside and the other Benedictine monasteries of modern England, which hardly applied in the centuries before the great dissolution by Henry VIII. Before the Reformation the activities of the Benedictines were almost wholly those of the choir and the cloister, though much modified, for the richest abbots, by the claims of politics, and of estate management for those who held certain offices in the communities. Teaching, except for the training of novices, and of a few boys whose singing diversified that of the monastic choirs, was no part of the duty carried out by the Benedictines, or by other monks. But the circumstances of penal times, and of post-penal Catholicism, led them both to the keeping of important schools, and to the serving of parish missions both close to their abbeys and in more distant places, Liverpool for instance and Beccles in Suffolk in the case of Downside. So apart from the great church, itself shared by the monks and the boys, most of the many buildings at Downside are there because of the school, with lay masters as well as monks on its teaching staff.

The feeling of Downside blends ordered, devotional quiet with the carefree clatter of a no less ordered school community. The monastery block, the more solemn cloister passages, and the monks' refectory have their more relaxed counterpart in the classrooms, the buildings for entertainment and recreation, and the linked boarding houses of the school. Still in a key position, commanding from its windows the main courtyard of the school buildings, the mullioned late Stuart mansion was once a somewhat gloomy place, but has been well renovated to house such things as the school office and the quarters of the headmaster. Alone among Downside's older buildings it stands a little outside the high Gothic tradition. But for connoisseurs of nineteenth-century buildings, and of the more tasteful work which followed Victorianism, Downside is a choice delight. Goodridge, Charles and Edward Hansom, Garner, Walters, Comper, Leonard Stokes in school buildings whose design and detail are particularly good, and Giles Scott are all represented. More recent buildings for the school, and a new library for the monastery's fine, hitherto dispersed collection of books and records are by Lord Esher and Mr. Francis Pollen.

But the heart and centre of Downside, immensely impressive in its solemn peace, is the great vaulted church which must rank among England's grandest works of the Gothic Revival; not everyone realizes that in size it exceeds Truro Cathedral and some smaller English cathedrals surviving from before the Reformation. Here in the main structure, and in the varied chapels, is some sort of modern version, cleaner, better lit, and better heated than in olden times, of what Glastonbury and St. Mary's at York may have been before their wreckage at the Reformation. It may be copyist Gothic, but in the local conditions it is wholly convincing. Yet in one respect Downside Abbey has always parted company from the arrangements of a great medieval cathedral or abbey church. Being used, simultaneously on such occasions as Sunday High Mass, alike by the boys and the monks of a fairly large resident community its nave and its choir limb are opened out into a long, narrow, single unit; in this respect a sub-divided church like Gloucester Cathedral or that at Wells is closer to the original. But an important reordering has now been carried out to make the great church more conveniently usable under liturgical conditions which include services in English and a closer participation, by all present, in the action of the Liturgy The High Altar has been moved closer to the crossing, and the monks' choir and the abbot's throne fill what was once the spacious sanctuary. Strenuous efforts are being made, in these post-conciliar days, to make the best of a geometrically awkward worshipping space. More fortunate, one feels, will be the Benedictines of Downside's one-time dependent monastery at Worth in Sussex, where a new, and still unfinished, circular church presupposes, from the beginning, liturgical conditions for which neither medieval nor pseudo-medieval churches were ever laid out.

Beyond Downside the Mendip countryside stretches on, past the quarrying village of Gurney Slade, and past Old Down Inn with its memories of Parson Woodforde, of hungry and thirsty travellers by chaise and stage coach, and of the regular gatherings, at so convenient and hospitable a crossroads, of such bygone personages as country justices and parish overseers. Not far away is the lonely, high-set, well kept church of Emborough, while the

Mendip scene: Crook Peak
Mendip scene: behind Cheddar

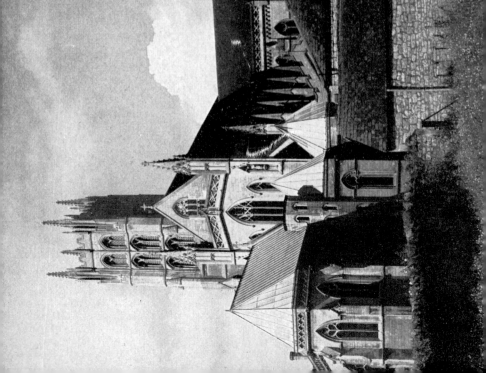

Emborough ponds are natural sheets of water, not a reservoir. They are better shrouded with trees, and more picturesque in the accepted manner, than one would expect in such a landscape, or from the exposed, windy fields of this plateau country. The plateau slopes easily down, to Ston Easton with its massive Georgian mansion all glorious, inside, with fine Rococo plaster-work of the Bristol school, and to Chewton Mendip where the village nestles snugly in the consolation of its dip in a bleak landscape. But its church, with a superb tower, built soon after 1500 and among the best and most elaborate in North Somerset, stands high on its hillside so that its pinnacles at least can be seen from afar. Here in Chewton the very ancient family of the Waldegraves made their home. Their primevally simple arms, *party argent and gules*, adorn the famous heraldic roll which bears their name and appear on the signboard of Chewton's inn. Here, and to the south of the village, we reach the line of the easy stage coach road from Wells to Bristol; beyond it, for our later exploration, is the 'gruffy' territory of the old lead mines of Western Mendip.

The main road from Croscombe to Wells skirts Dinder, where a watercourse charmingly lines the one-sided village street, and the pastoral, unravaged side of Dulcote Hill whose southern flank is frightfully marred, and veritably eaten away, by what must surely be one of England's most offensive quarries. Yet from one end of this ridge there is the most romantic, theme-setting view of the four towers, and the Victorian church spire, which rise over the distinct districts of Somerset's cathedral city.

No place in England has so utterly the atmosphere of traditional cathedral calm as Wells. It was something of an accident that it ever became the seat of a bishopric. For when in 909 the large diocese of Sherborne was split up, and when a Somerset diocese was created it was a considerable problem to find a central and convenient headquarters for the new bishop. Glastonbury was in monastic occupation. Somerton, though central, must have seemed small and remote. Bridgwater did not, as yet, exist, and Taunton was firmly in the possession of the bishop of Winchester. So this country site, under the lee of the Mendips, was chosen; the copious streams whence the new city took its name amply furnished these Anglo-Saxon cathedral clergy with a pure and limpid water supply. The later history of the bishopric,

Modern Gothic; Downside Abbey
Medieval Gothic; Wells Cathedral

and of its cathedral, was not wholly smooth. For a time Wells lost its status to Bath; only in the thirteenth century, after a ding dong struggle, did things settle down to the joint bishopric of Bath and Wells, with Wells the cathedral more favoured by most of its bishops. The clergy at Wells, as one can still tell from the spacious Close and from the loose disposition of their residences, were secular canons, bound neither to dwell together nor even to keep continued residence.

The cathedral quarter of Wells, with its mellow stonework and great lawn, hemmed in by gateways and crowned by its three towers, is wondrous in its quiet, lightly motorized perfection. The cathedral, unlike most of those in England which have come down from before the Reformation but in this respect like those of Lichfield and Salisbury, is wholly Gothic, superseding whatever cathedral may have served Somerset before about 1190. It was built on a modest scale, being a smaller church than that of Glastonbury Abbey; it survives, nowadays, as the chief medieval building in Somerset. The early Gothic of its transepts, of the oldest part of the choir, and of the first bays of the nave, is historically important as well as being most beautiful in the clustered piers and moulded arches of its arcades, in the carven delicacy of its capitals, and in the creamy purity of Doultings stone. For here, and not in the slightly later, more uniform cathedral at Salisbury, we have the first cathedral in England whose design, from the time when the masons first worked on it, was wholly Gothic. The nave's western bays are later than those next to the central crossing. The western façade, as spectacular as its builders meant it to be, is much admired, despite the insignificance of its doorways and the somewhat blatant way in which it comes less as a logical ending to the nave's structure than as an operatic showpiece for its tiers of canopied statues; above it the two early Perpendicular towers, subtly different yet designed as a pair, fit a little awkwardly above the older design. More awkward still, though structurally ingenious and splendid from outside is the central tower put up in the fourteenth century. More fascinating, to my mind, than its beauties of detail are the devices whereby the masonry below it was stiffened to take some thousands of tons of stone never intended to press down on the central piers. Some arches of the adjacent arcades were made narrower, and

at the triforium level the masonry was stiffened and filled in.
Above all, one had the famous, technically effective, yet unlovely
inverted arches (or St. Andrew's arches from the cathedral's
dedication) which span three of the crossing arches and emphasize
the division of such a church, beneath a single roof, into two main
worshipping spaces.

More delicately beautiful is the eastern limb, with a complex,
unifying vault to cover the rectangular choir whose real composition, as at Lichfield, is that of a short early Gothic choir lengthened
out at a time of more elaborate architecture and cleverly joined,
in work of pure delight and brilliantly unified space, to what was
at first, a separate, elongated octagon of a Lady chapel. Here in
its easternmost fastness, amid a wealth of thin columns, vaulting
ribs, bosses, and secluded chapels, is the most delicate master
work of Wells Cathedral. Incidental, and of much interest, are
the tombs and the cagelike chantries, the glass of the fourteenth
century, the modern, largely heraldic tapestry of the stall-backs,
and the quaint, yet sculpturally sophisticated misericord carvings
beneath the seats in the choir.

The moated palace, and the associate buildings of this gem
among the secular cathedrals, are what give Wells its specially
Barchesterian charm and its lovable renown. The palace, fortified,
with its great ruined hall, its chapel, and its early Gothic main
living block, tells clearly of the feudal standing of the prelates
whose prestige, and whose well scattered residential manors, made
them barons as well as bishops. No less famous than the defences
are the swans which glide round the moat, and whose readiness
for a dole from the porter makes them raise their beaks to sound
the gateway's bell. Visitors from all over the world have admired
them, not least the American soldiers who were in Somerset not
long before D-Day; some of them 'guessed' that these Wells
swans were as 'cute' as anything they ever saw in England. Nor
are modern tourists the only people who have seen how 'cutely'
these swans ask for their snacks. For some old glass now at
Nailsea Court suggest that the birds have been at their tricks at
least for five hundred years.

The cloisters at Wells serve none of the vital purposes of those
built to link the domestic buildings of monasteries. They do not
even connect the cathedral with its chapter house. For this

splendid octagonal room, on an early crypt, is on the church's northern side, up steps which Bishop Bekynton conveniently prolonged to reach the covered corridor, above the Chain Gate, which gave constant access to the houses of the vicars choral. The deanery, the one-time archdeaconry with a very early wheel window in one end wall, and the other houses in the Liberty and near the cathedral are what one can expect in the precincts of a non-monastic cathedral. So too, as at Lichfield, Chichester, and Hereford, is Vicars' Close. But the sheer quality and atmosphere of this housing area for minor clerics, wholly practical in its taut planning yet dreamily secluded, and ethereally quiet in our rushing age, puts the buildings erected for the College of Vicars Choral at Wells in a place of esteem which is all its own. It is sensed as one strolls past its Georgianized medieval houses, revelling in its almost car-free peace and stopping to caress the placid cats, Siamese or otherwise, which can loll content on the walls of its little gardens.

Yet despite their delights the Vicars' Closes of such cathedrals as Hereford and Wells are late medieval witnesses of the breakdown of a system which was started in optimism but which historic circumstances nearly turned into a farce. The theory was that the canons of these cathedrals should reside for most or all of their time; only in their separate eating and sleeping would they much differ from communities of monks. But as things turned out many who drew the incomes of their canonries resided only at long intervals or not at all. The money from many canonries swelled the incomes of ambitious clerics, or financed the non-ecclesiastical activities of ordained court officials or civil servants. But the choir services in the cathedrals had still to be kept up. So the absent canons' places were taken, often permanently, by the *vicarii chorales*. Not all of these chanters needed to be priests, and some were in minor orders. But priests or not, they needed housing. At first they were in lodgings, peppered about the towns. Better order and discipline came when they were gathered together, in 'colleges' or unified living places, which one found in the cities of 'secular' cathedrals. Here at Wells the college arrangement was started, in 1348, by Bishop Ralph de Salopia. The hall and the lodgings came first. The chapel, the library above it, and various improvements to the vicars' houses,

came later. There were two ways in which one could set about
such a job. The Close could be laid out, as in Hereford and in the
quads or courts of Oxford or Cambridge colleges, on a more or
less square plan. More often the little houses were put on each
side of a long, narrow enclosure. This, as thousands know, was
how the task was carried out at Wells. Bishop Bubwith, about
1420, had the front gardens screened off. Despite many changes
in such items as doorways and windows the effect of the Close
is still that of a carefully planned street; in its own town the work
foreshadowed the important medieval terrace of the *nova opera*
with which that prolific builder Bishop Bekynton tidied up one
side of the market place.

The cathedral's towers at Wells are not the only ones in the
city, nor are they, to my mind, as satisfying as the superb western
tower of the city's one medieval parish church. St. Cuthbert's
is, by dedication, a strange Northumbrian exotic here in deepest
Wessex. It was, from an early date, a large, important building,
much transformed in the fifteenth century when its early Gothic
arcades were heightened and when the clerestory windows, and
the splendid roof, now gay again with bold colouring, were
placed above the nave. This was also the time, with the city's
clothworkers a prosperous body, when the church's noble
western tower was built, sturdy in plan, brilliantly vertical in
the continued upward rise of its panelling and windows, aestheti-
cally successful because here, as in Somerset's other western towers,
a new composition, with its whole height from the churchyard
to the top of its pinnacles was readily seen from almost every angle
of vision.

Many old houses, picturesquely medieval and Tudor, or more
disciplined in the dignity of their Georgian fronts, stand close to
the cathedral quarter and in the quiet Liberties north of it. The
inns, the cafés, and the curio and postcard shops combine to give
the atmosphere one most associates with a cathedral town. Wells,
moreover, with between seven and eight thousand people, has
remained smaller than England's other old cathedral cities.
Tucked away beneath the Mendips it is off the country's main
highways of traffic and exchange. Nowadays it has no railway.
though for a few Victorian years this small rural city had no less
than three separate stations and thus has its well-marked niche in

railway history. Despite its past share in the cloth trade, with almshouses, not far from Bishop Bubwith's in Chamberlain Street, for "old decayed wool-combers", which may have given Trollope an extra tip for Hiram's Hospital, it has never become obtrusively industrial. Yet this quintessential Barchester has its Hogglestock side. Though they are numerous its hotels and restaurants employ a mere fraction of the city's people. Shops, transport, hospitals, the professions, and building account for far more. Small engineering concerns between them have a good number of workers, while the great concern of Unigate, in Wells as in other places in Somerset, gives work to many people who turn out cheese, baby foods, and other products from the milk of the county's lush pastures. Less expected in such a place, yet since the late war the leading employer in a city so famed for its medievalism, Electrical and Musical Industries have established, on the city's fringe as one travels towards Wookey Hole, an important electronics establishment, busied on research, the evolution of prototypes, and on some production work. Their activities show how the old and the new can both lie within a single small city, over a thousand years old, which must still make its way in our own century's late decades.

The stream from the copious springs which gave Wells its name flows down, below the market and then, in divided form, along the side runnels of High Street, towards what can well be called the country of the little hills. For the Mendips, like the Cotswolds north-west of Winchcombe but on a smaller scale, have a string of nubbly, picturesque little outliers, towering sharply from the beginnings of the moor country and happily diversifying the scene. Some of them stretch out, past Wookey village and Yarley, well towards the Isle of Wedmore. More distinct are Knowle and Lodge Hills, some lesser knolls and, towards Cheddar, the rocky islet of Nyland Hill which stands sentinel over the moors, and over the winding River Axe which has burst out into the light from its chain of dim caverns.

Wookey Hole attracts its visitors for two contrasting yet interlocked reasons. Caves and papermaking are the things which distinguish it, and as the caves are owned by a member of the family which once ran the upper, and older, of the two paper mills which span the Axe, the connection is now more happily reinforced than when, in the early years of this century, the paper-makers found their business much hampered by the leady pollution of the water, starting near the smelting works up on the high plateau and coming out from the successive abysses of the caves.

I must confess that the Mendip caves are not an aspect of Somerset which overwhelmingly interests or attracts me; I am, I suppose, what one must call a spelaeophobe. Yet these caverns are important in their own county. Like those in Derbyshire and further north they can be explained by the geology of the limestone rocks which make up the escarpment of the western Mendips and which enshroud their sandstone core. They have had much attention from geologists, potholers, and cave explorers, and they have a copious literature of their own. Those at Wookey Hole, and at the foot of Cheddar Gorge are the most frequented; a yawning contrast exists between their entrances from the outer daylight. Of Wookey Hole one can still say that its quiet wooded approach, past the upper paper mill and its strongly flowing leat, is as "extremely picturesque" as it was in Collinson's time, and that its surroundings are still "wildly magnificent". Many paintings, of Collinson's date and far into last century, show that picturesque charm long marked the valley just below the caves at Cheddar. A careful look at its old cottages, and at the stream as landscaped by the Bristol Waterworks Company, still reveals much of that earlier beauty. Yet one can also be appalled, as at many other 'beauty spots' by the harsh commercialism of what is certainly one of Somerset's most favoured, and enjoyed, haunts of day visitors.

Though Cheddar's caves tend, nowadays, to be better known than Wookey Hole the cavern which contains the Axe's underground headwaters gets many visitors and certainly finds a greater place in our early topographical writings. The early Christian writer Clement of Alexandria almost certainly had Wookey Hole in mind when he spoke of the hillside cave in Britain with its sound, like that of clashing cymbals, caused by the inrushing wind. William "of Worcester", that father of English topography, describes it; so does Camden in his *Britannia*. Early in the seventeenth century Drayton speaks poetically in his "Polyolbion", of "Ochy's dreadful hole". By the end of that century, and from the time of Queen Anne, we have matter-of-fact, illusion-free accounts by topographers who were no more than moderately impressed by the cave's legends, or by the likenesses seen in its admittedly impressive rockforms, stalagmites and stalactites. Celia Fiennes, the lady traveller who journeyed through England in William III's time, has a passage of fair length in Wookey Hole; she compares it to Poole Hole in Derbyshire's similarly limestone Peak District. Daniel Defoe also visited both of these caves, and makes the obvious comparison. The Poole's Hole he calls "another of the wonderless wonders of the Peak", enlarging considerably, but with evident scorn, on a phenomenon which had failed to impress him. He has a curt passage, with which I have some sympathy, on the "famous and so much talked of" Wookey Hole. He comments on its stalactites. But this general verdict, not, one assumes, that of the many modern visitors who admire its lofty recesses and cool, steel-blue streams, is that Wookey Hole had "nothing of wonder or curiosity in it". What one does notice, in this sequence of recesses in the Mendip limestone, is that there, down from the hollow swallets and not in such normally dry valleys as those of Ebbor Rocks, Cheddar Gorge, and Burrington Combe, are the streams which gush forth from these famous hills towards the flat moors and the muddy Bristol Channel.

With its modern Gothic church, its little bridge, and the prominent buildings of its ornately Gothic hillside school, Wookey Hole village is of real interest and secluded charm. Though it is now a set of mainly nineteenth-century buildings its paper mill still keeps an atmosphere of late Georgian industrialism, while in the village some terraces, rendered in the 'Arts and Crafts' manner and built of the dolomitic conglomerate also seen in the caves, were put up by the owners of the paper mill, to house some workers in a small 'model' community.

Cheddar Gorge, picturesque and romantic with its towering, dominant crags, is to my mind much more impressive than the caves which lie beneath its cliffs. It is up this valley, or up the more modest yet geologically similar rift of Burrington Combe, that one can best reach the gentle upland plateau country of western Mendip. A starting point for the fuller exploration of this countryside, much changed since the end of its mining and the taming enclosure of its ancient commons, is the present main road from Bristol to Wells.

As one leaves that road, where the gracefully rounded summit of Pen Hill just scrapes above the thousand-foot mark, the skyline is now offensively pierced by the tall, grey, graceless cylinder of the television mast which has lately been put up, and whose top is closer to the sky than anything in Somerset east of the Quantocks. Past Pen Hill there is a two-faced scene. The steep escarpment, still rough and rocky with its uncultivated upper slopes, commands splendid, revealing views over central Somerset and down south, beyond the county boundary, to Dorset's downland spine. The narrow, secret, tree-shrouded gorge of Ebbor Rocks, unspoilt and only passable on foot, snakes up, from near Wookey Hole, to the lonely farmland of the Mendip plateau. What must once have been unfenced pastureland is now a level landscape of corn and hay fields, split up, as in the Cotswolds, by low walls of the native stone and giving pasture to cattle as well as to its more expected sheep. Many of the long, straight roads of this stretch of country are of a fairly recent vintage, laid out since maps of 1817 showed the Mendip scene as it was when its ancient mineries were on their way to final decline.

The activities of the Mendip lead miners have been splendidly chronicled by Dr. Gough; almost all that can be known about them can be gathered from his pages.* The lead-mining area stretched from down towards Chewton Mendip to the district of Charterhouse not far below Blackdown. The deposits of ore, first reached by the shallow diggings which produced the tangled, pitted 'gruffy ground' still seen in this historic area, were exploited before the Romans came. Their knowledge of these British riches gave the Romans an economic, as well as a political reason for Claudius' conquering invasion. The main Roman minery was near the upland hamlet of Charterhouse, whose present name comes from the time when the Carthusians of Witham had it as an outlying, income-producing estate. The museums of Bristol and Taunton, and the leaden sheets which still line the bottom of the great Roman plunge bath in the bathing suite at Bath, have more vivid evidences of this ancient

* See J. W. Gough. *The Mines of Mendip*, 2nd edn., 1967.

mining settlement than what can be seen on the spot. The so-called 'amphitheatre', a small earthwork enclosure far too confined for such events as beast fights or gladiatorial displays, is unconvincing but may, perhaps, have been some place of local assembly. But for the appearance of Roman Charterhouse in its mining heyday an informed imagination is a better guide than anything now to be seen. The same, unfortunately, is true of the long period of lead-getting, with its ever deeper, often flooded workings, which for many years gave ample work to Mendip people and to adventurers from outside. The chief visible traces of Mendip leadworking are now near Charterhouse, above West Harptree, and not far from Hunters' Lodge Inn and the oasis-like hamlet of Priddy in its shallow hollow which gives shelter from the worst of the upland gales. For there one sees tumbled, ivy-clad ruins, flues, and the disused dams and mill ponds of the Victorian smelting works where the slags and slimes of an older industry were put into furnaces where more modern techniques could still get saleable lead from what earlier smelters had cast aside. These were the operations which, at the St. Cuthbert's works in 1908, were ended, in part, by trouble caused through the lead pollution of the stream running down to Wookey Hole.

Beyond Charterhouse the high saddleback of Blackdown is heatherclad in the manner of such moors as Dartmoor or Exmoor, and becomes a little boggy when the weather is wet. Its summit, 1,068 feet above the sea and a mere two feet below Cleeve Hill in the Cotswolds, makes it the highest point in the Mendips. The views, expectedly from such a summit, are magnificent. From here a walker soon drops down, past Tynings Farm and the thick growth of Rowberrow Warren, to another district of 'gruffy ground' and to the worked-out diggings of a metal more rare, and in its own time more important for local industry, than Mendip lead.

Shipham and Rowberrow were two of the Somerset villages, all but abandoned by their normal pastors, which were visited, schooled, and rechristianized by Hannah More. Their mining families, increased during the eighteenth century by the great demand for what they produced, were even tougher and more abandoned than the people of Cheddar or the district of the lead mines. What they dug from their scattered pits was calamine, a vital ingredient for the important brass and zinc industries of Bristol. Worlebury near Weston-super-Mare had produced this same material, but here, in this small area of Shipham and Rowberrow, was the main source of supply. Calamine, like lead, is now but an economic memory in Mendip. One should not, however, forget it while it is still possible, in such churches of the district as those of Wedmore and Axbridge, to admire the great chandeliers of the eighteenth century which remain among the best achievements of Bristol's vanished brassfounders.

The village of Cheddar, downstream from the gorge and the caves, and past an ugly belt of modern bugaloid development, deserves attention as well as the place's more famous attractions. Unlike its more obviously charming neighbour Axbridge it is a place where the medieval market cross still exists, and where the old parish church has better glass, and better brasses, than most others in Somerset. Among archaeologists, and indeed among all who take an interest in Anglo-Saxon building, Cheddar has gained much renown from Mr. Philip Rahtz's skilful uncovering of the postholes, and other foundation traces, of the palace which was used, when they hunted in the 'forest' country of Mendip, by the kings of Wessex and then, after Alfred's time, of a gradually united England. Despite its being in a stony district the main structure of the palace was a timber hall, long, narrow, and more or less rectangular. Other buildings, for such purposes as cooking, sanitation, and the milling of corn, lay separate but not far away. Then in Norman times a far larger hall, aisled and with great timbers like those still seen in the bishop's palace at Hereford, was built for the more ample accommodation of twelfth-century monarchs. The whole complex, with its successive halls, still tells of the building practice of a time when wood, even more than stone, was still normal for unfortified secular buildings.

Some of Cheddar's modern claims to fame lie in the realm of good eating. Back in the eighteenth century, when Defoe reported on the place, its people still made much 'Cheddar' cheese. Nowadays 'Cheddar' is but a name for cheese, much of it nutty and delicious, which, along with 'Caerphilly' (not made beneath the walls of the finest castle in South Wales) is still widely made in Somerset, but whose less passable imitations reach grocers from Canada and New Zealand. But Cheddar's other delicacy does indeed come from the gentle, sunny slopes, near the village and for a few miles on each side of it, which lie close and warm beneath the steep northward shelter of the Mendips. For the strawberries of the Cheddar district are as famous as those of southern Hampshire. Bristol is their closest market, but Midlanders rejoice no less in the fruit grown and picked, in a hot, backbreaking process, between Westbury-sub-Mendip and Axbridge.

Though church-trotters should visit Rodney Stoke, rich in Carolean woodwork and the fine monuments of the family whose other branches produced the great Georgian admiral, the more easterly parishes between Wells and the seaward end of the Mendips are of no special note. The same cannot, however, be said of the old borough of Axbridge, now freed, in its narrow main street, from the demolitional menace of road traffic by an avoiding road which runs, in part, along the disused Cheddar Valley railway first built to connect Yatton and Wells.

Axbridge, like Cheddar, was a royal possession and a resting place for hunting parties back from the chase on the high plateau of Mendip. Royal favour thus came to it; hence its grant, confirmed by later charters, of borough status and the feeling, in its small yet tautly girt square, of a small town. Its dignified little Regency town hall completes the impression; within it the ancient charters, the fine silver maces of 1623, the ale-taster's official glass, and the branding irons for marking stray cattle AX still remind those who see them of a status for Axbridge more dignified than its present position as a parish, and as the headquarters of a rural district made populous, like others in northern Somerset, by Bristol's gobbling overspill. Out in the square the old market cross has gone, and the houses have changed much in the past two centuries. But the noble church, cruciform and overtopped with its stately tower, still dominates the scene as one looks up, through a stepped gap in the houses at one corner of the square, towards its grey, rocky background of the hills. Traditional England is here at its best; no wonder that the television screen has featured the Christmas festivities in Axbridge's central square.

The villages, and the countryside, below Mendip's steep northern slopes are better wooded, shadier, and more romantic than what can be seen along the open, sun-baked fields of the

strawberry belt. The Harptrees lead on to Compton Martin
with its pretty pond, and with a parish church which has the best
Norman work of any in Somerset. Its clerestoried nave, its
vaulted chancel, and a pillar with spiral decoration in the Durham
manner make it of national, and not merely of local architectural
importance. Past Compton Martin is Blagdon, pleasingly
scattered on its hillside in a countryside much favoured by well-
to-do commuters into Bristol. Edwardian members of the Wills
family were among those who started the trend, in those days
before fast and reliable cars when they could travel from a
Blagdon terminus, along a convenient little Great Western
branch, to Bedminster station a few hundred yards from their
tobacco works. Below Blagdon village the reservoir, impounding
the waters of yet another Yeo and long famous for its trout
fishing, is smaller, deeper, and more picturesque between its
hills than the more recent Chew Valley Lake. As its verges are
apt to be inaccessible to all but fishermen it is best and indeed
splendidly seen from various hillside vantage points. Below
Blagdon, the traveller by road soon reaches Churchill Gate,
unpleasingly bungaloid and set amid the roaring traffic of A.38
which soon runs over the easy pass between the main range of
the Mendips and their last two hills of any imposing pretension.

At Churchill, as in so many areas of North Somerset where
the region's greatest city exerts its economic pull, we are in
Bristol's commuter country; the same is true of Winscombe,
still officially a village but untypical, with its commuters and
retired residents, of the county's villages whose people's living
comes from the land or from their daily journeys to factories in
the country towns. Winscombe's large population of educated,
middle-class people is swollen by those who teach, on the hillside
towards Shipham, at Sidcot School, co-educational and of
Quaker foundation though not, nowadays, confined to the sons
and daughters of Friends. Its origins go back just before 1700;
along with King's at Bruton and Downside with its predecessor
at Douai it is among the oldest boarding public schools in
Somerset. In its present form, with a core of Regency buildings
and many of more recent dates, it was re-established in 1808,
largely for Quakers of the western counties but with many pupils,
then and since, from elsewhere.

Not far beyond Winscombe Banwell seems largely suburban to Weston-super-Mare. But its village centre is attractive and its history is richly varied. Its 'castle' was, indeed, a product of Victorian romanticism, and its much altered 'abbey' never sheltered monks or nuns but was an often used residence of the medieval bishops of Bath and Wells. The good standing of pre-Reformation Banwell was shown in the splendour of its parish church. The stone pulpit survives, among several in this best of all areas for this particular item of church furniture. The wooden screen, splendid with its richly carved and vaulted rood loft, is the best in northern or eastern Somerset. With Henry VIII's arms in the middle it can be dated to 1522, a year when such an heraldic ornament could still be placed, below and subordinate to the Rood and so without religious controversy, on a church's most conspicuous piece of furnishing.

Sandford and Banwell hills are fair-sized westward outliers of the Mendips. So too, much more impressively, are the looming massif of Winscombe Hill, rising steeply above the tower and the good late medieval glass of Winscombe church, and Crook Peak with whose lovely, mountainous cone, over six hundred feet high as it towers above nestling Compton Bishop and the Lox Yeo's flat valley, we can say farewell to the range which we have traversed from Cranmore Tower.

CHAPTER VII

THE HEARTLAND

NOT far south of Shepton Mallet, and close by the straight, Roman alignment of the Fosse Way, a new feature of this part of central Somerset is the permanent site laid out for the Bath and West Show. Though the geographical scope of the society which runs it is far wider than Somerset it is more fitting that its best publicized activity should now settle, after a long history of shows in various places, in the county in which Edmund Rack, the Society's real founder, made his second home. Our notice of this spacious, gently sloping site can lead us, nearly two centuries after the Bath and West Society's first work for the West Country's agricultural and industrial 'improvement', to some thoughts on the general state of Somerset's agriculture.

By area, pastures and arable farming occupy far more land than any other activity in the county. Outside the towns the overwhelming impression is of an agricultural county. Even in their heyday the mines failed to destroy the agricultural aspect of the coalfield. Quarries, as one sees at Backwell and Dulcote, are a worse visual intrusion, while Puritan's Royal Ordnance factory, and the nuclear power station at Hinkley Point are reasonably merged into their immediate landscape. Only in some places near Bristol has much agricultural land been used up for urban demands. The flat, rhine-drained pastures of the moors, the mixed farming country of the north and east, and the hill farms of the Exmoor fringe are truely of the visual image of modern Somerset.

Yet it is surprising to find that the Somerset people who now draw their living from the land are far fewer than those who work in offices, or in certain forms of mechanical industry. Seventy years back the farmers, and the agricultural labourers whom they employed, must easily have been the county's largest working group. Four years ago those on agriculture and forestry, and the mere handful of Somerset's fishermen, numbered less than 10,000; they came fourth, on the Ministry of Labour's reckoning, of the county's broad groupings of manual workers. Those in the building trade, in 'professional' callings, and in shops or distributive jobs, were much more numerous. Somerset has moved far from the days of its traditional 'laughing Jarges' and from the besmocked and whiskered labourers who in this county, as in Hardy's Dorset, were its mid-Victorian economic mainstay.

Yet farms, and dairy farms above all, are a leading vital element in the life of present-day Somerset. For arable crops the county falls behind many others, including Wiltshire its eastern neighbour. But in its dairying it stands first, the more so since Cheshire, its nearest rival, was so fiercely devastated, in 1967 and 1968, by the onset of foot-and-mouth disease. In the numbers of its milk producers, and of its dairy cows, and in the gallons of milk sold by its dairy farmers, the figures of three years back show that the leading county was Somerset. Its dairy cows numbered a little over 170,000, ten thousand more than those of the far larger, but also dairying county of Devon. The best cheese farms, as we have seen, are in Somerset's eastern, more undulating reaches. Milk, especially that coming from summer milking in the pasturelands which are the last to go dry, comes in copious measure from the rich pastures of what were once the swampy moors. Such facts are the life's background, and the daily talk, of those who now come yearly, from all parts of Somerset as from elsewhere in the West, to the showground.

South from the Bath and West site it is an easy stage to the busy, somewhat formalized village of Evercreech, dominated by yet another of Somerset's finest vertically panelled towers, nearly a twin to that of Wrington between the Mendips and the Lulsgate hills. Then across what was once the line of the Somerset and Dorset Railway, and beyond the place where Evercreech Junction served many a train in that railway's heyday before 1914, the hills of Ditcheat and the Pennards invite the leisured wanderer to a quiet, sleepy countryside of utter rusticity, no more than intersected by the busy highway of A.37 and all the better for its not being the favoured stopping haunt of those who use that

Mendip Gorge: Burrington Combe

road as part of the Somerset corridor between Midland or Bristol homes and the English Channel coast. Yet Ditcheat's church is worth a detour and some delay. For it is excellent in a manner somewhat rare in the county. Its general aspect, and its sturdy central tower, are indeed of the Perpendicular period. But in its chancel it has excellent work of the fourteenth century and in the Decorated style, with a clerestory added above those lower windows; its heraldic shields suggest that this heightening job was done between 1472 and 1491. Ditcheat was yet another Glastonbury manor, so Abbot Selwood's arms are there, along with the coat of the Yorkist Bishop Stillington and the cumbrous cannon of Dean Gunthorpe who rebuilt the Deanery at Wells.

Past Ditcheat the more level terrain of the Brue and its feeder streams soon brings the explorer to the still busy Great Western main line to Plymouth, and to the hillier, attractive, countryside, with old houses charmingly tucked away amid its folds, which runs down from Castle Cary's outskirts towards Yeovil and the beginning of Dorset. Ansford, where in the eighteenth century the Woodfordes were both patrons and incumbents, and where Parson James Woodforde the diarist spent some of his pastoral years, comes first as one ascends from the junction of Castle Cary. It has long been closely allied to the larger place, and its Georgian houses merge with Castle Cary's northern outskirts.

Despite its name's feudal suggestions Castle Cary is a somewhat disappointing place; the main charm of its townscape comes from the scenic conjunction of its main street with the large pond whence the river flows out to give the rest of its name to the little town. The castle of the Percevals stood two sieges in the dreary civil war of Stephen's time, but thereafter was allowed, for the political purposes of the Plantagenets to fall into unmilitary ruin. Yet Castle Cary's markets, almost in abeyance by the time that Parson Woodforde and Collinson knew the place, made it something more than a village, and a slightly urban feeling still pervades the place. Its best building, put up in 1779 for £23, is its parish lockup, circular, of stone, and with a most graceful, pagoda-like roof. Somerset is less rich than north-western Wiltshire in these relics of a by-gone rural law enforcement. But here at Cary is one of a real aesthetic quality—unappreciated, one

Shepton Mallet: textile mill (Showerings' offices)
Street: Wilfrid Road, company housing

imagines, by those clapped in by the parish constables to cool off an evening's excess of scrumpy. Castle Cary is a quiet place nowadays, untroubled by the heaviest rush of modern road traffic. One firm in the town makes webbing, well away from Somerset's main area for this particular product. Cary also possesses a conventual rarity. Medieval Castle Cary had no establishment of monks or nuns. But now, in buildings once used by the contemplative nuns of the Visitation Order, the Sisters of Jesus Crucified have their one convent in this country. Where they stand apart from other communities is that they foster the vocations of women who are most of them, in some way, physically handicapped. At Castle Cary about half of the sisters are French, the Order having been started, in 1930 in France; the remainder are English and of various other nationalities. Their activities include the running of a printing press.

From Cary one journeys easily to the level country traversed, through the devastated stations of Sparkford and Marston Magna, by the railway to Yeovil and Weymouth, and to the tangled, beautiful, little known country of the Cadbury Hills. Compton Pauncefoot is the scenic gem of this rural landscape. Its 'castle', and that mansion's small parkland delightfully adorned, in the Repton tradition, by a tree-girt lake, are much too good scenically to be medievally true; it is what one would expect of a castle which turns out to be Gothic of the age of Nash, with none of Horace Walpole's genuine "rust of the barons' wars". A little to the west we have the contrasting marvels, medieval, Elizabethan, pre-historic, and Dark Age, of the two Cadburys.

North Cadbury takes pride in the restrained dignity and simple beauty of its Perpendicular church, built not by the clothiers who later put up, or enlarged, so many of Somerset's churches but by a high-born lady who planned its chancel as the worshipping place of a chantry college. She was Elizabeth, née Daubeney of a well-known county family and the widow, since 1391, of the first Baron Botreaux. Her new church, severe as are many of the early Perpendicular period, dates from about the year of Agincourt and not, like so many others in Somerset, from the Tudor end of the same century. Her college never functioned as she intended, while the nave's splendid bench-ends, with a mousetrap, a mouse, and a cat among their vivid subjects, are from the 1530s; bar their high-rising finials they foreshadow, here in south-eastern Somerset, those seen near Taunton and in the Quantock country.

Close by the church North Cadbury Court has a fair quantity of medieval work, and in other respects it is something of an oddity. For one side is Elizabethan, while out on the other side great changes were made, neo-Classical in the idiom of about 1800, to shift the mansion's scenic emphasis to the south, opening its social rooms to the sunlight and allowing a splendid prospect of the hill country by then reckoned, in the days of a flourishing romanticism, to be that of Camelot. But the house is, in the main, the Elizabethan creation of Sir Francis Hastings; in central Wessex only Longleat (whose mixed classical idiom it echoes) and Montacute can be held to surpass it. Among the house's best elements is its blood-proud profusion of armorial glass. Religious pictures would, to so staunch a Puritan as the aristocratic Sir Francis, have been taboo. But he did not disdain, in the windows of his hall, to display his good connections and to prove, in this array of many-quartered achievements, his kinship with as many as he could muster from among the Knights of the Garter. From such an heraldic galaxy one can see how such men as Shakespeare's Bolingbroke felt it if their "household coats" were spitefully torn from their windows.

South Cadbury village has its leafy, secluded charm. But what makes the place, raising it above the other parishes in this part of Somerset, is Cadbury Castle—in other words the great fort on its neatly isolated hill, first used far back in prehistoric times and abandoned in the century whose last years were prolific, under the Norman conquerors, with castles of the accepted medieval type. Add to its archaeological reality the strong antiquarian and romantic claim that here, and not in Cornwall, was the Camelot of King Arthur, and this is one of the county's places most worthy of a lingering inspection.

Though some of it is more shrouded in vegetation than Maiden Castle, and though Cadbury Camp is less stark and unencumbered than the superb hill fort near Dorchester, it is among the greatest of southern Britain's many-ramparted hill forts. Like Maiden Castle it was used by Neolithic man, while the Iron Age Britons, not long before the Roman conquest, were the men who first piled up its great ramparts, crowned them with palisades which have now vanished, and scooped out the deep, impeding ditches which could well entrap an attacking foe. On any historical reckoning Cadbury was outstanding as a prehistoric strongpoint. What tradition has claimed, and what archaeologists have recently hoped to prove or disprove, is that its greatest lustre came in that spell of relapse to the Iron Age which is known, if only for the dimness of its historic evidence, as the Dark Age, and which was the historic seedbed for the doings of 'King Arthur'.

The excavations carried out, since 1966, by Mr. Leslie Allcock are amongst the leading 'digs' of our time. Camelot or no Camelot they have told us much about the successive stages of the great ramparted enclosure's occupation. Extra light has shone both on the camp's Neolithic use, and on its comparatively minor Bronze Age phase. The Iron Age, in the last centuries before the Romans came, was certainly a main period in Cadbury's history. But it now seems, from the foundation traces of regularly designed, parallel rectangular buildings that some activity continued there in Romano-British times. But the obscure period after the Roman troops departed is the one to which we must look for any historic basis for Cadbury as 'Camelot'. The archaeologists have proved that the great hill camp was refortified and re-used about A.D. 500. From the scale of the work done to strengthen the place, from traces of buildings, and from smaller finds such as pottery fragments it seems certain that some leading chieftain, here at Cadbury in this troubled time of creeping invasion, maintained his refurbished stronghold. He may, perhaps, be claimed as an original for so great a figure of Celtic resistance as 'Arthur' is said to have been. Yet one cannot surely say, even on so prominent and large a site of Dark Age resettlement, that Cadbury alone inspired the notion of Camelot. Yet legend has here had no mean reinforcement from modern archaeology. What is certain is that Cadbury's defences were rougher and less elaborate than those which can be seen at such castles as Nunney or Raglan, and that those who lived there in the sixth century were a community very different from the chivalrous knights and ladies of medieval romance as presented, with such vitality, by Sir Thomas Malory. The ladies of this hilltop community would have worn clothes and headgear not at all like those seen in brasses of about 1470 or in Tenniel's drawings of the Ugly Duchess, and these resisting Celtic warriors would never have worn armour like that in which the Kingmaker died at Barnet.

More solidly historic, and no less exciting than what Cadbury has revealed of its 'Arthurian' phase, are the traces of this great hill fort's re-use, soon after A.D. 1000 when the invaders to be met were not Saxon but Danish. For Ethelred II ('The Unready') substantially reinforced the innermost rampart with a wall of stone. Within the enclosure he established a small mint; many of its coins went to pay Danegeld, and most of those surviving with the Cadbury stamp are in the Scandinavian museums. It would seem that here, deep in inland Wessex, the king planned some sort of a resistance from a well fortified town built on a site which had, some four or five centuries earlier, had a similar use. The *burh's* main entrance, from the south, received defences of special strength. Up on Cadbury's topmost plateau some other buildings were started, but never brought to completion. Foundations show that one of these buildings was to have been shaped as a Greek cross, with all its four limbs equal in length. Such a structure would, most probably, have been a church; had it been finished on such a plan it would, along with the first abbey church at Athelney, have been among the most interesting in Somerset. But the mint, and Cadbury's career as a fortress town, did not long outlast Ethelred's death and Canute's accession. By 1020 it was abandoned and its new ramparts were slighted, and it now seems that it soon had a spell of squatter or peasant occupation. But within late Saxon and Norman times it duly declined, within the quadruple circuit of its pre-Roman defences, to the status of an agricultural hilltop. Later, King John may have been the last monarch to leave a slight mark on Cadbury. For in 1209, when England lay under its papal interdict, and when the King's great conflict with the barons was drawing near, some royal money was laid out "towards the works of the castle at Cadbury". Pottery of about this date has come to light near the hill fort's highest point, and if this particular Cadbury is the one meant in the document there seems, at a date much closer to Malory than to 'Arthur', to have been a slight, uncompleted effort to build up a castle of the normal medieval type.

From the foot of the Cadbury hills, along the winding course of the Ivel, or Yeo, we come well into Somerset's central flatlands of rich pasturage and dairying. Near Yeovilton many conveniently level acres of what was once dairy land have now, for some thirty years, been the best known of Somerset's Service establishments. This is the Naval Air Station, famous in the Fleet Air Arm and throughout the Navy, whose planes noisily enliven the air for many miles around. Northover, with its roadside church, lies on the Fosse Way as it approaches Ilchester and comes, on the Ivel's right bank, before the unimpressive little town which was a Roman staging post. It was on this Northover side, till 1843, that the county gaol long gave damp, but reasonably planned lodging to the worst of Somerset's offenders. Before the seventeenth century the prison had been in the town itself and on an islet traversed by the bridge. So small a town as Ivelchester, long stagnant and bereft of the barge traffic which, in times of high water, crept up to it from Bridgwater via Langport, is livelier now as it meets the needs of motorists driving through Somerset. Yet it seems an odd locality to have been, for seven centuries, the holding place for those in the county who awaited trial, sentence, or punishment. Its status as a prison town came naturally enough from its long held position as the seat of Somerset's Assizes. For it was in this royal manor and in a town once larger, better provided with churches and chapels, and of much more consequence than it is today, that the king's judges found Ilchester's southerly, yet reasonably central site a good pretext for the holding of their Somerset courts. So when, in 1373, Bristol's busy merchants got the privilege for their town to be a county, and its own Assize town, it was Ilchester, along with Gloucester, that was mentioned in Edward III's charter as an awkwardly distant place for time-consuming journeys to the fount of justice. Geography and events thus combined to put Ilchester into the central, historic heart of its own county.

Though the flatlands of Somerset's moor country spread wide, and run deep from the coast towards the county's southern recesses they are not unbroken by sharply rising ground; hills of various heights are much more in evidence, as a background to Somerset's central level, than they are in the fen country of Cambridgeshire and the Isle of Ely. Bar Brent Knoll, the Isle of Avalon, and the steep little hills which lie nearest to the Mendips, these rising contrasts to Somerset's moors tend to appear in such ridges as the Polden Hills, the eastern promontory of the Isle of Wedmore, and the lean spur which juts out from near Taunton and is crowned, not far from its end near Langport on the Parrett, by Pitt's Burton Pynsent column and the large village of Curry Rivel. But on one fringe of these central levels a set of hills rises not as a narrow range but in a spreading massif, steep-sided where, as near Aller and Compton Dundon, it dramatically confronts the moors, elsewhere more gently sloping amid quiet farmland. Between the two main blocks of what can, perhaps, be called the Somerton Hills the River Cary meanders, in a narrow valley and almost apologetically, to make its course from the low country of the Fosse Way to the wider moors. Here in these hills near Somerton, or between Butleigh and the picturesquely varied scene at Compton Dundon, is the blue lias country, still yielding the blue-grey, easily worked stone which is the main material (sometimes beautifully blended with the more spectacular gold stone of Ham Mill) of its houses and churches. Here too, as some experts in place names claim, is the tract of country whence our whole county, from Bathford to the Bagworthy Water, has come to take its name.

Of many explanations of the name Somerset the one which I find most convincing is that given by Dr. W. G. Hoskins in his essay on the process whereby the Anglo-Saxons spread westward till the whole of what later became western Wessex accepted their sway.* Dr. Hoskins reckons that the Somersaetas—or the folk who settled in the summer—were Saxons who had, soon before or soon after their great victory at Dyrham in the southern Cotswolds in 577, gained possession of the Avon valley and of the Mendips, dividing the Britons west of the Severn from those who still held out in what is now the south-west of England. From the Mendip country these settlers may have moved down, in their search for richer pastures and for such islands of drained, agricultural land as they could find amid the swampy moors, towards the Yeovil area and the Bristol Channel. Though much of the moor country must, in those days, have been hopelessly undrained and waterlogged its many low islands would have been high and firm enough to give good grazing, in summer or for longer spells, to the cattle and sheep of men whose normal

* See W. G. Hoskins, *The Westward Expansion of Wessex*, 1960.

pastures were on higher and bleaker ground. The Isle of Wedmore was one such 'island', while up at the far tip of the northern moors the 'ea' of Nailsea was another. Better still, where the thin ridge of the Poldens widens out, beyond Butleigh and again well south of the Cary valley, the double massif of the Somerton country justified a lasting settlement, not merely a summer foray to lush grazing. Instead of the summer migrants to the other islands one could plan here for more lasting habitation. So here, on these firm commanding hills, the early settlers seem to have established their main holding in what is still a tract of unspoiled upland country.

For me, and perhaps for some others who know the county these hills near Somerton, and their adjacent lowlands, are essentially more of Somerset than anywhere else in the county. I know the district less closely than some other parts of Somerset, yet here, between Street and the Ivel at Long Sutton, at Burrow Mump or between Aller's wooded bluff and the Fosse Way, I feel, as nowhere else in Somerset, that I could be in no other county. Near Bath one is conscious of Gloucestershire and the Cotswolds, while on and round Exmoor one hardly seems, when one thinks of these central hills or of the flat moors of the Brue and the Parrett, to be in Somerset at all. Selwood Forest has its links with Wiltshire, while along the coast, when the weather is clear, the very different land of Wales is always in view. Parts of Somerset's marches with Dorset have much in common with the smaller county to the south, and the Blackmoor Vale, Tess's native district and Hardy's "Vale of the Little Dairies", starts well in Somerset. But the in Somerton country, and down in the most central of Somerset's moors, one is deeply unaware of any other shire.

Collinson's remark, of this countryside of the Dundon and Somerton hills, that the area was "finely interspersed with culti-vated hills and rich luxuriant vallies" is as true now as it was about 1790. My only variation on this report is that not all this fine upland area is 'cultivated'. Fine farming country does, indeed, stretch gently up towards the steep, indented escarpment of the Dundon hills. But the sharpest slopes, and some of the fertile plateau country behind their crest, are picturesquely shrouded with woodlands. Nowhere is this more true than around the highest point, above Compton Dundon, in Somerset's central massif. For there the dense undergrowth of Great Breach and Copley woods makes these hilltop and hillcrest thickets among the most impenetrable in the county, confining an explorer's superb views over the moor country to what he can get from a few stretches, each side of Windmill Hill with its column towering prominently above the trees, where woods mercifully give way to open downland.

The hilltops of Somerset are quite liberally capped with commemorative towers, columns, and obelisks which enhance their eminence and add to their scenic effect. Brown's Folly above Bathford, and King Alfred's Tower on the Stourhead estate are shared with Wiltshire, but several others are wholly within our county. The chapel tower on Glastonbury Tor was, one imagines, what started the fashion, Beckford's Tower above Bath commemorates an eccentric's last years, while those at Ammerdown and above Cranmore are deeper into the nineteenth century than one might normally expect. Some are typically Georgian scenic gestures; three of these, at Burton Pynsent, above Wellington, and here at Butleigh have their strongly historic emphasis.

The village of Butleigh, lying low beneath these central hills, gave its origin to one of England's well-known naval dynasties. Its naval connection started in 1741, when two sons of the vicar, the Reverend Samuel Hood, left home for sea. The two boys saw service of great, though not of supreme distinction. Both of them, as Viscount Hood and Lord Bridport, ended up as peers. The elder one, named Samuel after his father, was the most distinguished of the Hood clan. At the battle of The Saints he was Rodney's second-in-command; later as Commander-in-Chief in the Mediterranean, he was Nelson's good friend and superior officer. He is the Hood to whom, after his death in 1816, one might have expected to see some memorial erected close to his birthplace. But the Butleigh column, simple and unfluted Roman Doric, and fitly surmounted by the bold sails and ships' sterns of a naval crown, commemorates another and a younger Samuel Hood. It is splendidly placed on its hilltop, and well landscaped, with its approach avenue exactly aligned, as one looks away from the column, on to Glastonbury Tor.

Vice-Admiral Sir Samuel Hood, of the same family as the two

naval peers but their cousin and not born at Butleigh, achieved his measure of fame. To quote the wording on one side of the column's simple plinth he was "an officer of the highest distinction amongst the illustrious men who rendered their own age the brightest period in the naval history of their country". He was junior to Nelson, but like the other Samuel Hood he was his friend and colleague. He served under Nelson in the disastrous raid on Santa Cruz de Teneriffe, and as one of the ships' captains at the Nile. He held various senior posts, and then on Christmas Eve in 1814 he died, at Madras, as Commander-in-Chief of the East Indies Fleet. Aged only 52, he was cut off as he neared the peak of his career. Here at Butleigh, far away from the scenes of many of his actions, Sir Samuel Hood found due and conspicuous commemoration. For officers who had served under him, admiring the dead admiral's high qualities and "amiable virtues", in 1831 set up this column which rises high above the parish of their hero's clerical forbear.*

West of the site of Somerton this hilly refuge above the undrained moors was favoured, before ever there was any thought of Anglo-Saxons or Somersaetas, by Romano-British country gentry. Roman remains have been found at Pitney, now deep in an unspoiled rural peace, while at Low Ham the splendour of the mosaics, with the story of Dido and Aeneas among the subjects, suggested a sophistication akin to that which the Georgian gentry introduced, in rustic settings up and down England, into Palladian or neo-Classical country homes. More unusual, though not without some equivalents in its own county, is the church at Low Ham, Gothic of the seventeenth century with its embattled West tower, a mainly Perpendicular architectural idiom, a mixture of Gothic and Renaissance in its woodwork, and some admirable glass. It is, in its own shire, an opposite number to Leicestershire's famous rarity at Staunton Harold. Back at Somerton, from the earlier decades of the same century, the church has an opulent communion table, and other woodwork, of the most usual Jacobean type.

Though Somerton was once an important centre both in

---

* A monument in Butleigh church, with a long blank verse epitaph by Southey, records the careers of Sir Samuel and of his two naval brothers who long predeceased him.

Somerset and in all Wessex much of modernity has passed it by. No really major road runs through it, the main line trains to and from Exeter and beyond now roar past a shut and derelict station, and the little town seems to have no substantial industry. For those reasons it is a place of quiet charm, nearly all of it, as in Collinson's time, built of the local blue lias whose close-set blocks have now mellowed to a more ordinary grey. By modern standards its streets are astonishingly peaceful so that one can almost feel, on some quiet summer afternoon, that the pre-motor age has returned to Somerton; it is hardly a surprise, in the yard of the 'Red Lion' to find some repainted letters informing us that the hotel is "Licensed to let Post Horses". This inn, once the Ilchester Arms and still proudly displaying the Fox-Strangeways arms, looks out on to the market place, and on to what Professor Pevsner has rightly called "one of the most happily grouped urban pictures in Somerset". The church, with a transeptal southern tower rising to a delightful early Perpendicular top stage, the medieval market cross as rebuilt under Charles II, the old town hall, some excellent mullioned and Georgian houses there and in the wholly delightful Broad Street with its pollarded limes, all these combine to make 'The Borough' of Somerton a place of delight. The one great thing which is missing is the castle, the successor to King Ine's fortified royal 'burh', which must, for part at least of the Middle Ages, have dominated the market place on its southern side.

This royal control of so central a place in Somerset was the key to Somerton's long spell of major importance in its own county. A castle succeeded the Saxon fort; the site, as the terrain still shows, helped its own defence and made it easy to control the town. For on its northern side the castle overlooked the market and the church. Not far to the south the valley of Lower Somerton, with a stream which could have been dammed to provide strong water defences, protected it on the other side. It seems not to have had fortified use after Henry III's reign. Yet it still had its uses for the purposes of the Crown. Somerton and Ilchester were the only important royal manors in this central district of Somerset. For a time they alternately had the dubious honour of possessing the county's gaol; the well drained precincts of Somerton Castle must have given the county's malefactors drier lodging than they got down by the river at Ilchester. The White Hart, which is another of Somerton's many inns, is said to cover part of the site. But only the excavation of the more spacious ground at the back could tell much of what may, in its feudal glory, have been a fairly imposing fortress.

Islands of firm, fertile ground, rising clear above the mists and mud of the moors and making fine sites for settlement, were naturally attractive to the kings and thegns who followed Somerset's earliest Saxon settlers. After the Dundon-Somerton massif the largest and best of these 'eas', stretching for six miles between its blunt end near Weare and the tip of its narrow ridge which jabs out towards Wells, was the rich Isle of Wedmore. Like Somerton, and not surprisingly, it eventually fell to the kings of Wessex; it was for this reason that Wedmore found its place in our national history. King Alfred had a residence there. At Wedmore, in 878 and after his great victory over the Danes which had led to their leaders' baptism, he made the treaty which loosed the Danish hold on southern and western England, and which partitioned the country (only temporarily, as events proved) between Alfred and his successors and the invaders who stayed on in control of the 'Danelaw'. Wedmore's royal ownership did not permanently outlast its one great appearance in history. For Edward the Confessor transferred its lordship to the Bishops of Wells. By them it was passed over to the Deans, while the revenues of its church long helped to swell their income.

The parish of Wedmore was once far larger than it has been since the 1840s; churches such as that of the fittingly named Chapel Allerton, or of Mark where a slim and splendid tower rises conspicuously above the village and the low moor country, were once its chapelries. Even when these places had cut away the rich and fertile parish remained large; Collinson and Hannah More both remarked, in the 1790s, that it was the largest in Somerset. At the time of the Reformation it had contained some 1,500 people and its noble, spreading, cruciform church owed less to the woollen trade than did most Somerset churches of such size and splendour. Wedmore itself, as the Isle's natural centre, has a dignity above that of an ordinary village. It was a manorial borough, with a portreeve at its head and beneath him a train of such local funtionaries as bread weighers, haywards, and ale tasters. Wedmore still has the mien of a place more considerable than a village and its pleasingly urban central district, like that of Somerton, still goes by the name of The Borough. Its tradespeople have served, and serve, a population larger than that of the town, and Wedmore (some commuters and retired people apart) has long had its quota of what the 1831 Census analyses call professional and 'educated' people. But the isle's main character has always been deeply agricultural. The cloth trade and other forms of industry have avoided it, and with few employed nowadays on the land its population has dropped steadily. Its isolation, and the remoteness from the mainstreams of modern traffic which now give the isle its charm and distinction, have also had their social disadvantages. Hannah More, whose plans for a school met fierce hostility from Wedmore's high-handed and brutalized farmers, and who had a specially difficult time in this parish, found Wedmore "depraved and shocking". By now the place has socially improved, but the Isle of Wedmore remains something of a place apart.

Wedmore church, conspicuous as it rises above one end of a gently rising street, is reasonably well known. Less prominent, and some of them well tucked away, are the neat Georgian frontages of many houses; some of these, in the Borough, conceal much older work. Best of all are some houses round an open green south-west of the main settlement. Porch House, a long building of the seventeenth century with casement windows, and a large Georgian porch jutting boldly from its frontage, is the most imposing. More remarkable still is the little mullioned building to one side of it, inscribed with the name of "John Westover, chyrurgeon", and dated 1680. The Westovers were an old Wedmore family and John's father, of the same name, was also a surgeon. In one field of healing the younger John was a pioneer. For in those days of Bedlam's promiscuous horrors he took private mental patients, and it was for their housing, and more humane treatment, that he put up this stone house. He seems, in his small way, to have anticipated the work of those pioneering Quakers, William Tuke in The Retreat at York and Dr. Edward Long Fox on the outskirts of Bristol.

The best known, most far seen of central Somerset's 'isles' is that of Avalon. For some it typifies, and symbolizes, the whole county. From many viewpoints, it can be clearly seen, and Glastonbury Tor's natural height of over five hundred feet is enhanced by the late fourteenth-century tower of St. Michael's chapel on its summit. The town below the Tor has been much chronicled and recorded. Its history, and its religious fame, are familiar. It stretches for the best part of a mile, a blend of grey stone in its centre and of conspicuously ugly red brick and tile towards its commercial end where the canal once terminated, and where in the 1850s the Somerset Central Railway took over the main burden of local transport. The ancient centre is, for obvious reasons, the most favoured part of Glastonbury, of great interest and of many associations. The Perpendicular tower of St. John the Baptist's church is of a splendour outstanding even in Somerset. Yet the existence of that fine church, and of the smaller one of St. Benignus lower in the town, has helped to make central Glastonbury a strangely depressing place.

Medieval Glastonbury, with its great Benedictine abbey the richest, bar only Westminster, in all England, held a unique position. We can now discount the story that St. Joseph of Arimathea ever found his way to Avalon over Wearyall, or Wirral, Hill;* what mattered, in pre-Reformation Glastonbury, was that the legend was long believed as a focal point in the great gatherum of holy associations which clung to the place, and to the low isle of Beckery, not far to the west, where modern excavation has revealed very early graves and chapels. St. David, St. Patrick, and St. Bridget, to say nothing of King Arthur and Queen Guinevere, added their quota to Avalon's accumulation of holiness. Glastonbury could not, like Bury St. Edmund's or Canterbury, claim any single, powerfully attractive religious event or treasured relic. But its holy atmosphere, its place in the history of the country's Benedictine monasticism, and the sheer size and wealth of its abbey gave it a place unique among the monastic towns of Wessex. It was, moreover, an abbey whose community remained large, and seemingly observant, right down to 1539 when its dissolution was enforced, and when Richard Whiting, its last abbot, was dragged to his execution on the top of the Tor.

* This name, for a long hog-backed hill, is the same as that of the Wirral peninsula, with its similar silhouette, between the Mersey and the Dee.

Glastonbury's ancient heart has largely been torn out. The abbey site is its main element. The ruins, less impressive than they were three centuries ago, are now pathetically scanty, and as a monastic ruin Glastonbury is far less impressive than such monasteries as Tintern, Kirkstall, Castle Acre, and Cleeve. The best that one can say is that more survives of the abbey at Glastonbury than of some other great Benedictine houses—Ramsey for instance, Hyde Abbey at Winchester, Reading or Evesham—where the quarrying of ruins has been even more drastic than here in central Somerset. Yet a careful look at the ruins, and the foundation lines, of the great church of Glastonbury reveals its size, and the unusual elements in its plan.

Whatever may have been the origins of the monastery at Glastonbury the tenth century, with the donations and reforms of such men as King Athelstan and St. Dunstan, was when it came firmly, and lastingly, into historic light. The church seems then to have been somewhat unimpressive for so notable an abbey; its domestic buildings, on the claustral lines which later became normal, were probably more important. The whole church, bar the primitive wattle chapel of the Blessed Virgin, already existing to the west of it and specially holy in its associations, was replaced, as was normal in England's pre-Conquest Abbeys and cathedrals, by an impressive Norman Romanesque church. This Norman abbey, along with what must, by then, have been the ramshackle Lady chapel, was, in 1184, burnt down by a fire which seems, for Glastonbury, to have been even more of a disaster than that which had wrecked Canterbury Cathedral ten years earlier. The great new church which was soon started was that which, in the main, remained that of the Glastonbury Benedictines till Henry VIII's time. A new Lady chapel, an exquisite little building of the transition between Romanesque and early Gothic, replaced the wattle chapel. Nowadays it is the only convincing relic of the church whose main fabric, apart from this unusually placed Lady chapel and the 'Galilee' vestibule which joined it to the nave, was over four hundred feet long—the largest church in medieval Somerset and noticeably larger than the cathedrals at Lichfield, Rochester, Exeter, Wells, and elsewhere. Its style was the transitional Gothic of the last years of the twelfth century; as in the choir limb of the cathedral at Oxford the two lower stages of each bay in the eastern limb were both enclosed within the compass of a giant arch. The great church is pitifully ruined, but enough, astonishingly, remains to leave vestiges of its alterations. Thus one can trace the assimilation of its fourteenth-century work to the older design, the casing of the choir's interior, like that of the abbey church at Gloucester, with a cagelike skin of early Perpendicular stonework, the strainer arches which, as at Canterbury Cathedral about the same time, helped to sustain the weight of a great late Gothic tower which became the dominating feature in this monastic town.

By the time of the dissolution no part of Glastonbury's great abbey church was used by the parishioners, who had their two churches out in the town. None of it thus needed to be spread; the church, and nearly all the monks' domestic buildings, lost their lead, their timber, and their stonework as a convenient source of builders' materials. But most of the site remained clear of new buildings—hence the sad modern vacuum to the south and east of modern Glastonbury's streets. The abbey's peripheral buildings have fared better than those once used for the monks' worship and domestic living. The abbot's kitchen is the best preserved of those which stood within the precincts, while close below the Tor's lower slopes the barn of what must have been the abbey's home farm is as good an agricultural building as any to have survived from English medieval farming. It was built, as one can tell from its buttresses, and from its triangular, convex-sided, and traceried end windows, at some time about 1300, while its transepts were much altered, under that prolific builder Abbot Bere, about 1500.* Best of all, and giving emphasis to the building's one-time ownership by religious, are the sculptured symbols of the Evangelists which beautifully adorn the barn's four gables; similar plaques were put on the abbey's slightly later estate barn, now roofless after a recent fire but structurally intact, not far away in the village of Pilton.

Glastonbury Abbey still leaves its mark on the buildings of the town. In the High Street the Tribunal, of the fifteenth century and with its frontage renewed during Abbot Bere's early Tudor régime, was the building where, as the local agents of the Crown,

---

* The dating of this barn is a point on which a correction must be made in Professor Pevsner's generally excellent book on South Somerset buildings.

Central landscape: the Dundon Hills

the abbot's officers dispensed justice in Glastonbury Hundred. Down the road the George Inn, with its lovely late Perpendicular façade, was rebuilt, for visiting pilgrims, not long before the dissolution removed the need for their journey. Round the corner, past a convincing early Victorian market cross, the best buildings are more secular. The town hall is no surprise, for such a building is normal in so old a borough. It has a simple, refined late Georgian ashlar façade of 1818, unsensitively violated in recent years by the insertion, over its pediment, of a projecting, two-sided clock. More surprising, and jutting out at right angles to Magdalene Street past the large modern Catholic Church, a pleasant little building, boldly built in the vernacular Georgian of the 1750s, was put up as the pump house of Glastonbury's short-lived, but locally popular spa; its water came from the 'Chalice' Wall near the foot of the Tor.

With rather over six thousand people Glastonbury is now a busier place than in its somewhat stagnant early Victorian days. Many of its people work elsewhere, at Street for instance with C. and J. Clark's. Down by the disused station, and the old head of the canal which reached the town in 1833 the timber yards, once getting their stock by water or rail, are of more than local note. The most important of Glastonbury's industries, making it the chief town in England for its particular trade, has its main place of activity at the town's westernmost tip.

The tanning of sheepskins, and the making of sheepskin clothing and footwear, is the industry for which Glastonbury is now best known. Some small firms pursue the craft in or near the centre of the town, while out towards Beckery and the boundary with Street the first of the two tanneries which a traveller from Glastonbury encounters is the smaller and older of the two which sprawlingly dominate this outer part of the town. It is that of Baily's, now part of a larger group but at work on this waterside site for over a century. The buildings, and in particular its well detailed brick chimney, are worth noting by *aficionados* of Victorian industrial architecture. A much larger concern, nearly a century old and employing over a thousand people here, and a few hundreds in its much newer factory at Highbridge, is that first known as Clark, Son, and Morlands.

In 1870 John Morland, a young Quaker of Westmorland

Castle Cary: Georgian house and lock-up
Somerton: an earlier townscape

origins but more recently at work near London, came into partnership, here in central Somerset, with his father-in-law James Clark and with William Stephens Clark who was his brother-in-law. The new combine was planned to take over the sheepskin rugmaking so far done as part of the activities of C. and J. Clark's of Street. Kinship apart, John Morland's attainments as an analytical chemist were most useful in such a firm. The site of Clark, Son, and Morland's had already been used for a tannery, and it included (and includes) the early Tudor fulling mill which once belonged to the abbey. The business soon progressed, and many members of the Morland family have always been active in it. Footmuffs for use in open motor cars, slippers, and sheepskin garments duly joined rugs among the items of Morlands' production. Morlands' rivalry with Baily's their neighbours was not merely confined to the quality of the two firms' goods. It was also linked to their use of water from the adjacent stream; in addition it had a political tinge. For the Bailys, unlike the Liberal Morlands and Clarks, were staunch Conservatives, so that some local farmers of the Tory persuasion would only sell skins to their sympathizers. Nowadays, however, British sheepskins form only a part of the million and a half skins which are annually treated, by Morlands' alone as Europe's largest firm in this particular business. Many of the best are used locally, on the wide, fascinating, and extremely beautiful range of garments turned out in these Glastonbury works. Other skins are sold, after tanning, to other makers. Morlands' origins, as a business once mainly preoccupied with the skins of sheep which had grazed in the fields of Wessex, cannot really be parted from the story of C. and J. Clark's of Street.

The parish of Street, now largely filled with its industrial buildings and its shops, and with the scattered homes of a township of over seven thousand people, has come far since, in 1801, the first census gave its population as 540. It was another of Glastonbury Abbey's possessions, its old church has better work of the fourteenth century than is usual in Somerset, and out at the Polden Hill end of the parish the ancient house of Ivythorn Manor shows important building improvements of Abbot Selwood's time. Here and there in the more populous part of Street, and towards the Poldens, some blue lias houses, mullioned or Georgian, date from the years before the great transformation of a scattered village into Wessex's best example, bar Swindon, of a 'company town'. The farmers and graziers of late Georgian times, some of them Quakers or the adherents of other Nonconformist bodies, could never have foreseen that Street would one day be the main centre of Britain's largest footwear firm, and the headquarters of an industrial empire with many branches overseas. That, however, is the position which C. and J. Clark's have created in this interesting, not wholly unattractive mid-Somerset town. Street is, moreover, the focal point of a great boys' and girls' boarding school of much more than local fame. It certainly ranks among the most significant places in Somerset.

The origins of the Clark family lie in the farming community, and in the long-established Quaker meetings, of the Polden country. Both factors, and in particular their Quaker traditions and outlook, have vitally affected the story of their firm, and of Street as it has grown with the rise of trade. The year 1825, when Cyrus Clark ended his partnership with Arthur Clothier, and set up his own business as a fellmonger, wool dealer, and rugmaker, is reckoned as the firm's foundation year. Cyrus' brother James joined him as an apprentice, and in 1833 as a full partner. By that year he had started to make wool-lined slippers, using pieces of the short-woolled skins which were unsuitable for rugs. It was from this homely pioneering that C. and J. Clark's started as a shoemaking concern; by 1870, when Clark, Son, and Morland took the rugmaking across the Brue to Northover, the making and sale of shoes dominated the Clarks' business. From then onwards, and still more since 1904 when the family business became a limited company, C. and J. Clark's grew, with an ever increasing impact on the life of Street whose population had risen, in the first eighty years of their operations, from about 800 to a little over 4,000. True to their Quaker faith, and to their strong interest in social, political, and cultural affairs, the Clarks deeply concerned themselves with such things as local government, workers' housing, education, and welfare, and what they felt to be the best forms of recreation and amusement. Their late Victorian and Edwardian business was smaller, more concentrated, and more intimate than it can be in the present days of a large industrial empire. This was the time of a close, and perhaps over-emphasized paternalism of the type already seen in the North, at such places as Saltaire, and paralleled, by other Quaker employers, at Bournville. Strict temperance being among the Clarks' beliefs the number of Street's places of alcoholic refreshment was lessened by the buying up, to extinguish their licences, of several inns and beer shops. Less controversial, as one still sees in Street, was the gradual growth of the factory, the considerable sprouting of company-provided houses, and the building, by 1885, of the large working men's club which is fittingly named the Crispin Hall.

By 1939 C. and J. Clark's had become a reasonably large firm, still concentrated at Street and specially known for women's and children's shoes, and for their own chain of shops under the name of Peter Lord. But the years since the end of the Second World War are those which have seen the most exciting spell in the firm's history. They soon found that the demand for their goods could not be met from the labour available in Street and in the villages reasonably near it. So while they still organized a network of buses to bring workers to and from Street they have also burst beyond the confines of the area where they started their business; in so doing they have much affected the entire economy of Somerset. Starting with factories at Shepton Mallet and Bridgwater, they went on to open others at Weston-super-Mare, Radstock, Midsomer Norton, Ilminster, Yeovil, Bath, and Minehead and, outside their own county, at Barnstaple, Plymouth, and elsewhere. Subsidiary companies deal with such matters as shoemaking machinery and supplies to the shoemaking trade. The firm has also moved overseas, with factories, and selling organization, very far from central Somerset. In their own county they have some five thousand employees, making them Somerset's largest private employer. In non-rubber footwear they command some 5 per cent of the home trade, and they count as Britain's largest shoemaking concern. C. and J. Clark's, are still, moreover, run by members of the founding family, with its senior men living, in or very near Street, in houses of a modesty remarkable for the leaders of so great a modern industrial empire.

By contrast to the Victorian period, little outworking now occurs in Street's footwear industry, and C. and J. Clark's large factory, and the administrative offices which now employ more people than the production blocks, rise high, with their late Victorian clock tower, above the middle of the town. Though most of these buildings are fairly modern they include one block as old as 1829. Inside, the shoe museum has a fascinating, though not wholly complete collection of the footwear of many peoples, while next door to it the old office, with many furnishings and items of desk equipment surviving from last century is, in its way, as entertaining a bygone working place as Hardy's reconstructed study in the Dorchester Museum. The factory and offices have now spread over the site of James Clark's modest home; a few yards down the road the Friends' Meeting House, replacing an older building, is in its style a late Georgian survival of 1850. Out at Bullmead, on Street's western edge, the firm's newest buildings, proving the extent to which their activities have grown, is the centralized, largely automated dispatch depot for the supply of the home trade.

In the town, and as far as the edge of the countryside, one is often aware of what C. and J. Clark's, and individual members of the Clark family, have done for the place. Two of the town's schools, and large additions to the County Library, were built by them. So too, in the area near the church where much recent development has occurred, and where the modern buildings of a secondary modern school and the technical college have arisen, the Strode Theatre makes the best venue in central Somerset for such activities as drama and music. Close to the factory, the admirable Greenbank swimming pool was laid out with money left, over thirty years ago, by Alice Clark, a member of the family who was a personnel manager, and a director, of the firm. The pool's entrance is in Wilfrid Road, where one can best see C. and J. Clark's earlier efforts towards company housing.

Architecturally speaking Wilfrid Road is among the more characterful parts of Street; on its small scale it is a local equivalent of Bourneville or Port Sunlight. Its terraces are in a restrained version of the 'Arts and Crafts' Tudor which became popular in the last two decades of the nineteenth century. Wilfrid Terrace, boldly dated 1885, is the oldest; Lawson Terrace, on the same side of the road, is six years later. The most imposing range, with its central cupola and vane, is dated 1889; its name of Cobden Terrace reflects its sponsors' Liberal and Free Trade beliefs. In the Grange Road area on Street's northern fringe most of the company-built housing has more arboreal names to accompany its gables and simple mullions. The names of Brutasche and Grange Terraces lie outside the general pattern, but one also has the Acacias, the Chestnuts, The Lilacs, and suchlike; the dates here range from 1892 to 1903. Elsewhere in Street houses put up, before 1914, by the Urban District Council, on which the Clarks were prominent, display something of the same taste.

The Arts and Crafts Tudor of the late nineteenth century was not restricted to Street's company housing. It appears, in a more manorial vein, in house which William Stephens Clark, who then managed the firm, built for himself in 1889. He called it Millfield; the name has lasted as that of the well-known school which Mr. R. J. O. Meyer has brought into being, and whose headquarters are here on this spacious, and now much changing site.

Mr. Meyer started the school, as a small private coaching establishment, in 1935. Though Millfield grew both before and during the war its spectacular growth, and main fame, have come since 1945; in the upshot Street has become the focal point of one of England's largest public schools. Its mixture of boys and girls, with the girls now increasing in numbers, is one unusual feature. Millfield's concentration on group teaching, with few pupils in each class, means that there are more teachers, in relation to pupils, than in almost any other school. Millfield's policy whereby excellence, in any field, is intensively nurtured, has led to scholastic successes and some remarkably high athletic achievements. As only a few boarders live at Millfield itself the remainder, in separate houses for boys and girls, are scattered in several country houses, at Street, Glastonbury, and elsewhere; the school's presence in central Somerset is thereby much increased. Great changes are now in hand on the central site, and Millfield is now passing through a transition from the physical facilities of a large coaching establishment to those of a co-educational public school, centralized for teaching and social purposes yet also much dispersed. The Nissen huts which have so far housed much of the teaching are making way for modern blocks; two of these, by a Bristol firm of architects, were in use, with such items as classrooms, subject libraries, and a fine language laboratory, by the end of 1967.

Hemmed in between Avalon and Street, the Isle of Wedmore, and the Poldens, the moor country of the Brue and its connecting waterways runs flat, and for the most part fertile of grazing, towards the river's mouth at Highbridge. These flatlands have long benefited from important ventures. They are among the Somerset River Authority's busiest scenes of activity; we have seen how the Huntspill River, whose outflow has lessened damaging floods along the Brue, has been the Board's most spectacular achievement.

Of the villages in this tract of moor between the low hills of Wedmore and the Polden ridge, the best known is Meare, set on its own low island above the moors and now a drier, better drained place than it must have seemed when the mere, whence it took its name, was a watery reality. Archaeologists know it for the relics of its Iron Age lakeside settlement; recent digging has suggested that this habitation had two phases, the first with peasant farmers, the later one by people who pursued a good range of crafts in metal and weaving. More certain still is Meare's long history, in the days of its shallow, far-spreading pool, as a provider of monastic fish. It was yet another Glastonbury manor and it was from Meare, not from the somewhat puny fishpond near the abbey itself, that the large community of monks and attendant laity mainly met their Friday and Lenten needs. The abbey's fish house, now set among cow pastures but once near the edge of the great pool with its teeming fish, its swans, and its waterfowl, was the home of the abbot's fisher bailiff and the place where he stored his gear. Up in the village the manor house, like that at Downham near Ely where the bishops of that rich see had an alternative residence, was a country retreat, not too far from the cloister, for the abbots of Glastonbury. Though altered, like so many other abbey buildings and properties, by Abbot Bere it is, in the main, a first-class piece of manorial architecture. The village is now trim and pastorally inclined. But though Locke saw, in this large parish, a golden field for his pet pursuit of agricultural 'improvement' Meare long remained beset by the misty miasma of the moors. An old survey, quoted by Collinson, tartly remarks that its air was "not very holsome, saving to such as have continued long therein".

There are still parts of these moors north of the Poldens where drainage is still less than complete. The word 'heath' still fitly applies to some of the country, near Ashcott and Shapwick, which was once crossed by the primeval section of the Somerset and Dorset Railway.* Peat, not pasture, occupies the minds and aids the incomes of some dwellers in this little known tract of Somerset. The peat of these moors has had its importance as fuel, for as late as the Second World War it was sold, in such places as Bath, as a quick-burning, somewhat costly, but useful addition to the coal then available. Now, however, it is mainly welcome for gardening and potting, and horticultural peat, from the long-drawn cuttings and their dark, attendant stocks, is a valued product of central Somerset. Its dankness has helped to preserve the oldest of all the county's transport relics, far older than the Glastonbury Canal and the Somerset Central Railway which, successively, ran straight through this moor country between Avalon and the Severn sea. For here, in the ground crossed by what has been mistakenly called the 'Abbot's' Way, is some of the country which the prehistoric dwellers on the nearby hills traversed on their timber trackways, laid down with birch or alder logs, or in some cases, in the manner of fascines, with bundles of birch twigs, and secured by thousands of birch pegs. Some stretches of these early anticipations of the duckboard paths of the Somme and Passchendaele have been known for a considerable time. Others, Neolithic or of the Bronze Age and running north or south from the low hillocks of Burtle and West Hay, have been recently located. Sixteen at least had been found by the late spring of 1969; nowhere else in Europe has boggy country disclosed so great a system of prehistoric tracks. Radiocarbon tests now date the oldest of them at least as far back as 2,900 B.C. Their first users must have plodded along them as parts of a complex, sophisticated system of paths giving them reasonably dry transit between the Mendips, the Isle of Wedmore, the Poldens, and the faintly perceived, yet acceptable isles of firm ground not far north of the course later chosen for the Glastonbury Canal.

---

* A short piece of this line, from Highbridge to Bason Bridge, is still open to serve the dried milk factory at the latter place.

CHAPTER VIII

MORE ON THE HEARTLAND

ȚHE lowlands of central Somerset are strangely intersected by the straight, low ridge of the Polden Hills. They have no counterpart in the Lincolnshire or Ely fens. Only once, at Righton's Grave above Edington, do they rise up above three hundred feet; only at their western end does the peak of Knowle Hill faintly compare with Brent Knoll or Avalon. Yet the Poldens sharply bisect the main expanse of the Somerset moors. Their northern slope, with such villages as Catcott and Shapwick, is gently subdued, and the whole ridge makes a firm basis for arable farming. The Poldens' steep escarpment is to the south. In that direction, and very specially from such vantage points as the Georgian windmill tower on Walton Hill, the Poldens give their best views of the southern moors, of the hills which shut in those levels on their eastern side, of the glint off water in the straight rhines which drain and intersect them, and of the rough, unsurfaced 'droves' which give access to the pastures for farmers and their animals. Above Stawell and Bawdrip the prospect, much changed since 1685 in the alignment of its rhines and in the pattern of its agriculture, is over the battlefield of Sedgemoor.

The night battle in which James II's small regular army defeated and scattered Monmouth's quickly raised, and by then diminished forces is by far the most dramatic event in Somerset's more recent history. What happened at Athelney, at Edington on the Poldens (if this place, as some claim, is the site of Alfred's great victory over the Danes), and at Wedmore may have had a deeper, more decisive significance. But for poignant drama, and because we know so much about the battle of Sedgemoor, the military débâcle of the Monmouth episode holds the field of our attention. The trouble is that the tactics of the battle are now hard to reconstruct, or to make convincing, from the more tamed and more inhabited scene now found between Chedzoy or Pendon Hill and the village centre of Westonzoyland.

The Monmouth Rebellion was an intensely Somerset occasion.* Though its objective lay in high national politics, and though this rising in the West was meant, by Monmouth and his confederates, to be but one of at least four converging attacks on the new king, Somerset was actually more involved than anywhere else in a venture which had, in the absence of Whig victories elsewhere, a slender chance of success. Though Monmouth landed and was captured in Dorset, and though his army briefly marched into eastern Devon, the county of Somerset was his main recruiting field, his chief theatre of war, the scene of his final disaster, and the home country of most of those who died or were transported for their share in the rebellion. Taunton and the other clothing districts, with their old Puritan and Nonconformist sympathies, were the places whose weavers, fullers, and dyers sent the Duke his most devoted fighters. It was here in the levels, amid rhines and meadows much unlike the swifter streams and rolling meadows of the clothing countryside, that some fifteen hundred of them died before the royal cannon, bullets, and sabres.

Whether a visitor to the battlefield comes out from Bridgwater, or along from Middlezoy over what was once the Royal Air Force airfield of Westonzoyland, or down from the Poldens to Bradney whence the rebel army stepped stealthily on to the open moor, he must realize how hard it must be for any modern student of battlefields to sense the feeling or recognize the key points of that strange encounter on a July night. He is, for one thing, unlikely to attempt the excursion by night. But the darkness of night was the setting for a battle wherein neither side could see its enemy. The King's Sedgemoor Drain, now the district's dominant water course, was not cut till the 1790s, and the Bussex Rhine, tactically vital in the whole battle, has long been filled in; the rhine by the battlefield memorial did not exist in Feversham and Monmouth's time. Westonzoyland village is larger, and no doubt more trim, than it was when it housed Lord Feversham's headquarters. The open ground, north of the village, where the

* For more about it, see Bryan Little, *The Monmouth Episode*, 1956, and Charlse Cheuevix-Trench, *The Western Rising*, 1969.

royal army encamped is now filled with houses, orchards, and gardens. Westonzoyland church, with its slender tower and the late Gothic nave where many captured rebels were kennelled for the night, has alone, among the things to be seen in 1685, changed comparatively little. The most convincing picture of the battle (if one allows for the darkness in which most of it was fought) is what one gets from the fine model in the Blake Museum at Bridgwater.

The town of Bridgwater started as the best crossing point of a river which could not well be forded; mud, or rather its avoidance, was the underlying cause of its being. Bridgwater duly became the main port of entry and outlet for much of central and western Somerset. Taunton, Langport, Ilchester, and even Yeovil sent out and received goods through the estuary of the Parrett, along that river and its feeders, and by the canal made to Taunton and beyond. Bridgwater is still a coasting port, but its riverside quay below the historic bridge is bare of the sailing brigantines and ketches which once lined it, the dock with its admirable warehouses receives fewer vessels than it did, and most of the ships which use the port of Bridgwater come no further than the wharf at Dunball and the berths, a little higher upstream, where dredgers disgorge what they have sucked up from the sandbanks of the Bristol Channel. It is as a shopping centre, as a well diversified, intensely industrial town, and as a place with rich remains of its historic past that Bridgwater must now be reckoned.

Bridgwater's great castle has almost disappeared, so that its church, with a graceful stone spire which can be exactly dated to the year 1367, is the town's best medieval survival. Yet the church's architecture is less notable than some of its contents which go back to the Stuart and Georgian periods of Bridgwater's prosperity, when the future Admiral Blake was a young man in his native town, and when the Parrett, and its links inland, had made Bridgwater a thriving centre of the coasting trade. The screen, re-erected in a side chapel, is richly Jacobean and some opulent mural monuments are of about the same date. In the chancel, the visitor has his eastward gaze arrested by what must surely be the finest painting in any church in Somerset. Its subject, dramatically and brilliantly rendered, and almost certainly by some Italian painter of the Baroque *seicento*, is the Descent from the Cross. Lord Anne Poulet, of the well known county family from Hinton St. George, long Member of Parliament for Bridgwater and a godson of Queene Anne who got his Christian name from his godmother, gave the picture to the church. It was said to have been captured from a French ship; it could also have been brought home by some gentleman on the Grand Tour. Not far away, a Georgian zone recalls the doings of a greater eighteenth-century magnate than Lord Anne Poulet. He was the wealthy, magnificent Duke of Chandos, who in 1721 bought Bridgwater's manorial lordship and formed ambitious commercial schemes for making the town Bristol's trading and industrial rival. He failed to shift the larger, more conveniently placed port from its well entrenched position. But some houses remain of those built for the merchants and harbour officials who were to throng the duke's port. The Lions, a lately renovated Baroque house, stands close by the Parrett's grassy and muddy left bank. The best group is in the placid thoroughfare of Castle Street, of brick and stone and sloping gently down, to the Quay, from King Square which is the site of the castle's keep. The street's early Georgian atmosphere is intact, and even if one allows for strong competition from Bath there are few more perfect Georgian streets in Somerset. Elsewhere in the town some good buildings of the Greek Revival proclaim the early nineteenth-century period when Bridgwater's prosperity was renewed. The best, familiar to all those who make their way up the main street, is the nicely balanced forebuilding of the Market Hall, started in 1826 and distinguished for the rounded, Ionic-colonnaded, and domed central section which now houses the Post Office. Before it, the statue of Robert Blake, the Commonwealth's 'General at Sea', commemorates one of the country's greatest men. Born in Bridgwater, educated at Somerset's own Oxford College of Wadham, a respected townsman and in 1640 the borough's Member of Parliament, Taunton's defender in the Civil War, Blake was steeped in the life of Somerset before ever he saw his great sea service against the Netherlands and Spain.

Modern Bridgwater is a thriving, well varied place of industry and commerce. It may be reckoned among Somerset's most completely industrial towns, and with rather over 26,000 people it slightly leads Yeovil as the county's fourth most populous place.

A few years ago the Blake Bridge was opened, a short way upstream from the more historic Bridgwater Bridge; its existence
has freed the town centre from much of the traffic which once made
it a notorious blockage point for travellers on A.38. Ancient
manufactures, such as that of bricks and tiles, are on the wane, and
wire ropes give work to fewer Bridgwater people than once they
did. But many other trades are at hand to make up for those
which are flagging, and Bridgwater, like Bristol, is happy in its
industrial diversity. Several light engineering concerns operate in
Bridgwater, and one such factory employs some eight hundred
people. Furniture and wooden fencing are also in evidence, while
the town, and the nearby villages, get much benefit from the
dispersal policy of two of Somerset's largest industrial concerns.
For C. and J. Clark's make shoes at Bridgwater in their large
factory near the railway station, while in Bailey Street shirts and
collars are turned out by a branch factory of Van Heusen's whose
main base we shall notice at Taunton. Most notable of all, and
Bridgwater's largest employer, is British Cellophane with its
large factory out to the north of the town. Here Bridgwater can
claim an industry of national note, for on this Sydenham site is
Britain's largest plant which produces a new, and by now important material. In its silhouette and its detail the factory is ugly,
but this matters comparatively little in a district where the main
railway line runs close, and where light industry and storage
depots have anyhow made the first stretch of what is now the
main Bridgwater to Bristol road one of the least attractive parts of
Somerset. What comes as a pleasing surprise is the cellophane
factory's blend of industrial modernity with some ancient and
distinguished domestic architecture. For this essentially modern
factory contains, within its actual borders, the old house of Sydenham Manor, admirably kept up as a company guest house and
staff dining place. The core of it was built, very early in Henry
VIII's reign, by members of that well-known county family the
Percevals. Soon after 1613 it was much expanded; it well shows
the transformation of such a building from a yeoman's home to a
small squire's residence.

Back on Bridgwater's deserted quay one again thinks of the
town's past as the gateway to the county's main network of
inland waterways, and of Defoe's notice of its standing as the

point of distribution for all manner of goods from Bristol, and for coal from the Swansea end of the Glamorgan field, sent over by sea as part of the cross-channel trade which was long important both for Somerset and for South Wales. Barges no longer ply up the Parrett or along the placid canal to Taunton. But down by the quay, in buildings which include the watergate which is the one good relic of Bridgwater Castle, are the offices of the Somerset River Authority whose activities, no longer concerned with inland navigation, are still of vital concern to the county's farmers, and to all who must live and move within range of the rivers' floods.

In the far north of Somerset the Bristol Avon River Authority is the body which maintains the course and the banks of the Avon and some of its tributaries. Elsewhere in the county the Somerset River Authority, the present-day successor of the Drainage Commission which started work in 1880, cares for almost all the rivers and streams, and of some stretches in Dorset where the Parrett and the Ivel have their headwaters in that more southerly county. Geology, and the lie of the land in the hills and plains, have given Somerset an awkward blend of high rainfall in its western hills and of a slight, slow fall of water in the rivers which creep through the flatness of the moors. Extra trouble comes from the strong inward surge of the Bristol Channel's high tides. Severe flooding is thus a constant hazard; it has often been made worse by the defective, unscientific drainage efforts of earlier times. Mr. Louis Kelting and his staff, at Bridgwater and out in the field, have a great task on their hands. It is much to their credit that the ravages of the floods are far less now than they were as little as forty years ago.

For obvious reasons the drainage of the levels has long preoccupied the people of Somerset. Some sort of a start must have been made in Saxon times and later in the Middle Ages. But specially fierce fresh water floods, combined with inroads from the sea, must often have reminded Somerset folk how much their living turned on the control of the waters. The disaster of 1607, when floods joined high tides to drown thousands of acres along the Severn estuary, and to flood the low-lying centre of Bristol, was a particularly dire visitation. This was the age, in the Thames estuary and in the eastern counties, of diking and drainage ven-

tures under Dutch engineers. Cornelis Vermuyden, an expert
from Zeeland in the Netherlands, was the practical genius behind
this partly successful effort. Nor did he confine his efforts to eastern
England. Since James I's reign schemes had been afoot for what
the King called the "religious" work of draining and parcelling
out the main Somerset moors. Much of King's Sedgemoor was
allotted to Crown ownership. But as in Exmoor during the nineteenth century the Crown was itself unwilling or unable to
develop its portion. So in 1632 Charles I made over the four
thousand acres of Crown moorland to Vermuyden and a London
merchant whose interests included Fenland drainage. The Dutch-
man, so it seems, was in any case the leading spirit in this move to
develop Sedgemoor. Nothing was done before the onset of the
Civil War. But in 1655, after what were referred to as "the late
distractions", Vermuyden again took up his case, seeking Crom-
well's permission to enclose what had been the "boggy and
unwholesome" royal part of Sedgemoor, and obtaining some
local support for his scheme. But nothing came of it; had the
Dutch engineer got leave to go ahead the later cutting of the
King's Sedgemoor Drain might not have been required.

The channel of the Brue, with various rhines and drains connecting with it, and the fairly new, broad channel of the Huntspill
River are the Authority's chief responsibilities in the moor country
north of the Poldens. Inland from Bridgwater the rivers which
most concern it are the Tone, the Parrett and the Ivel, and the
Cary whose lower course is now deflected, and merged in the
King's Sedgemoor Drain. There is also the watercourse,
straightened out and tamed as the West Sedgemoor Drain, which
irrigates the rich belt of pasture between the low ridge of Stoke
St. Gregory and North Curry and the steep, wooded escarpment
of the ridge on which Fivehead and Curry Rivel stand. Straight
rhines, in a great though well ordered complex, drain the flatlands on each side of the Parrett; among the most important is the
North Moor Main Drain which serves a large tract to the south
of Westonzoyland and close to Brunel's railway line of the Bristol
and Exeter. Imposing sluices, on the rivers and on such important
rhines as the King's Sedgemoor Drain, aid the work of the
numberless rhines. So too do the Pumping Stations where the
old steam engines have now made way for diesel pumps. Some

old machinery, among it two gleaming, well painted steam pumping engines built, in 1869, by the London engineers Eastons, Amos and Anderson, are still reverently preserved in the little museum formed, alongside more modern plant, in the Pumping Station at Burrowbridge. At Oath the great sluice on the Parrett, with its gantry silhouette adding a Netherlandish touch to the flat landscape, replaces a lock which once aided the barge traffic between Bridgwater and Langport.

The avoidance of flooding, and the comfort of those who must dwell in Somerset's moor country, is an obvious purpose behind this system of drains, pumps, and sluices. So too is the convenient livelihood of Somerset's farmers, particularly those who are in the dairy trade. The needs of these people differ from the requirements of those who till the drained expanses of dark earth in the Lincolnshire or Ely fens. In those eastern counties of corn and sugar beet the great fields must be so drained that they remain unflooded and reasonably dry. But in central Somerset what dominates the farmers' minds is abundance of milk; dryness such as one needs, and finds, in the Fens would never suit those whose living comes from this westcountry grazing. What the River Authority at Bridgwater must do is not only to control winter flooding which can, like the high Nile, be a boon if it does not last too long, but also to keep some river and rhine water back from the Bristol Channel to refresh the summer pastures. If they are too successful in the banishment of floods they can get complaints from farmers, for whom some temporary inundation brings the promise of lush grass, that their pumps and sluices are starving them of fertilizing water. What can help the townsmen of Taunton or the villagers along the Parrett's banks can harm those who look forward to brimming churns.

From Bridgwater a few miles' journey up the tidal, muddy, navigable yet un-navigated Parrett takes us up to Burrowbridge, where Burrow Mump rises steeply over the river's crossing, and whence the main road from Glastonbury to Taunton passes close by the larger area of Alfred's refuge at Athelney. Cadbury and Glastonbury have their links with 'King Arthur' who may have his basis in the broad sweep of history but who lacks the solid proof which authentic documents can give. King Alfred, from proven records, is a more certain figure.

Down in the Moors: near Godney

Alfred's marshland base for his counter-attack on the Danes falls neatly into two districts which are separated by the Parrett. To the west the low, yet noticeable Isle of Athelney could have sheltered some hundreds of men. East of the river Burrow Mump—the hillock which has named the bridge—is higher and more sharply visible. Like Avalon it is of Somerset's very essence. A modern writer gives its older name of "Tot Eyot"—the look-out island;* as such it could have well served the Wessex king's tactical purpose. For much of its modest height it may be artificial. The ruined chapel on its top has medieval origins, yet most of what is now there is in the Gothic of the eighteenth century. The Mump's views over the moors, as Alfred's watchmen must have found, are conveniently superb. The Cary's curve once flowed round its base; it is girt, nowadays, by the traffic of a busy road. Over the bridge the longer and roomier Isle of Athelney stretches west above the low flatness of the drained moors. It lies in the parish of Lyng, whose village is at the far end of the isle, and whose Perpendicular church tower, in the soft light of a summer evening, is a specially lovely stone concerto in silvery grey and mellow gold. This is the tract of land where Alfred and his friends must have found refuge, and the legend of the calcined cakes is rooted here among the fields and withy beds between the Taunton road and the Tone as deepened, straightened, and widened by the River Authority. Here too, on the top of the low ridge where farm buildings and a Georgian monument now stand, King Alfred made his visible act of thanksgiving by founding an abbey. Athelney Abbey should have been important, but after its Saxon beginning it failed to flourish as it could have done. Other Benedictine houses overshadowed it, Glastonbury above all, also the more modest Muchelney on its low isle six miles away. Nothing is left of it above ground, and the building activities of Athelney's abbots are better seen in the court house, mainly of the fourteenth century though altered in 1658, whence they controlled their manor at Long Sutton. But their earliest church, small and timber-supported if not wholly built of wood and wattle, seems to have been of rare architectural interest. For William of Malmesbury, who could have been told of it as a

* W. H. P. Creswell, *Dumnonia and the Valley of the Parrett*, 1922, p. 74.

Georgian streetscape: Castle Street, Bridgwater
Restoration frontage: Tintinhull Manor

structure recently standing, says that four timber piers held up the main fabric of what may have been a square nave, and that four round-ended *cancelli* (a chancel and three chapels) led out, in a version of the Greek-cross plan, from the sides of the nave. So Byzantine a plan may perhaps have derived from what Alfred himself could have seen on his boyhood visit to Rome.

Modern Burrowbridge is largely the creation of the time when it served as a river port. For till the railway came to this part of central Somerset, which was not till 1853 when the Bristol and Exeter opened its line from Durston to Yeovil, waterborne transport was the lifeblood of this countryside, and of such towns as Yeovil. A step forward came in 1836, when an Act of Parliament opened the way for the 'improvement' of the Parrett and the Ivel, for the navigation of the lowermost reach of the Isle which flows down from above Ilminster, and for the cutting of a short new canal whose charming terminal at Westport we shall duly encounter. But despite the claim of the Act's sponsors that the Parrett navigation had lain "in a most miserable state" it had long been important. For Collinson (or more probably Rack) speaks of "large barges" coming up to Langport. On Burrowbridge he is more specific, mentioning an 18-foot depth of water at high tide, and an easy passage for coal barges of as much as 40 or 50 tons. But I doubt that such vessels could have cleared the ancient obstacle which was removed in the 1820s. This was the three-arched bridge of stone, mentioned by Collinson and shown in an excellent drawing which hangs in Mr. Kelting's office. It had deep cutwaters, and pointed arches whose tips were almost reached by the water of the high flood. The fourteenth century seems likely as its building date and it was perhaps, a joint venture of the Athelney Benedictines and of their Glastonbury confreres who were manorial lords in the next village of Othery. The plan was made, in 1824 and before the bridge's replacement, by a surveyor named Philip Ilett. He, perhaps, designed its successor which was better both for turnpike traffic and for flood prevention. It is a graceful, single-arched structure, dated 1826 and engraved with the name of its builder, one Johnstone of Yarcombe in East Devon. Some of Burrow-bridge's houses are of about this date, but the church at the foot of the Mump, by Richard Carver of Taunton who designed the octagonal one at Blackford near Wedmore, and several others in the county, is of the year of the Act which really tackled the navigability of the Parrett.

I. K. Brunel was one of those who reckoned that the river could be made more navigable from Bridgwater to Langport, and who considered the Isle valley favourable for building a canal. It was obvious that much needed to be done. Shoals and other obstacles caused delay to barges, and the towing path had become so bad that horses were sometimes hurt, and horse-boys were drowned, in frenzied efforts to get past points of collapse. In three years from 1836 much was done to make things better. The river's bed was made easier to navigate and four locks, one of them at Stanmoor near the junction with the Tone and another at Oath which the great sluice of 1927 has now obliterated. Little remains of what was done in the first few miles above Burrowbridge, but a riverside cottage was once the King William Inn whose name honoured the sovereign in whose reign the enabling Act was passed. This riverside area is also a main centre for the growing, and still more for the 'managing', of the basket willows which are specially linked with this part of England.

Willow-growing was once widely spread in the moor country of Somerset, and little withy beds were found, among the enclosed pastures, in such northern moors as those of Nailsea and Clevedon. But the trade has now declined and is still shrinking. Almost all the growing, and such basketmaking as is still done in the county, are concentrated in and south of Bridgwater. Yet what remains of an old Somerset calling is full of interest, lending character to the scene along the Parrett and in the Isle of Athelney. The country's acreage of basket willows, now standing at between 800 and 900 acres, accounts for nearly three-quarters of all England's willow-growing.

The willows used for wickerware are the saplings which would, if allowed to grow, become the trees which attractively line the roads and rhines of this watery countryside. They are planted in rows 26 inches apart; some 17,000 sets, or plants, grow in an acre. The sticks of those cut at the largest size can be used for such things as the legs of wicker chairs; for baskets and other wicker goods the required thicknesses vary greatly. The rods, after their cutting and 'managing', make up the bundles which are set out for drying, and which are conspicuous to those who drive through this district of the willow-growers.

Most Somerset-grown willows are sent to basketmakers elsewhere; the Black Mole and the stouter Champion are the best favoured strains. The growers number some fifty in all; as many more people earn their living as employees of the growers. A few growers work as such for the whole of their time; others combine their growing with the dairy farming which is everywhere important in these lush pasturelands. More interesting, in some ways, is what local people call the 'managing' of the cut crop. Mr. S. W. J. Gadsby, who both grows willows and makes baskets, has his managing plant by the Parrett at Stathe. His warehouse seems first to have been a timber store which would have been well placed for any wharf that may here have existed; the hamlet's name, going back to the Middle Ages, implies the early presence of such an unloading facility. Stathe has long been a great centre of the willow trade, and Collinson's history makes the point that over £6,000 worth of what he calls "willow withes" were annually grown there. The river, in his time and still more after 1836, could have served to freight the coal then, and later, needed for the boiling and steaming of the cut rods. The management of the willows is a process whose variations depend on the precise colours needed for the different sorts of wickerwork. The darkest, chocolate-coloured shoots are steamed with their bark on them, those which appear nearly white are cut and stripped as their sap is rising, while some of those which are sold away, or locally used, in a reddish-brown hue are boiled before stripping, so that the sap of their bark soaks in to tint them. Boiling, the soaking of cut willows in pits of water, and the bundling of 'managed' willows for dispatch are processes seen at Stathe and elsewhere. The most picturesque, once done through special gauges, and by hand, but now by machinery, is the stripping which takes the bark from the rods. Basketmaking, as it is done in central Somerset, is also a picturesque, unmechanized country craft. No women are employed, and the men sit at their work on box seats, or on low wooden platforms (known as planks). Nowadays these are heated from underneath, and the men work on them with the continued use of such traditional tools as cutting hooks, and thick bodkins to pierce ways for the handles of the baskets.

Past Stathe it is an easy journey over the main railway line to Plymouth, and across one end of West Sedgemoor, to what Collinson calls the "finely waved and indented" slopes of the Curry Rivel ridge. These hills, from their stem near Hatch Beauchamp, through Fivehead and Curry Rivel and almost to Langport, form a part of Somerset which I know less well than I should like to do. Near the top of the steep ascent of Red Hill one does, however, get an agreeable encounter with History. For here is the mansion of Burton Pynsent, for some years the provincial country retreat of William Pitt the Elder, in the last years of his life the Earl of Chatham. The statesman had got the estate by a curious chance. For Sir William Pynsent, of Urchfont near Devizes and of Burton Pynsent, the second baronet of that name and an eccentric, crusty old gentleman, had fallen out with nearly all his relations. He was, however, a great admirer of Pitt's patriotism, and when in 1765 he died he left the Great Commoner most of his property. Pitt thus got the chance of a substantial country estate. Urchfont he sold, using much of the money to add to his new home at Curry Rivel. But he set aside £2,000 to commemorate a benefactor whom he had never met. 'Capability' Brown was his architect for the stone column, 140-feet high, Roman Doric, and with a simple urn on top, which rises high above the green flats of West Sedgemoor and is far seen in many parts of southern and central Somerset.

Nor is Pitt the Elder the only prominent man of affairs who had a link with this low yet prominent hill ridge. For at its eastern tip Herd's Hill was the home of some of the Langport Bagehots, whose best known member gained renown, among many other achievements, as the author of *The English Constitution*.

South of Langport the low, reasonably spacious isle of Muchelney lies in the angle made by the Parrett and the Ivel. Before the days of better drainage it was "frequently insulated by the stagnant waters of the surrounding moors". Agues, one imagines, must have been a standing hazard of Muchelney life, and Domesday has a truly fenland touch with its reference to the manor's two fisheries which annually produced six thousand eels; the Muchelney Benedictines need never have gone short on Fridays or in Lent. The abbey was of Saxon foundation and was never, by Glastonbury standards, of more than modest size or wealth. Its best relic, surviving from a long history as a farmer's home, is the abbot's house, nearly all of it early Tudor of the last phase of England's pre-Reformation building. More interesting, in their way, are the lately revealed foundations of the Saxon abbey church, well proving how modest, and simply planned, were the first churches of what later became large monasteries. The village is an oasis of quiet charm. Many stones from the abbey are built into the walls of its farmyard, its ancient vicarage is well known among priest's houses of medieval days, and the ceiling of the parish church's nave has the rarity of a wooden ceiling, gaily painted in the vernacular Baroque of the Laudian age. Back towards Langport, and indeed on the very fringe of the little town which started as a commercial settlement the end of the ancient royal manor of Somerton. Huish Episcopi has a church tower which is splendid even by the standards set by Somerset's parish churches. It is, perhaps, the finest of those whose design lays less emphasis on continuous vertical height than on the tower's horizontal division into storeys or stages.

From the top of the town, where the 'hanging' chapel is attractively poised above an old gateway, to the riverside district down by its bridge, Langport is still a place of character and charm. Some good Georgian houses survive from its rising days as a centre of river traffic and of distribution out into the countryside, and a town hall of the eighteenth century reminds us of Langport's status as something more than a village. Yet one can say, as Collinson did in 1791, that this old borough was "anciently more celebrious than now". Its great days, before the improvement of the Parrett and in the following years when the river traffic was at its peak, were when the merchanting and banking activities of the Stuckeys and Bagehots largely dominated central Somerset's economy.

As a trading concern, both in coastal and river navigation, Stuckey and Bagehot's went back to the reign of Queen Anne. The two families were connected both in business and by intermarriage; they combined to form the commercial, and later the banking oligarchy which overshadowed Somerset's central lowlands. Stuckey's Bank, much favoured by the farmers and in

time the chief bank in all Somerset, started here in the river
port of Langport. Thomas Watson Bagehot, the great economist's
father, managed the Langport branch and it was here, in a town
more commercially focal in 1826 than it is today, that his son
Walter was born. River navigation was already locally important; the Act of 1836, and more improvements authorized three
years later, made it even more so till the railway took over.
The rich records of the Parrett Navigation, well guarded in the
Somerset River Authority's headquarters, tell us much of this
by-gone barge traffic, of Langport as its main centre, and of
Stuckey and Bagehot's domination of the trade of which, in 1839,
they had a good two-thirds. Back in 1836, when evidence was
being heard in support of the earlier bill, Thomas Watson Bagehot said that, even then, before the Parrett's improvement, some
50,000 tons of goods had annually reached Langport by river;
he added, in a strangely precise statistical estimate, that 53,473
people got "almost all" their supplies through Langport, and
that "a great variety" of goods reached 41,000 more folk from the
same source. The goods carried, as one finds from the particulars
of the boats and their cargoes, included such regular items at
bricks, blue lias stone from Pibsbury wharf which was convenient
for the Somerton quarries, coal, culm which was solidified
anthracite dust from South-west Wales, salt, willows, cider,
sugar, corn, flour, and wool. Flax from southern Somerset and
from Dorset was another cargo, while machinery occasionally
features in the lists. The books also tell of the tonnages carried in
each barge. The boat owners (predominantly Stuckey and
Bagehot's) are also named, so too are the boatmen—John Gore,
Joseph Bell, William Sharman, James Lenthall, James Pearce,
and others—who kept this river traffic going in early Victorian
Somerset. A boatman could move on to a more responsible post.
So Francis Kuhlman, who had served Stuckey and Bagehot's as
a boatman for over twenty-four years, settled down, by 1845,
as the keeper of Langport Lock, collecting the tolls due to the
Parrett Navigation Company and taking the money up the street
to his old employer's bank.

One great obstacle on the river at Langport was not cleared
away till about 1844. Langport Bridge had long been an imposing
stone structure, of nine arches including those which supported

the causeways by which it was reached. It must have been picturesque, but it impeded both the passage of flood water and the transit of riverborne goods. Packages, and sacks of coal, had to be carried from barge to barge, beneath the bridge's dry arches, on planks or on men's shoulders. The bulkier consignments, hogsheads of sugar for instance or large baulks of timber, could not be moved at all past the bridge's row of medieval arches. So in 1839 plans were made for its replacement by the noble bridge, with its three wide, elliptical arches, now seen and used at Langport. The designer, whose drawings I have seen, was William Gravatt, the Principal Engineer of the Parrett Navigation. He had, under I. K. Brunel, done civil engineering work for the Bristol and Exeter and Bristol and Gloucester Railways; earlier still he had worked in Yorkshire for the Calder and Hebble Navigation. Though his bridge at Langport is early Victorian in date its style looks back to late Georgian Regency.

Higher up than Langport, and on the stretch of the Ivel which was made navigable to Ilchester, an ancient bridge was less drastically handled, for the needs of barges and their boatmen, than the one at Langport. The medieval Load Bridge spans the Ivel between Long Sutton on its northern bank, and Long Load which was once the commercial end of Martock parish. All that was done to ease the passage of boats was the enlargement of its central arch. A few traces remain of the wharf which once handled goods on the Long Sutton side; across the muddy stream a wharf and a goods depot were once managed by the well-known Yeovil firm of Bradford's. For Long Load, at the far end of the road running down from Martock, was once a port for that ancient town, and also for Yeovil and other smaller places in southern-most Somerset.

CHAPTER IX

THE SOUTH

FEW of those who know Somerset would suggest that Yeovil is among the county's most attractive towns. Yet it has its good points. Set in a delicious countryside and now grown so that it has something over 25,000 people, it may become more populous if developments occur which are hoped for in that corner of the county. The town provides work, shops, and some amusement for people in many surrounding villages, not all of them in its own county. Despite modern rebuilding, and much drastic change in the townscape of its old shopping and industrial centre, Yeovil has, in its somewhat tangled, triangular historic core, some attractive houses, both Georgian and older. Its parish church, set in a spacious churchyard and with an eastern crypt of the Decorated period, or perhaps earlier, was almost wholly replaced, in the late decades of the fourteenth century, by the work which makes it outstanding. It was the first of the county's major parish churches to be so completely rebuilt. Its early Perpendicular dating makes it contemporary, on its more modest scale, with the main fabric of St. Mary Redcliffe in Bristol, with the nave of Canterbury Cathedral which was put up in Chaucer's time, or with William Wynford's recasting of the great Norman nave at Winchester. Few of its medieval fittings remain, and what must have been a specially splendid Georgian altarpiece, stately with its Corinthian columns, clouds, roses, and cherubs, has also disappeared. But for those who, like myself, much prefer desk to eagle lecterns a great treasure in this noble church is its brass lectern, made about 1450 and on both of its flat sides engraved, in the manner of the monumental brasses more normally found on church floors, with an inscription and a half-length figure to commemorate Brother Martin Forester.

A glance at the map shows that Yeovil, more than most places in Somerset, is a border town. Beyond Pen Mill Station, on the old Great Western line from Castle Cary down to Weymouth, and past the new, wide-spreading, and efficient leather-dressing works of C. W. Pittard and Co. Ltd., the Ivel, by now a winding stream of no great size, forms the boundary with Dorset; a short way to the South Yeovil Junction Station, on what was once the London and South Western line to Waterloo, lies on the very border. Yeovil's economy concerns Dorset as well as Somerset. For many people whose homes are in North Dorset villages come to work in Yeovil's shops, offices, and factories. Some Yeovil people, moreover, find their way to jobs in Sherborne and elsewhere in the neighbouring county. Yeovil, like other towns which lie close to the edge of their particular counties, shows how little, in these days of flexible road transport, a county boundary can mean in terms of daily living. Yeovil, like such other towns in Somerset as Bridgwater and Street, has played its part in giving work to dwellers in villages which once lived far more completely within themselves than they do today. Yeovil's industry and commerce, as in the county's other towns of small or moderate size, has partly come to depend on villages whose people once busied themselves on outwork sent from the towns.

Like many other towns in Somerset, Yeovil was long on cloth-ing. But by Defoe's time, and still more by the end of the same century when Collinson wrote, it had swung over, for its main manufacturing activity, to leather gloves. Yeovil and Worcester eventually settled down to a long career as England's chief gloving centres; they were aided by the decline of London's glovemaking. Yeovil itself became the centre of a large gloving district in southern Somerset; the trade also flourished at Milborne Port, at Tintinhull to the north of Yeovil, and in a more westerly direc-tion at Stoke-sub-Hamdon and Martock. Some of the work was done in small factories, but more was found in the humbler houses of Yeovil and in cottages in the villages, with men, women, and children hard at work, for long hours, on the needful cutting and stitching.

Gloving is still a well-entrenched trade in Yeovil, and in the district near the town. A craft which came later than glovemaking, and which has been locally in evidence for less than two centuries, is the dressing of fine leather, much of it for use in gloves, but much also for such goods as handbags and leather dresses. Some firms combine glove-making and leatherdressing. Others are purely leather-dressers, especially Pittard's, easily the leading local firm in the trade and England's largest producer, for use in England and for exports, of high-grade leather. It was largely through its having its own dyeing and finishing plant that the firm·grew, from small beginnings over a century ago, to so great an expansion in modern times. Starting in Middle Street, in those days on Yeovil's eastern outskirts and reasonably spacious for the laying out of new premises of their particular kind, they duly moved to a larger site, a little way up the hill in Sherborne Road. They duly outgrew this factory. Being anxious to move to a site which was, among things, much better for the discharge of waste fluids, and which made it possible for them to offer the best possible working conditions in what is now a highly mechanized, though inevitably somewhat unpleasant trade, they have now moved to their new factory down by the river and the Dorset border at Pen Mill.

The leather-dresser's craft has itself changed much since it started in Yeovil. Though the skins originally used by the Somerset glovers were those of local sheep, the craftsmen soon changed to those of the less woolly sheep of such countries as Italy and Asia Minor. Nowadays the leather-dressers go further afield, for the most part using the skins of the hairy, scraggy sheep which graze scantily in Abyssinia, Somaliland, and the Cape. Techniques have also changed, so that such crudely vigorous, picturesque operations as fleshing by hand, with much strength needed to run the curved, specially designed fleshing knives down the skins' inner sides, have made way for fleshing by machine. Modern chemical processes, have, moreover, replaced homely techniques which were once used in the treatment of the skins.

Yeovil is also the headquarters of the company (now merged into the far larger entity of 'Unigate') which oddly canonized the local river to give the name of 'St. Ivel' to its cheese and other dairy products. Nor are Pittard's the only Yeovil firm in the front rank of production for their particular goods. For the largest local employer is also, among many other activities, in the country's top rating as a maker of helicopters. Westland's, a firm once mainly known for its propeller-driven aircraft, has in recent years added helicopters to its list of products, and it is for these machines that it is now specially known. The Westland works are prominent on the western fringe of this town of aircraft production, leather and gloves, general engineering, marketing, and of dairy products closely linked to the fine pastures of the countryside which still surrounds it. These industrial concerns draw their workers from a wide geographical range, not least from the exquisite villages, melodious with such proud, two-worded names as Sutton Bingham, Preston Plucknett, and Hardington Mandeville, which dot the South Somerset scene.

Towards Crewkerne and Ilminster the villages, close-knit with their old churches and mullioned cottages, are heart-warming in their frequent use, in doorways and windows and more and more in complete structures, of the golden Ham Hill stone whose quarries are near at hand in the modest hills which overlook the lower land of the Parrett's basin. Many of these places are outstanding for their beauty and rural charm; a few are famous for the fine architecture of their best buildings.

Past Preston Plucknett with its fine manor barn one soon reaches Montacute, and what is, in all likelihood, the county's most visited 'stately home'. But there is more to Montacute than an outstanding, though moderate-sized Elizabethan mansion, less vast than such 'prodigy houses' as Longleat or Hardwick, yet of an excellence, within the somewhat hybrid terms of Elizabethan design, which gives it a place in many books on this country's architecture.

The name of the village came readily from its topography. For the shapely peaked hill, now shrouded with trees and less obviously a *mons acutus* than it must have been in the feudal days of its castle, rises neatly above the village on its western side. The tower which now caps it is, predictably enough, a fancy of Georgian romanticism. From its top, so Collinson tells us, the tower's owner in the 1790s flew a pennon of the imposing length of fifty-six yards; below that great flag lay the district of Montacute's long feudal and monastic history.

The Mortains, that proud Norman family who got the manor at the Norman Conquest, built a castle on the hill at Montacute and then in the first decade of the twelfth century, made over the manor, with the village which is still called 'The Borough' to the great Burgundian abbey of Cluny. A subject priory was founded, much later to become independent of Cluny but still within the Cluniac family of the Benedictines. From what we know of the Cluniacs' architectural habits its church, and its other buildings, may well have been outstanding in their splendour. But as the site has not yet been excavated the church's plan and details remain obscure. The only relic of what was probably a stately priory is its dignified gatehouse, late Perpendicular and datable, from the heraldry of Thomas Chard the Prior of Montacute who was also an assistant bishop in the Bath and Wells diocese, to the years between 1514 and 1532. Soon after the gateway was built the Cluniacs had gone, and laymen owned the site. Twice it changed hands, but within thirty years the property's owner was Thomas Phelips, of a local family which had already risen some way in early Tudor officialdom. Thomas Phelips, like many others who obtained monastic property, lived within the monastic site, perhaps in what had been the prior's house. But when Edward, one of his sons, a prosperous lawyer under Elizabeth I and in James I's reign the Speaker of the House of Commons, came to make his country home at Montacute, he abandoned the monastic precincts, starting a new home some hundreds of yards away. On his easy, level site he was free, with no impediment from older buildings or foundations, to employ the Renaissance ideas of symmetry and balance which were already in evidence, not far away, in the more completely Gothic, early Tudor mansion of Barrington Court.

With gables and rounded oriels, large transomed windows, artless statues, and classical balustrades Montacute House is mellow and serene in its Ham Hill colouring amid the peaceful South Somerset countryside. It is one of the most favoured properties of the National Trust; a good café in some of its outbuildings adds to its relaxed attraction. For those who like Elizabethan architecture better than I do it is a gem; it is certainly more restrained, and less vulgar in artistic bastardry, than some other buildings of its time. So well-known a building needs little description here, and a few points of explanation must suffice. The later Phelipses never rose as high as the mansion's first builder.

Their position, their finances, and perhaps their inclinations never urged them to extend the house, or to make it fashionable in the Georgian classical taste. When in the 1780s the then Edward Phelips wished to remedy the inconvenience of the Tudor mansion's narrow main block, and to give himself a new porch, and a set of corridors to link up his rooms, medieval and Tudor buildings were again coming into vogue. So instead of putting up a classical forebuilding, or some 'Horace Walpole' Gothic addition, he went, just across the Dorset border near Yeovil, to the earlier Tudor mansion of Clifton Maybank which was then for sale. He bought the splendid porch, and much of the stonework of the adjacent façade, dismantled them and carefully built them up again as an addition to his mansion of about 1590. Not only was the operation a success, but this more evidently Gothic work from the Horsey family's mansion is to my mind a good deal better than what the Elizatbethan Phelips had built on his newly chosen ground. Here in this attractive addition we see late Gothic with a dash of Renaissance decorative taste. For more purely Renaissance design at Montacute it is best to stroll, past the classical screen in the hall, out into the spacious front garden, there to admire the charming little circular Tuscan *tempietti* which punctuate the balustrade of what must have started not as one smooth lawn but as a formal pleasance in the Italian manner.

Hamdon Hill and its quarries adjoin the peak of Montacute and its Georgian tower. The views from the hill are superb, and its steep brow is crowned by the short obelisk which stands as the war memorial of the village below it. The upper plateau, within Iron Age ramparts, is dramatically pitted with disused workings of the great quarries which long yielded West Country builders their tonnage of yellow Ham Hill stone. Some of it is still worked on this famous hilltop, for restoration jobs and a few new buildings still make their demands. Below the hill lies Stoke-sub-Hamdon, a village of note as a gloving centre and for much of its architecture. A fair way from the main village, the church is unusual, in mainly Perpendicular Somerset, for the variety of its styles. For good Norman work is there, also portions from each one of the Gothic periods, starting with the last years of the twelfth century and proceeding, through Early English and the Decorated of about 1330, to the Perpendicular Gothic more extensively, and more brilliantly seen, on the other side of Ham Hill, at Norton-sub-Hamdon. In the village the fortified manor of the Beauchamps of Hatch, once proud with its collegiate 'Free Chapel' and the tombs of its feudal lords, has totally vanished. But the priory (more correctly the provostry) which houses the provost and the junior priests who served the Beauchamps' chantry college still adorns one of the village streets. Despite reorganization, and architectural changes, in Bishop Bekynton's time the house, and its farm buildings, are in essence those built for the foundation, piously intended but wasteful of priestly manpower, made by Sir John Beauchamp in 1304. Particularly eloquent of those early days are the rooms in which the provost and his four assistant clergy were all to sleep, and leading off it the little oratory with the piscina of its altar also serving as a squint. The house, long the home of tenant farmers and once partly a butcher's shop, is now the home of the National Trust's tenant. The barns still serve their agricultural purpose of nearly seven centuries; behind them the circular, unhappily roofless dovehouse is outstanding of its type.

Medieval domestic architecture put up for the use of churchmen is also seen at Martock, downstream from Stoke-sub-Hamdon and beyond the main road from London to Exeter and the far South-west. The old parish filled much of the angle between the Parrett and the Ivel, so much so that Collinson, who comments with disfavour on its low, flat, heavy-soiled site, tells us that it was sometimes, in olden days, known as Martock *inter Aquas*. But the Treasurer's House, built for the parish's rector who also held the post of Treasurer at Wells Cathedral, is but one gem in yet another place in Somerset which is something more than a village yet not quite up to the size and dignity of a town. An endowed Grammar School, founded largely for "schollers of the towne and hundred" and a neat Georgian Market House raised Martock above the normal run of villages; they are buildings which still add to its distinction. Long Load is now separate from Martock, and the modern village is split between the main settlement and the more southerly hamlet of Bower Hinton, traditionally the craftsman's zone and long a centre of Martock's Nonconformists. In this direction, linking up with the flax growing once common on the

local farms, one finds the canvas and tenting works of Yeo
Brothers, Paull. Gloving, in the workshops of Martock itself
or sent out from Yeovil, has also flourished in the little town whose
chief scenic glory is in the neighbourhood of its noble church.

As the chancel at Martock is clearly Early English, with five
lancets in its eastern wall, it is something of a rarity in Somerset.
The church's western tower is a little less splendid than one
might expect at the West end of so fine a building. But the late
Gothic nave is a splendid clerestoried hall, built early in Henry
VIII's reign and finely covered, in 1513, with a typically Somerset roof, low in pitch, supported by tie beams with low king
posts above the central point of each beam, and liberally adorned
with angels and rich panelling. Yet the design of the nave itself
makes it an exotic here in Somerset. For it is as if a late Perpendicular pair of arcades had strayed down from the eastern counties,
while the panelled spandrels above the arches recall Saffron
Walden, Great St. Mary's at Cambridge, or Lavenham in
West Suffolk, which is like the nave at Martock as being a
reminder of money made in the cloth trade. The church at
Martock has lost many of its adornments, among them a superb
late Georgian altarpiece, put up about 1785 by a local man, John
Butler, who had done well in Nova Scotia. It must, from its
likeness to the classical reredos which survives as a screen in
Christ Church, Bristol, have been made in that city. But some
seemly Georgian monuments adorn the walls, among them a
tablet to an exemplary vicar who died in 1763. For not only
did the Rev. Thomas Bowyer reside, and diligently visit his
parishoners, but he observed the feasts and fasts of the Church,
held weekly catechism classes, and celebrated Holy Communion
at the then unusual rate of once a month.

Martock has a good share of Georgian houses; the best, very
close to the church, is one with a rich 'Gibbsian' doorway of
about 1750. More entertaining, and next to this house, is the
long, low, mullioned building which once housed the grammar
school. This was founded, in 1661, by William Strode of Barrington; his arms are above the late Gothic doorway which still
seemed natural in such a building. Strode's educational ambitions
for the boys seem to have been somewhat advanced. For an
inscription describes it as a Trilingual School, and the word

Greenham Barton, near Wellington
Contrasted towers: North Petherton; Wells, St. Cuthbert

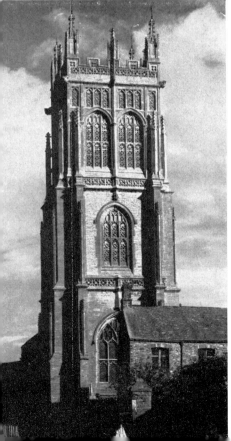

'God' is written up in Hebrew, Greek and Latin. More homely, and to the point in this workaday countryside, is the founder's advice in the words "Neglect Not Thine Opportunities".

From Yeovil's western outskirts, and from the top of Hendford Hill on the A.30 main road from London to Crewkerne and Exeter, one soon approaches the Coker country which was once famous for its sailcloth. East Coker, moreover, combines rare beauty as a village with an important literary link. For this is the village whence T. S. Eliot's Puritan ancestors migrated to New England. The village gave its name to one of the author's long, well-known poems, and the heart of the devout high churchman T. S. Eliot is buried in the church which is well set near the varied mansion (now a school) of Coker Court, and above the charming Carolean almshouse row at the top end of a village which is, even in this gracious Ham Hill country of the Somerset and Dorset borderland, much lovelier than most.

East Coker was once busy on the making of sailcloth, the raw material being the flax which was widely grown in this southern sector of the county. West Dorset was also heavily concerned in this same attractive trade. East Coker's sailcloth works closed some ninety years ago, but the name 'Coker Cloth' was, and is, well known to denote canvas of good quality made anywhere in this district. For the area was once important, for the ships of the sailing navy and for the sail-driven merchantmen of the nineteenth and earlier centuries, in the same way that the marine-engineering firms of northern England and the Clyde have become for the ships of more modern times. Merriott and the Chinnocks were once specially important in the flax and canvas trade. But the largest place in the district to have much concern with it was Crewkerne; in the Napoleonic War, so a Directory of .1830 tells us, £50,000 was made each year by the sailcloth makers in and near the little town. Woollen cloth had once been its mainstay, and as in Wellington Crewkerne's clothiers once sold many serges to the East India Company. But sailcloth and webbing replaced cloth as the best known product of the town and its industrial outskirts.

The centre of Crewkerne, contrasting with more industrial zones on two sides of it, is typical of an ancient market town. Its modern industrial picture is, moreover, a more varied one than

Blackdown Hills; the Wellington Obelisk

that of a town given over to textiles. Light engineering employs
men in the town itself and at works in Yeovil and Chard. Gloves,
shirts, and pyjamas are made in this little town of some four and a
half thousand people. Near its centre, and in a district of quiet
streets and placid old houses, the church, nearly all of it Perpendicular, is one of the county's best. Its plan, and a little of its
fabric, reflect an earlier building whose shape was cruciform, and
whose transeptal plan, as at Axbridge, Wedmore, and Yeovil,
remained that of the later church, showing that a great parish
church of the later Middle Ages need not be based on the design
of chancel, rectangular nave, and western tower. Crewkerne's
central tower indeed gives the church its chance, well taken in the
early Tudor years, of a western façade of minsterlike quality,
far surpassing those normally found outside abbeys or cathedrals.

The more recent industrial story of Crewkerne has largely
lain in the town's northern and southern outskirts. The process
started over a century ago, and it was no accident that in 1851
the most populous streets were those of the workers' little houses—
North Street, and South Street down as far as the almost separate
industrial hamlet of Viney Bridge; some of Crewkerne's Nonconformist chapels were also in these areas. The making of sailcloth was at first a home industry, with its weavers often sitting
outside their cottage doors. But it later became mechanized in
mills; in the town itself it has now, in the main, made way for the
manufacture of webbing, an industry small in its manpower yet
large enough, in this southern Somerset town, to make it the
country's main centre of this particular, and very varied, trade.

Picturesque scenes of Crewkerne's present industry are down the
long, straggling highway of South Street which leads, over
Viney Bridge across a headstream of the Parrett, to the town's
somewhat distant station on the railway to Waterloo. The first
of two mill groupings which one encounters was built last century. It was long a webbing factory, and many of its early Victorian buildings, refurbished for their new use, are still there.
Nowadays, however, it houses some activities of the great textile
concern whose headquarters we shall encounter at Taunton. For
Van Heusen's have now been in Crewkerne for some fifteen years.
Some of their shirts are produced there; more important, and
giving work to most of the people, from Crewkerne and nearby

villages, who work in what was once Bird's mill, they have centralized their stock and dispatch arrangements for all their home market.

At Viney Bridge a terrace of houses, dated 1880 and at a fair distance from the other homes in South Street, must have been built to house workers in the nearby webbing factory. But the mill itself has a much longer history. By 1797 the firm of Sparks and Gidley produced girth webbing there. It was, of course, a water mill in those days, and the waters of its little stream were retained, in the brook's narrow, steep-sided valley, by a long, narrow, pond which must also have been deep. The block nearest to the stream was built late in the eighteenth century. Its pedimented Tuscan doorway, with its fanlight in the 'Adam' taste, could as well be in some elegant street in Bath and is Somerset's most stylish surviving piece of industrial architecture. A block parallel to it is a little later, perhaps from the days of the Napoleonic War boom when the Nelsonian Navy was voracious in its demand for high quality sailcloth made here in southern Somerset. The Viney Bridge mill's present production, carried out in this later Georgian building and in a more modern weaving shed, shows a wide variety; the oldest block is still at work on the final inspection and dispatch of the goods now made in this factory of the company known as Crewkerne Textiles. The Richard Hayward element of that combine is the one now operating at Viney Bridge. Sailcloth is produced there, nearly all of it now of Terylene and no longer of flaxen or cotton canvas. The ships which it drives are no longer the frigates or 74s of Nelson's time, or even the once numerous sailing merchant ships. But yachtsmen have, for many years, used canvas from Viney Bridge, among them Sir Francis Chichester and several contestants, American and British, for the *America's* Cup. Chair canvas, and webbing for an astonishing range of uses, are also turned out in these truly historic works. A most colourful item is the webbing, in the wide though diminishing range of regimental colours, which goes into the making of Army belts.

Past Crewkerne on A.30 the main feature of the countryside is the massif of Windwhistle Hill, a rarity in Somerset in that here, in this southernmost strip of the county, the upper part of a hill ridge is largely made of chalk. Despite the busy traffic along its spinal main road, the country to each side of that road is quiet and remote. Some of the Windwhistle streams, like that at Cricket St. Thomas, flow south to the valley of the Axe. Here, in southern Somerset, there are swift waters whose destination is East Devon, and whose final outfall is in the English, and not in the Bristol Channel.

Beyond Martock, and just short of Crewkerne on the Great West Road, the Parrett makes a slight division between two tracts of agricultural countryside, the western of which ends in the valley of the Isle, and at Ilminster which takes its name from that unimpressive stream. It is a land of mixed crops and pasture, and of villages so little modernized as to keep many of their mullioned cottages wholly built, in this favoured region, of Ham Hill stone. Among them the unquestioned gem is Hinton St. George, not far past Crewkerne on a by-road to Ilminster. It is unblemished in its mixture of an ancient church, of houses of various periods, and of a great mansion which was, till lately, the home of the Pouletts. One hopes, since its recent sale, that its architectural splendours will become widely known; it has already been fully photographed by the National Monuments Record.

Further north the first place of attraction beyond the Parrett is South Petherton, an ancient, trim little town, of royal foundation from as far back as the early Wessex kings and long instinct with a dignity beyond that of the villages round it. Its church is another major one in Somerset which is cruciform, and its crossing piers and tower vault still date back to the early thirteenth century when the place was still a royal manor. Above those sturdy piers, and upheld so it seems without trouble to their structure, the tall central tower is octagonal, as are some others in the county; it dates from earlier in the Perpendicular period than many other fine towers in the county. Its terminal is a rarity in these parts, for it is a short, leaded spirelet, of the type known as a 'Hertfordshire Spike', which is common on the skyline of Cambridgeshire and the county which adjoins it to the south. South Petherton church, more than most in Somerset, is good for brasses; the two canopied figures of Sir Giles and Lady Daubeney, being on a raised tomb and not on the floor within range of tramping feet, are unusually intact.

If South Petherton smacks of a somewhat early medievalism, at Barrington Court we have Gothic on the verge of the Renaissance. For when, in the first years of Henry VIII's reign, Lord Daubeney built his new mansion the idiom which his builders employed was the simply detailed, mullioned and transomed late Gothic which was still normal for England's larger houses. Only in the twisted spirals of some pinnacles and of the chimney stacks is the French Renaissance spirit in evidence; no Renaissance detail crept into the main fabric of the house. But the general symmetry of its design, conceived in a single plan and with each flanking wing and gable balancing one on the opposite side, clearly heralds the mathematically balanced spirit of the Renaissance, and the architectural symmetry which was, in Elizabethan mansions like Montacute, and still more in the neo-Classicism of Inigo Jones and his followers, eventually to capture English taste. In later years the Strodes owned Barrington Court and theirs, by way of contrast, is the red brick stable court, in the idiom associated with Wren and his contemporaries, and a new building when in 1680 Monmouth paid the Strodes his angling political visit.

The Act of 1836 for the improvement of the Parrett navigation mentions "a close in the parish of Barrington" as the proposed terminus of the short new waterway which came to be known as the Westport Canal.* For in the northern end of Barrington parish we are down again at the level of the moors, and rhines reach close to the charming little canal port which is here set in these southern Somerset meadowlands. The canal itself, two and a half miles of it to Westport from its divergence from the navigable Isle, was planned on generous lines. Despite the simultaneous planning and cutting of the Chard Canal, serving Ilminster as well as its terminal town, the project for the Westport Canal was well supported. The Stuckeys, the Bagehots, and others interested in barge traffic on the Parrett very naturally backed it. So too, despite their nearness to the sea and their new harbour at West Bay, did the rope and twine makers of Bridport. But they had, by now, obtained a market in the United States; for these customers the best English port of shipment was Liverpool. The

* In the Act of 1839 for the Parrett's further improvement the extremity of the new canal is styled "Newport".

most convenient way of sending Bridport goods to the docks was by canal and river to Bridgwater, thence by coaster up the Bristol Channel to Bristol, from that port to be forwarded, by the Severn and the West Midland canals, to the Mersey for loading into ocean-going ships now thronging the growing northern port. So bales of rope and cordage, destined perhaps for American clippers or New England whalers of the type which feature so vividly in *Moby Dick* would go overland from Bridport to start a waterborne journey, here among the meadows of Barrington and Curry Rivel, which would end in Boston or New York.

William Gravatt's drawings show that the short canal to Westport was to be wide and capacious, with a guaranteed depth of four feet and amply large for the barge traffic of those days; it was, indeed, to provide deeper water than the Parrett. The cost, so its promoters reckoned, was to be £11,553; this sum was much exceeded. By the end of 1840 the canal was open. In three years' time the Stuckey and Bagehot boats alone took over 10,000 tons of cargo to Westport. Inward goods, such as coal, culm, slate, salt, bricks, and drainpipes were like those carried on the Parrett; their greater cheapness must have been a boon to the small builders and poor cottagers of those times. Elm timber, willows, flax, and wheat were among the downward cargoes. But from 1842, when the opening of the Chard Canal gave the Ilminster district its second navigable waterway, the Westport Canal's decline was all too likely. The railways dealt it another blow; despite dredging and improvement it was surprising that it lingered on almost to the 1880s. More unexpected still, after the disuse of many decades, is the charming survival if its terminal haven.

Nowadays the broad channel of the Westport Canal is dry. But some neat stone bridges, well preserved by the Somerset River Authority, take roads and farmers' droves over its empty bed. At Westport itself the canal ends. Two terminal limbs, and ample space for the turning of barges, comprise the harbour. The local inn is no longer the building where the boatmen and the wharf workers must have slaked their thirst, but as late as the spring of 1967 a row of derelict cottages recalled the housing of boatmen. Of the surviving warehouses two are excellent buildings, in the plain, assuming Regency tradition of storage architecture. One is of brick, on a stone base, with recessed arches. Another, of stone, is now a house. But its iron crane still projects over three loading doors, built one above the other in an imposing confrontation with the water of the canal. Some distance away another house, perhaps built for the wharf keeper, adds a touch of the early Gothic Revival.

As I have never climbed up the Burton Pynsent Column I do not know just how much can be seen from the platform below the urn which caps it. But the top of this column put up by Pitt the Elder should give a view of some parts of the park, and perhaps of the house, which belonged to another, less successful Georgian Prime Minister. For Dillington House, not far above the valley of the Isle and on the fringe of Ilminster, was the property, by his marriage to one of the Spekes of nearby Whitelackington who had owned the house, of Lord North, England's Premier at the time of American Independence and for his last two years the Earl of Guilford. Here, like Pitt at Burton Pynsent, he would reside as a Somerset country gentleman; in 1774 he became the county's Lord Lieutenant. What was once the country home of a politician, and later of less prominent gentry, now serves the cause of education and culture.

The house itself has seen some interesting transformation. Its northern half, though much altered inside, is manorial early Tudor, built by the Bonvilles before the Speke neighbours bought it. In Lord North's time the house was unsymmetrical if appealing; its southern end was a strange jumble of elevations and styles. Then at the very beginning of Victoria's reign that end was built up, and made equivalent to the older portion, by James Pennethorne; though the new work was begun in the year of Victoria's accession its rectifying balance make it classical in spirit, the achievement of a man who had been Nash's pupil and whose training was that of the Regency. The stable court is more committedly Victorian and it is there, after ingenious changes and adaptation, that much of Dillington's work is now done. For the house is occupied by the County Council, as their residential college for courses in adult education. But the activities pursued there give pleasure and benefit to many local people as well as those who come from afar to attend the courses and savour the fellowship of the place.

Ilminster is a quiet little place, industrial in its lower outskirts but in its centre very much the traditional country town. A pillared market hall, single-storied and with no town hall above it, fills much of the central square; up the street a Unitarian chapel of the early eighteenth century is among the oldest in the county. Over the street the 'George' is palpably a coaching inn, and it was in the era of stage coaches and private chaises that it had its most famous customers. For its inscription proclaims that Queen Victoria once visited it. We need not, however, conjure up grandiose visions of the retinue of Victoria Regina, the Widow of Windsor, or the Queen Empress of her serene last years. For Victoria was but a baby girl, less than a year old, when in the winter of 1819 she stopped at Ilminster, the Duke of Kent her father being on his way to what he hoped would be a long, and needfully economical stay among the trim villas of Sidmouth. The future Queen Empress must, at so tender an age, have been blissfully unaware of the lustre she conferred on a sleepy little South Somerset town.

Its church, however, is the outstanding glory of Ilminster. Any religious community that may have worked here in the valley of the Isle disappeared long ago, yet its cruciform plan, and its tautly integrated design, still give it a monastic feeling; despite the alteration, in 1825, of its nave arcades it is still the best knit, and the most convincing of the county's transeptal parish churches. Its tower, unlike those of most parish churches in Somerset, is specially good for architectural students. For the arrangement of its pinnacles, and the planning of its wall surfaces, are closely modelled on those of the central tower, some hundred and fifty years old by the time that this one at Ilminster was built, of the Cathedral at Wells. Inside, and specially in its brilliantly ornate northern transept, the Walronds and the Wadhams, who were once great in Ilminster, are worthily commemorated. The most historic of these tombs, with its inscription recording their foundation of the Oxford college which trained Blake and Wren, has the fine Jacobean brass of Nicholas and Dorothy Wadham; their statues, dressed very much as they here appear in their Somerset parish church, adorn the main feature inside their college's late Gothic quad.

Beyond Ilminster the main road west from Salisbury and

Yeovil spans the Isle, and then soon climbs and impinges on the lonely, secluded country of the Blackdown Hills and the Devon border. This countryside, bar its clothing towns, seems often to have lain somewhat aside from the main stream of the county's life. It was certainly so in Rack and Collinson's time about 1790; their descriptive sentences on these parts speak of such things as meanly built, single-storey cottages, some of them with the cob walls also common in the next county. Here and there, however, things were somewhat improved. For at Donyatt, on the Isle and now almost merged with Ilminster, they give vivid details of a Jacobean almshouse built, as so often happened, by some local man who had made good in London, and of a labourers' benefit club whose members, in a place of fewer than 300 people, numbered eighty-four, and whose contributions, only 2d. a week per member, for the labourers' mutual support in old age and illness, made this parish's poor rates much less of a burden than they were in other villages around. From Donyatt it is no great distance, up the derelict course of the Chard Canal or along the now silent railway route from Taunton to the most southerly town in Somerset, and the last place we encounter in this southern perambulation.

Chard is an ancient town, of Saxon origin, a borough since the thirteenth century, and still with a Mayor and Corporation to administer rather over 6,000 people who live there. More than most places in the county it is a town of light industry, and much interlocking occurs between its economy and that of Ilminster. Its townscape, moreover, is so conditioned by the configuration of Chard's site that it is unique in Somerset.

The best known part of Chard lies along the steadily rising line of the Great West Road; at its upper end the houses lie higher above the sea than those of most Somerset towns except for Bath. But tucked away to one side of the main highway the Old Town is far quieter, and reveals much by its names. The old church is there, a long, low building, mostly Perpendicular and a little unimpressive for so historic and genuinely important a place. It is Chard's only building still standing from so distant a date. For in 1577 the town was almost wholly burnt to the ground; the disaster must have been as drastic as the great fire which in 1731 wrecked Blandford. Mullioned houses, such as the charming

Manor House, and the picturesque building of the grammar school, with its projecting porch and some little rooms above it, were put up in the years shortly following the fire. So a few buildings, about a century old when Monmouth came to Chard on his political reconnaissance and during the campaign of his rebellion, help to adorn the long, wide, steadily climbing Fore Street which gives Chard its special character. No other town in Somerset has quite this alignment, and it is common nowhere in Wessex, though Dorchester comes to mind as an obvious parallel. Another Dorset town may have given Chard's townspeople their idea for the jutting façade which proudly dominates the central sector of its chief street. For the town hall-cum-market house, boldly projecting in advance of the normal building line, gives Chard the fine focal point which Bridport gains from its own, similarly projecting and two-tiered town hall of the 1780s. Here at Chard the classical order is Roman Doric, and the age of the admirable town hall is some fifty years less than the one which is Bridport's pride. But its Georgian cupola, and its assertive projection are as one finds them in the attractive West Dorset town.

Chard has had its flourishing cloth trade, and has long been a manufacturing town. Shops, inns, and cafés apart, and apart also from what it does to meet the needs of many passing motorists, its people make a largely industrial living. They work not only in the main town, where fine late Georgian mills, once on cloth and later busied on the making of lace net, now house other callings, but in the borough's southern reaches and down as far as Chard Junction on what used to be the main line of the Southern Railway. Engineering is now Chard's leading trade, dairy products are what one expects in so pastoral a locality, and a little glovemaking links Chard with towns further to the east. Shirts and collars now maintain Chard's ancient textile traditions, giving it an industrial kinship with the much larger town of Taunton.

CHAPTER X

TAUNTON AND SOUTH WESTERN

A TRAVELLER to Taunton from the East can take his choice of approach routes. He can come in, from Hatch Beauchamp with its fine Georgian mansion and its old canal (and then railway) tunnel, through a belt of somewhat uninteresting country which will bring him to the county town's suburban outskirts. He can reach these same outskirts from Bridgwater, by the gently undulating road whose chief landmark is at North Petherton, where the church's splendid tower resembles that at Huish Episcopi in its emphasis, by horizontal bands of panelled decoration, on its storeyed construction, till at the top it bursts out in a proud riot of gargoyles and pinnacles. He can, however, approach Taunton along lower ground, over the moors by rail from Bridgwater or Langport, along the towpath of the peaceful, still filled canal, or up the Tone's newly scoured and improved course till he reaches that workaday part of Taunton where timber and coal were once unloaded from barges to the great convenience of the townsmen. This river approach is the most traditional and the most revealing of all. It runs close past Athelney, and so nearer to Taunton past Creech St. Michael where the toppled, battered arches of the Chard Canal's aqueduct cross the flat yet narrow campagna of this wedge of Somerset's moor country. Nearer Taunton, above the river and its gaily foaming weir, the peaky little hill of Creechbarrow is as conspicuous as Alfred's Burrow Mump. At its foot the spreading, modern buildings of the Navy's chart factory produce navigational aids of a type unknown in Alfred's ships, reminding us of new crafts which now vary Taunton's long-standing industrial scene.

One of the most pleasing things about Taunton is its skyline, well seen as one comes in by train from Bristol or London.

Church towers and steeples rise high, in a fine mixture, above the buildings of the town. The towers of St. Mary Magdalene and St. James are genuine Perpendicular, though rebuilt last century. Out to the East, in an artisan quarter of the town, the stumpier tower of Holy Trinity is very early, pre-Tractarian Victorian. St. John's, very near the County Hall, has a fussy Victorian spire, by Sir George Gilbert Scott, above an unattractive main building. The fine tower of St. George's Catholic church, by Benjamin Bucknall and seen as the high-rising terminal of a street, is Decorated in its detail but joins in spirit with Somerset's great tower-building achievement of the fifteenth and sixteenth centuries. North of the railway, the humbler broach spire of St. Andrew's completes a group which would give distinction to any place. Nor are church towers the sum total of the good architecture in this truly historic county town.

Taunton's origins go back to a date very early in the eighth century, when King Ine of Wessex pushed his westward advance far up into the Tone valley, establishing Taunton as a fortress both to guard what he had conquered from the Britons and as a springboard for a deeper westward advance. But the kings of Wessex soon handed over the manor, and large estates round the town, to ecclesiastical owners. These were not the bishops of Sherborne who had, by now, taken western Wessex into their new diocese, but the holders of the older, more important see of Winchester. For over a thousand years those bishops owned Taunton Castle and were the lords of the great manor of Taunton Dene; their holdings in western Somerset were among the riches of their wide possessions. The long control of Taunton by the bishops of a somewhat distant diocese does much to explain the place's medieval history. The Somerset bishopric, when the time came for its creation, could hardly be set up in a town so much the possession of another prelate. Royal power, moreover, was long overshadowed in a town which might otherwise have durably held the position it now holds as Somerset's main scene of judgment and imprisonment. So Ilchester and Somerton, more central than Taunton but in themselves far smaller, had their place as prison towns, with assizes often held at Ilchester. Parish churches apart, medieval Taunton was more obviously an ecclesiastical town than it has been since Tudor times. The castle, as

Bishop Langton's late fifteenth-century gate tower still proves by its heraldry and the crude Arabic figures of its dates, was often altered by Winchester's bishops; the square bulk of its great Norman keep, probably built by Henry of Blois, King Stephen's powerful brother who was both Bishop of Winchester and Abbot of Glastonbury, must have dominated central Taunton as no building now does in that part of the town. Nor is the castle's keep the only thing now missing from the local skyline. For some way north-east, and conveniently placed at no distance from the running water of the river, a large area once contained the buildings of the Augustinian priory. A bishop of Winchester founded it about 1115. It was the first of Somerset's Augustinian foundations, and was clearly meant to continue the work long done in the town by a small community of secular priests. The priory became one of fair size and wealth, and as its church was finished about 1342 it must have contained work in the Decorated style. It may, with a cruciform plan of the type normal for the churches of religious communities, have been the largest and most imposing in the town; the laity's churches of St. Mary Magdalene and St. James were its dependencies. The whole priory's destruction has been sadly complete. But Canon Street keeps its memory alive, while some Decorated tracery now adorns the Regency gate piers of Priory House. Behind St. James's vicarage another building is a survival of the canons' outer premises. It may have been a barn, but in one of its end walls two excellent windows, displaying the plate tracery of about 1250, may have been moved from some more dignified part of the priory. They clearly suggest high architectural quality.

The highlight of Taunton's medieval history came in 1497, at the very time when the town's prosperous clothiers were building, at St. Mary Magdalene's, what turned out to be the tallest, most vaunting of Somerset's parish church towers. It was now, in Henry VII's reign, that Taunton made its first acquaintance with armed rebellion. It was twice entered by rebel armies, first by the Cornish insurgents on their way to defeat at Blackheath, then in a few months more by Perkin Warbeck whose rebellion, oddly anticipating Monmouth, collapsed at Taunton itself. But no scenes of massive execution followed this pretender's pathetic attempt. Taunton's townsmen were left in peace to get on with their chief church's splendid panelled and pinnacled tower. The whole work of rebuilding, so a date on the south porch suggests, ended in 1508, the last full year of the first Tudor sovereign's reign.

Taunton settled down as a clothing, and eventually as a strongly Puritan town. Its staunch Puritanism led to its being a Parliamentary stronghold in the Civil War, isolated in Royalist territory, beleaguered, but never taken. Robert Blake, as a military colonel and not yet a naval commander, bravely led its defence. Puritanism, and Nonconformity claimed many of Taunton's clothworkers, and Defoe later noticed that the town had long been reckoned a 'seminary' of Dissenters. In such a place it was natural to find strong support for the 'Exclusionist' cause which sought to keep the crown from the proclaimed Catholic James, Duke of York. Support in Taunton was thus a main factor in the calculations of the Duke of Monmouth. His rising in the West has largely to be seen in terms of Taunton; the town and the clothmaking districts near it were a key factor in that short campaign of 1685. Lyme Regis became Monmouth's landing place because it was the nearest port, on the English Channel coast, to Taunton. The Taunton area was 'Prince Perkin's' chief source of recruits. It was in the Market Place at Taunton, amid houses, as Celia Fiennes found in another ten years, still "mostly timber and plaster", that he unwisely allowed his proclamation as king. But Taunton's leading townsmen were now unexpectedly chary of their full support. Royal cavalry forces soon successfully harried his outposts in the country towards Ilminster and the Blackdowns, and Monmouth's stay in Taunton was far less than the time which he needed to train his weaver and peasant recruits into true military shape. Then in the autumn, after Sedgemoor, the pursuit and rounding up of the rebels, and the first, summary executions by Colonel Kirke and his 'lambs', the county town, along with Wells, was the chief scene of the inevitable Assizes. Jeffreys, and his colleagues on a specially strengthened bench, sent some hundred and fifty of Monmouth's followers to their deaths, and many more to the hardly less lethal punishment of transportation to the tropic fevers of the West Indies.

The Monmouth tragedy interrupted, but did not end, Taunton's prosperity as a clothing town. It was such when Defoe came there; the author reckoned that it had more people than York which he made the birthplace of Crusoe. A leading clothier told him that 1,100 looms were all busy at work in Taunton, adding the grimmer point that no child of five or over, in Taunton and the villages round, could fail to earn its living if it had been well brought up and taught.

Such was the prosperity of Taunton in Queen Anne's time or under the early Georges. But well before the end of the eighteenth century Taunton's cloth trade was almost dead. Silk weaving to some extent replaced it, but the town had to find what compensation it could from its development as Somerset's social centre and assize town. The prime mover was a Tauntonian who had made good as a banker in London, sat as one of his native town's Members in Parliament, and did much for Taunton's improved appearance. He was Sir Benjamin Hammet, who gave his name to the brick-built Georgian street, now full of the offices of lawyers and other professional men, which neatly links the Parade to the western side of St. Mary Magdalene's great tower. It is a good foil, with its sober neo-Classicism, to the late Gothic glories at its far end. The effect survives, though hatefully marred on one side of the street's Parade end, by the unmannerly scale, and bulk of a recent shop block whose building caused the demolition of some of Sir Benjamin's houses. The street was laid out in 1778, five years later than the building of the bulky, dignified Parade Rooms, once flanked by arcaded market houses and giving Taunton better social facilities than it could have had in the old pillared market house which Monmouth and Celia Fiennes saw. Hammet also brought about the charming, Georgian Gothic refashioning of some living quarters in the castle. His are the buildings used, in their pleasingly mock-medieval state, as the headquarters of the county's Archaeological and Natural History Society; it is that society whose museum, throwing light on many aspects of Somerset's past life, fills much of the rest of the castle. Nor were Sir Benjamin's efforts the end of ordered elegance in Taunton. For out on what was then the town's western fringe, the shallow-curved, brick-built Crescent is a sweeping, simple group of 1807, built as a residential rampart to overlook the farmland which still crept close to the centre of the county town. At one end of it the Victorian Club became the rendezvous of the county gentry. At the other end a charming Ionic façade was at first that of Taunton's Catholic chapel, replaced by St. George's in the 1860s, and now a Masonic hall. Across from the Crescent an open site seemed suitable, in Victorian times, for the oldest part of the Shire Hall. By the 1830s the demands of county administration caused a need for far more accommodation. So a large, well-sited extension was built, neo-Georgian by Mr. Vincent Harris and somewhat cliché-ridden. This in its own turn has proved inadequate, so that some of those who now administer Somerset work in far more modern buildings within the County Hall site, or in some rented space, somewhat closer to the river, in Taunton's most important 'contemporary' office block.

Modern Taunton, with some 37,000 people, is a busy, characterful blend of county town, shopping centre, place of education, and industrial community. All these sides of its life make their contribution to its present appearance; one thing that the town lacks is an agreeable riverine scene. For the Tone, bisecting the modern town and with its ruddy, turgid waters once spanned by an old bridge of three arches, for the moment lacks charm. Yet it seems, once the work of deepening, widening, and embanking the town's name stream is finished, and once the Tone's newly improved course has settled down, that this vital part of Taunton will have made a better contribution to the whole town's amenity.

Taunton's buildings, and the simple layout of its main streets, are familiar to those who live there, and to many thousands who come in, week by week at least, to shop and do business in their county town. To any appreciation of Taunton's present state one must add the great flow of motor traffic which is apt, despite ingenious and well-marked avoiding routes to the North and South, to stifle the town at week-ends and in the West Country's main holiday season. As a shopping rendezvous Taunton serves many who live, elsewhere in Somerset, well away from the town or its nearest villages. The shops and offices of busy Taunton are natural haunts for those who dwell in the lightly peopled, intensely unurban Quantock or Brendon country. A few of the town's shops are those of the high quality dealers, in such things as Continental foods and fine cheeses, which one is apt to find in any county town. More obvious, and invading the town centre

On the Bridgwater to Taunton Canal
Recent ravage: Hammet Street, Taunton

with 'contemporary' store architecture of a kind common in many others, are the large, more standardized buildings of some multiple concerns.

Pride of place, in any account of modern Taunton, must go to the town's position in as the main centre whence the affairs of Somerset, outside those reserved to itself by the County Borough of Bath, are administered by the County Council. The officials of the county, of the borough, and in the local offices of various Government ministries make up the largest block of those who work in the town. We have seen how the County Council's offices dominate the once open district to the west of the Crescent. The modern office block in which some county administrators have perforce to work also houses, in a policy of dispersal from London, much of the day-to-day administration of those great shopkeepers, the Debenham Group. 'White collar' jobs, in a town long busied on the making of those very articles of wear, loom as large in the prosperity of Taunton as they do in the economic well-being of Bath.

Yet Taunton also has its long-standing industrial life. For centuries it was a clothing town and silk, for a considerable time, followed woollen cloth as the mainstay of its outward trading. It is fitting, and no real accident, that Taunton is still busy, along with paper-making and a fairly strong engineering trade, on the making of things to wear.

Taunton's shirt and collar trade is of fair antiquity; *Kelly's Directory* of 1875 lists four concerns of this particular kind. The water of the streams flowing down from the Blackdown Hills was long ago found to be good for the dressing of collars, and the collar trade was useful to local people because it gave work, much of it in their own cottages, to the agricultural labourers' women-folk. Shirt and collarmaking are not, nowadays, the monopoly in Taunton of the firm best known for their production. But the British Van Heusen Company, now part of the large federation of Viyella International, has become specially famous in this attractive trade. Unlike Wellington, and unlike the area round Exeter, Taunton has no ancient trading link with the Netherlands to explain so Dutch a name for a concern which, like C. and J. Clark's, is important for the well-being of more places in Somerset than its headquarters town.

Cleeve Abbey, the eastern range
In Watchet Harbour, Minehead beyond

The Van Heusen who gave his name to Taunton's chief collarmaking firm was an American, of Dutch extraction and of an inventive turn of mind. He evolved a method whereby multiply collars could be made out of curved fabric. He first started his manufacturing organization in his own country and then, soon after the end of the First World War, came to England, formed Van Heusen International, and planned to make his collars under licence. After a temporary change of name the firm became British Van Heusen in 1951; by then its activities were a well-established part of Taunton's industrial life. The town, with its tradition of collarmaking and plenty of its people well skilled in that particular work, had been seen by Mr. Van Heusen as an excellent place in which to set up his manufacture and exploit his patent. For the first few years all work was done on collars. A few shirts, for export only, were made about 1930; from then onwards the firm set out on gaining its present great share of the shirt market at home.

Van Heusen's Taunton factory and offices are now on a site once partly filled by R. M. Moody's who had long made collars and shirts, and who had also made Van Heusen collars under licence; they are still in business as collarmakers in Bridgwater. This south-eastern area of Taunton, with Viney Street the one against which the *Directory* of 1900 listed Moody's, is that which contains Holy Trinity Church, and whose spiritual needs the church was built to serve. This district of houses was created early last century, and the new Union Workhouse was put up in that part of Taunton. The *County Directory* of 1840 calls it "almost a new town"; it was, from the start, a district of craftsmen and artisans. Many of those who now work on Van Heusen's greatly enlarged output, nowadays mainly of shirts with their collars attached, still live close to the firm's headquarters. But many others come to Taunton, by car, from well outside the town, so that the creation of car-parking space now looms large among the managers' problems. Nor, despite their employment of over six hundred people here in Taunton, is this number enough to meet demands on what has now become one of Somerset's larger industrial concerns. As with C. and J. Clark's at Street, dispersal has been the only remedy, so that Van Heusen shirts and collars are now made elsewhere in western Somerset, and down in

Cornwall at St. Austell. I have shown how production and warehousing both take place at Crewkerne. The first place to benefit from this spreading out of Van Heusen work was not far from Taunton, in the trim village of Bishop's Lydeard, in the Vale of Taunton Dene and below the superb red sandstone and Ham Hill tower of the local church. Watchet came next, with shirtmaking established in what had once been a cinema. The most recent of Van Heusen's dispersals is at Bridgwater; less than half of their employees in the county now work in Taunton.

Taunton and its outskirts, now well spread to the north of the railway as well as in the direction of the steep Blackdown escarpment, have things of note beside the shops, the haunts of administrators, and the town's trading and industrial zones. Of its more prominent churches I have spoken when mentioning the town's attractive skyline. For historic reasons, and indeed by the restraints of the law, the older Nonconformist chapels avoided towers and steeples. Yet one of them, behind a dull Victorian frontage, survives as one of England's finest meeting house interiors. Mary Street chapel is now Unitarian, but its early Georgian work dates from its Baptist days as one of Taunton's main strongholds of a still entrenched Dissent. Two massive pillars, square, fluted, and Corinthian, support the ceiling, while galleries, a richly garlanded pulpit, old pews, an original communion table, a brass chandelier of 1728, and some Georgian mural monuments complete an ensemble of the type which must once have been fitted out by many Nonconformists after their disappointment over Monmouth and happier days after Dutch William's Act of Toleration.

Education, along with shopping and industry, flourishes briskly in Taunton. Huish's Grammar School, in new buildings now though Jacobean in its foundation by a Taunton man who had made his pile in London, is what one expects in such a town. So too are the County Council's schools and Bishop Fox's Girls' Grammar School which now benefits from some of the endowments once enjoyed by the boys' grammar school started by the early Tudor Bishop Fox of Winchester. More remarkable is Taunton's possession of no less than three boys' public schools, between them instructing some 1,400 senior pupils. Queen's College has a Methodist background while Taunton School, starting, like Queen's College, in the 1840s, was first called the West of England Dissenters' Proprietary School. Originally it took pupils from various Nonconformist homes, and had large gifts from those keen Congregationalists, the Willses, in their earlier days as tobacco magnates in Bristol. King's College, by way of contrast, started in 1879 when Canon Woodard bought the Gothic buildings which, for a few years on Taunton's southern outskirts, housed Bishop Fox's Grammar School. As a Woodard School King's has naturally had High Anglican traditions. Together, these three schools, all in Victorian Gothic main buildings, give Taunton an educational position unique in its own county.

Out past Queen's College it is but a short distance to the village of Trull, and to a church whose interior splendidly introduces a special glory of western Somerset. Fine bench ends, of those years in the sixteenth century when great religious changes were impending, are not, as one sees at Brent Knoll and North Cadbury, confined to West Somerset. But this far end of the county, along with many places in Devon and also in Cornwall, is superbly rich in this aspect of church furnishing. Intense rivalry, from parish to parish, must have helped, for the most part in the 1530s but sometimes a little later, to bring about this passionate urge to refurnish. There must also, somewhere in the West of England, have been the team of craftsmen who could satisfy the demand; the name of Simon Werman, on a bench-end at Trull which is dated 1560, must refer to some later carver. Here at Trull the wealth of carving, crudely vernacular yet effective in its vigour, is specially exciting. For the bench-ends include scenes from a religious procession of the type that was soon to end, and there are ancient screens both across the entrance to the chancel and in the side chapels. Rarer still, and unusual even in western Somerset with its riches of early Renaissance woodcarving, the wooden pulpit has canopied niches, and in those niches five statues of St. John the Evangelist and the Latin Doctors of the Church.

The Vale of Taunton Dene stretches on above the county town, a rich wedge of agricultural country between the Quantock and Blackdown foothills. Fruitgrowing has long been practised here along with dairying and the growing of arable crops. It is no surprise that cider is still made there on a more than domestic scale, on the main road between Taunton and Wellington and at Norton Fitzwarren where the branch railway to Watchet diverges from the main line which continues to give Taunton its importance for railway travellers.

Up Taunton's vale, and before the infant Tone flows down from the Brendon foothills, the chief places are Wiveliscombe and Milverton. Medieval Wiveliscombe contained an episcopal manor, much visited by the Bishops of Bath and Wells when on pastoral duty in this far end of their diocese. Nowadays it is a quiet, unexciting little town, and its old church has made way for a late Georgian Gothic building which is among the larger, more interesting churches by the prolific Somerset architect Richard Carver. At Milverton, long a clothing town which sent many recruits to Monmouth, the medieval church survives, mostly early Perpendicular but with a glory of early Tudor bench-ends, increasingly Renaissance by now and with portrait roundels which could have been drawn from some pattern book by a contemporary of Dürer or Holbein. Here at Milverton one can leave the Bampton and Barnstaple road, cutting across to A.38 and the Devon border through tangled West Somerset country whose antiquarian glory lies in the two manor houses, late medieval and in some ways alike, of Greenham Barton and Cothay. Members of the Bluett family, not long before the end of the fifteenth century, built the main portions of both houses. Despite changes and additions both manors, deep set in the folding hills of the West and both of them near the Tone and the Devon border, convincingly survive as good examples of the 'manor house' homes put up, in their particular period, by the rich clothiers and small gentry. Greenham and Cothay, like the medieval manor house of Lytes Cary in central Somerset, long lay unregarded as tenant farms. For their Georgian and Victorian owners they were sources of income, but not chosen fields for fashionable, post-medieval refurnishing and improvement. They thus awaited their sensitive and sympathetic restoration much closer to our own time. Both are highly picturesque in the most accepted sense. Cothay in particular, very close by the Tone, gains much from the ensemble of ancient stonework and the still surface, just outside its gateways, of the large pond.

South of Taunton, past the early Tudor mansion of Poundisford Park, past Pitminster church with a good octagonal top to
its tower, or through Somerset's more westerly village of Blagdon,
an explorer soon comes to the dramatic, well wooded escarpment
of the Staple and Blackdown Hills. Here, running lengthways to
the Vale of Taunton and in constant view from the nestling villages,
are the northern precipices of a great massif of remote hills which
stretches deep into Devon and whose spurs, each side of Sidmouth,
verge steeply on the English Channel. Here again some small tracts
of Somerset have streams which run south, away from the direction of those which water the flat moors and lose their waters in
the silty swirl of the Bristol Channel. Much of this countryside,
yellow in spring with wild daffodils and a resort of gipsies,
lies clear of most main roads and is strangely unknown. Part of it,
the parish of Churchstanton between the topmost reach of the
River Otter and the Culm's headwaters, was in Devon less than a
century ago. The lonely valley of the Otter itself (now a long,
narrow reservoir) was the county boundary. For Church of
England purposes Churchstanton is still in Exeter diocese, and its
hillside church, with no village grouped near it, has fine nave
arches and a waggon roof of the type which is more of Devon than
of most of Somerset. Churchingford, not far above the Otter
valley, is a tauter, more concentrated hamlet, with old mullioned
houses among its buildings. Between it and Churchstanton the
tableland, well cultivated and high above the sea, is flat and of no
great charm. But below Churchstanton, in the misty, lonely
country between it and the escarpment, the well timbered
valley of the infant Culm is of a quiet peace and beauty hard to
rival elsewhere in the county which has acquired, from neighbouring Devon, this territory behind the Blackdown crest.

For some three miles the road along the wooded, bracken-
grown edge of the hill is the county border. It is also, in the holiday
season, a favoured diversion route whereby cars coming to and
from Cornwall can dodge the blockage points of Taunton and
Wellington. Near the place where a road drops sharply down
towards Wellington a passable track turns off, towards a steep
promontory of the hills, to the point where a superb vantage
point is crowned by the great obelisk set up, within a few years of
Waterloo, to honour the battle's victor.

As the Wellesleys had some slight connection with Wellington in Somerset their most famous member chose this town, and not Wellington in Shropshire or the Herefordshire village of the same name, as the title for his peerage. Though the Iron Duke neither owned land nor lived in the place, so tactical a site above the town seemed suitable for the lofty memorial which now stands so conspicuously in western Somerset. The Egyptian style was in vogue at the time, so that on one side of the base of what is, in any case, an Egyptian art form a winged device in the Egyptian manner adorns the doorway to the stairs inside the slender shaft. The obelisk was meant to support a statue of the Duke. But this, most happily for its tapering and pointed purity of outline, was never set up. The designer, a Barnstaple man, was Thomas Lee who had studied in London under Soane. He much enhanced this Blackdown bluff, making it a place worth visiting for more than its superb views and its own heathland charm. Below the monument, strung out along A.38 and with an important suburb running down towards the Tone, the town of Wellington shows up somewhat harshly in the rural landscape.

The railway approach to Wellington from Taunton is worth while for its glimpses of the course, and of the engineering works, of the canal which once continued the line of that from Bridgwater to Taunton. This waterway reached as far as Tiverton, and was meant to be part of one of the West Country's most ambitious canals. The Grand Western Canal, from the Parrett's estuary to that of the Exe, was planned to enable late Georgian merchants to send heavy goods by water from the Bristol to the English Channel, so dodging the hazards both of gales and adverse winds off Land's End and of French privateers hovering for prizes along the Cornish coast. But as the stretch from Exeter to Tiverton was never cut, and as the upland portion through the Somerset and Devon border country turned out to be far more tough and costly than the promoters expected the Grand Western took its place in the annals of frustration and failure. But for the commerce of Wellington the work of the 'navigators' turned out to be a boon.

Wellington's main road is A.38, bringing much congestion to the town till such time as a bypass or a motorway again makes of it a place whose streets have to cope with no more than the burden of local traffic. The old church lies out at the town's eastern end—good, clerestoried clothiers' Perpendicular, and also important for the lofty monument of a Wellington man whose fame goes beyond his undoubted eminence as a lawyer, and as the judge who presided at Guy Fawkes's trial. For Sir John Popham, Lord Chief Justice when he died in 1607, is here buried in a stately tomb—freestanding and with a towering, Corinthian-pillared canopy in the full Renaissance taste. He was one of those who was, in his own time, most interested in colonization, and in the criminal punishment of transportation to which Jeffreys duly consigned several Wellington men. He, and Sir Ferdinando Gorges who hailed from Wraxall at the other end of Somerset, were those who, in the years just before the colony of Virginia was lastingly founded, sponsored voyages, from Bristol, to explore the chances of settlement in what eventually became New England. Then in 1607, the year of Popham's death and of the founding of Jamestown in Virginia, they made a move, as it happened without lasting success, to place a colony on the Kennebec River in what is now the State of Maine. Popham Beach in Sagadahoc County commemorates the Somerset lawyer who was largely behind a settlement of which his own brother was Governor and some of whose members did, indeed, come through the rigours of a Maine winter between 1607 and 1608.

Modern Wellington widens out, each side of its central cross-roads, into broad streets, with a few Georgian houses and of an urban spaciousness not unknown at each end of many country towns which expanded in the eighteenth century. The classical town hall stands close to the centre, dominating the scene yet less effectively so than its almost exact contemporary at Chard. Wellington's people now number some eight thousand and its economy is partly that of a shopping town. Light engineering, and the making of such varied goods as mattresses, bricks, and animal medicines give work to some Wellington people. A small public school, on a road leading south towards the Blackdowns, is another of its assets. More historic, and important both for Wellington's prosperity and that of some other places each side of the county boundary, is the concern whose activities now make it Somerset's last industrial producer of woollen cloth.

The firm of Fox Brothers is among the old Quaker businesses of the West Country. Its history goes back for the best part of three centuries. Since 1803, after a move from the middle of Wellington, it has been on its present Tonedale site. The firm started in the days of handloom weaving in cottages or small work sheds. The Weres, a family of Wellington Quakers, ran it for some hundred years. Serges were their main line of production and much of their trade, like that of clothiers in Tiverton and Exeter, lay with Continental customers. The cloth went, by waggon, to the Exe estuary, being shipped from Topsham, much of it to Rotterdam and other Dutch ports whence it reached central Europe. The Weres, more considerate of their market than many of their competitors, often stayed some years abroad, learning languages so that they could, unlike many English businessmen both then and now, correspond in their customers' own tongues. Thomas Fox, a grandson of Thomas Were who long ran the business, did likewise, so that letters in the firm's fine records make the point, in 1777 and later years, that they corresponded, if need be, in Dutch, German, and French. Their Dutch correspondence, in particular, is full of interest; letters during the American War of Independence refer, with Paul Jones and other privateers in mind as threats to the firm's North Sea shipments, to *Amerikanse Zee-roovers* and "Congress gentry". Coming nearer home the wool books have details of Were's dealings with small farmers in the rough country of the Brendon and Exmoor foothills.

The Weres did not long stay in their family business, and in 1796 Thomas Fox, already a partner, gained complete control. A spell of change and development then set in. At Uffculme, over the Devon border and well down the Culm valley, a water mill which had once been used for grinding corn was bought and fitted out for clothmaking. This was in 1797–8; in another three years Thomas Fox's bought, and soon converted, the flourmill down towards the River Tone which they renamed Tonedale and which is now the company's main scene of activity. Water power was the mill's driving force, provided not by the Tone but by a leat which diverts water from a stream running off the Blackdowns. But the leat itself was soon landscaped, as a long, narrow pond, to make the ornamental water in the grounds of Tonedale House, built as an 'on the spot' residence for Thomas Fox and those of his young sons who helped to manage the firm. That house, somewhat altered about 1830, survives as a home. The original mill, burnt down in 1821 which was the year of Thomas Fox's death, was soon rebuilt, in brick and with its floors in part of that same fire-resisting material, with iron columns of the Doric order to uphold them. For the large weaving shed, which they built in the 1850s, the Foxes re-used masonry from the locks of the now abandoned canal. A little earlier, Tonedale had seen an even more interesting act of re-use. Fox's had not used a steam engine till 1840, but in another ten years they bought two oscillating engines from the South Devon Railway, redundant when the atmospheric system of propulsion was given up on that interesting line between Exeter and Plymouth; their first power looms, presumably driven from those engines, started work in 1852. Thomas Fox's sons were not, in those days, alone in Wellington in the running of a cloth mill. For a little over a mile away, on a leat running off another of the Tone's tributary brooks, the Elworthy brothers were yarn spinners and serge-makers at Westford Mill whose somewhat forlorn building is well seen from the trains which soon plunge into the Burlescombe Tunnel that takes them into Devon.

Fox Brothers, as they operate nowadays at Tonedale and in other places, are a fully integrated concern. All clothmaking processes, including the dyeing of wool, are carried out at Wellington, while some of them are to be seen in the firm's works elsewhere. For some seventy years the company has had a small factory at Wiveliscombe. Weaving and mending are done there, also in buildings at Cullompton in East Devon. Uffculme, as I have said, is a very old branch establishment, at work for Fox's longer, in fact, than Tonedale itself. For some of its workers at Tonedale who live well away from Wellington the company provides buses which take them to and from their homes each side of the Devon border. Being a smaller firm than C. and J. Clark's they have made more modest 'social' provisions than those which one finds at Street. But a building of about 1840 was put up as a school, while a nursery school is kept in a little Gothic building erected, about that date, for the purpose which it still serves. Sixty years ago a large, unattractive building was provided for such things as a welfare centre, a club, rest-rooms, and a clinic, while the firm built some houses, and two schools, for the convenience of Tonedale workers in this place which stands well away from the middle of Wellington.

Records apart, some of Fox's most interesting and historic possessions are in the company's board room. A pair of iron 'Armada' chests may well be much older than the Weres' origins as sergemakers. Long ell cases, their covers gaily marked with the Royal arms and cipher, recall Thomas Fox's trade, through the East India Company, with customers in China. Some old leather fire buckets are still marked 'Fox'. Best of all, a fine standing clock, of the eighteenth century and by an Exeter clockmaker, has an upper dial which once showed the times of high water at Topsham Bar. I doubt, if one allows for the slowness and hazards of Georgian freightage by road, that such a device would have been of such immediate use to these Quaker sergemakers of Wellington as it must have been to their confrères in Exeter. But it can serve to remind us, far down in western Somerset, that we are in a part of the county which has looked, and looks, as much to Devon as it glances back to the flat moors or the Mendips.

CHAPTER XI

THE FAR WEST

BEYOND Bridgwater the countryside of western Somerset soon seems to be in another world from that which, within the same county, contains the Mendips and the moors. All the way down from Clevedon the gently sinuous, romantically viewed Quantock skyline, and the more distant, cloud-wrapped outlines of yet higher hills, have beckoned with their fascinating contrast to the more urbanized countryside near Bristol, or to the flatness of the great expanses each side of the Poldens. A sharp change from northern or central Somerset is what one expects, and hopes for, in the romantically challenging terrain of the Quantocks and of the hills towards the Devon border. Nor is expectation denied; the change is so pronounced that a visitor may be forgiven who feels himself no longer in Somerset.

Yet for the first few miles west of the Parrett the scene is not unlike that of the agricultural areas in some other parts of the county. Close by the river's tidal course, each side of the little haven of Combwich which once served the villages of the Quantock foothills, and down by the Parrett where it becomes an estuary, the country is as flat as anything in the moors behind Berrow's dunes or the sea wall which ends near Wick St. Lawrence. Further inland, and on each side of the busy, picturesque main road which leads, round the Quantock's northern bluff, towards Watchet and the further West the rolling, red-soiled land of tillage and pasture resembles much which lies in the South of the county. Down by Bridgwater Bay the farming land ends in a lonely, little known coastline of low cliffs, mud-caked rocks, and cloudy sea. Shurton Bars was a spot which Wordsworth and Coleridge knew. A little way to the east the Bristol Channel's coast is now punctuated, and has been given a vast man-made scenic feature, in the bulky rectangular blocks, for all the world like the twin keep of some great Norman castle, of the Atomic Power Station at Hinkley Point. From near at hand their modernity reveals itself. From afar, for example from the Esplanade at Burnham as they appear against a backcloth of hills and evening sky, they enhance their lonely landscape. Here, in a setting which was, only recently, one of primeval peace a site, well placed for the drawing in of cooling estuary water, and for its discharge after use, serves homes and industry by the application of the most modern technology.

Past Bridgwater, on the main road to the coast, the first place of any note is Cannington, a trim village on a sharp, right-angled bend which helpfully slows down the cars which pass its Georgian houses. In the road's angle the County Council's Farm Institute has an obviously important part to play in a county where agriculture, in its area if no longer in the sheer numbers of those who work on the farms, has so much significance. Its buildings are, perhaps, unique in England, for twice over they have been those of a Benedictine nunnery. For despite alterations in the seventeenth century the quadrangular buildings which stand close to the parish church are still, in essence, those of the small priory which was founded in the twelfth century, and which was dissolved in 1536. In Charles II's reign the estate became a property of the Catholic family of the Cliffords; Cannington was one of very few Somerset villages to have a Catholic congregation in penal times. Then in 1807, and for nearly thirty years, the Court became the home of the community of Benedictine nuns who had, in penal times, resided in Paris, who came to England at the time of the French Revolution, and who moved to Cannington from a temporary home at Marnhull in northern Dorset. The chief relic of their stay is the splendid polygonal chapel, domed and with Corinthian pilasters round its walls, which the nuns built between 1830 and 1831. Designed by a Wiltshire architect named George Peniston this one-time chapel is now a hall of assembly for the students of the farm institute.

At Stogursey, nearer to the coast in this gentle, rolling country the church proves a monastic history some years longer than the claustral story of Cannington Court. For early in the twelfth century William de Falaise, the Norman magnate who had obtained the estate at the Conquest, followed the pious example of many of his fellow adventurers who bestowed estates on abbeys at home with which their families had links. The abbey which got Stogursey was Lonlay. Its abbots established a small dependent priory on these Somerset estates, and the previous church was so extended as to make of its eastern portion the best Norman church building still seen in the county. In the Hundred Years' War Stogursey Priory, being the only one of these 'alien' priories in Somerset, was suppressed, not on religious grounds but as being 'enemy property'. The Crown did not, however, for long retain it, and Henry VI made it over, so as to swell the endowments of what was no less religious a foundation, to his new college at Eton which long kept the manor. The living quarters of the few monks sent over from Lonlay have gone. But the entire church remains, cruciform and of great merit not only for its Norman Romanesque architecture, but for its splendid set of early Tudor bench-ends, and for another of the fine brass chandeliers made in the Georgian age by the Bayleys of Bridgwater.

Along the main road the best known village is Nether Stowey; bar an excellent Georgian gazebo its interest comes less from its visual charms than from a great literary association. For this village, for nearly two years from the end of 1796, was the home of Samuel Taylor Coleridge, and the place where he wrote "The Ancient Mariner", "Christabel" and others among his best known poems. He already knew Nether Stowey; what drew him there was not so much the congenial, romantic beauty of the Quantock scene as his friendship and admiration for Tom Poole, the prosperous, politically radical tanner who was also, despite his simple yeoman background, a man of deep reading and wide culture. It was in 1797 that William Wordsworth and his sister Dorothy came to live, three miles away, and much closer under the lee of the Quantocks, in the larger house of Alfoxton Park. The poets were already firm friends, but now, with the romantic scenery of western Somerset and North Devon to inflame their inspiration, there followed that vital spell of close literary kinship which in a few more months blossomed out in *Lyrical Ballads*, not of course the first written expression of romanticism but the chief literary harbinger of the Romantic Revival.

South of the main road the northerly, steeper escarpment of the great hills is deeply and frequently scarred by the Quantocks' famous series of wooded combes. Back towards Bridgwater the entrancing, unsullied countryside of the foothills has its group of attractive villages and two country houses of note. Spaxton, conspicuous in this century for its somewhat turbulent history of religious eccentricities and disagreements has a typically splendid set of mid-Tudor bench-ends; among their subjects a working fuller and his tools remind us of the textile background to the glad provision of so much opulent furnishing in the churches of the West. More entertaining, for its blend of historic association and Augustan eccentricity is neighbouring Enmore where the park and the church stand close by the relics of what must, in its time, have been among the more odd of Somerset's great mansions.

The builder of Enmore Castle was no medieval baron but a Georgian nobleman of antiquarian tastes and some political prominence. He was John Perceval, a member of a family whose roots lay in Somerset, Member of Parliament for Bridgwater, and from 1748 the second Earl of Egmont in the Irish peerage. For some years he was First Lord of the Admiralty, and his name was given to Port Egmont in the Falkland Islands. He was learned and an expert genealogist. Horace Walpole tells us that, though he "did not dislike mirth in others" he never laughed himself and was only once, and that when playing chess, observed to smile. Walpole added the point that, although he was humane and friendly, "his heart wanted improvement rather than his head". He was, moreover, so Dr. Johnson said, much addicted to "romantic projects and airy speculations". Among the "speculations" were the attitudes of mind which led him, once he had bought the Enmore estate, to the building of his Somerset castle.

Egmont's medieval antiquarianism went deeper than a visual taste for Gothic. He was keen that feudal tenures should be revived, and proposed an Act of Parliament whereby they should be reintroduced. But as the political climate of Britain was against so backward-looking a scheme he hoped that some land across the Atlantic would suit his book. He asked for a grant of the Isle of St. John (now Prince Edward Island) in the Gulf of St. Lawrence. He hoped that there, away from the obstructions of Georgian England, he could found his feudal Utopia. Again he was disappointed: he thus fell back on the architectural expression of his yearning. For in addition to his advocacy of a renewed feudalism he believed that the use of gunpowder would one day be forgotten, and that medieval conditions of warfare would return. Pursuing this Georgian version of our modern ideas of nuclear disarmament he built, in Enmore Castle, a great castellated pile of dark red sandstone. It had massive corner towers and a great internal courtyard: it appears, in the landscape background, in Reynolds' double portrait of Lord Egmont and of his second wife who was the mother of Spencer Perceval, the Prime Minister who was murdered in the House of Commons. Not much is left of this Georgian nobleman's feudal refuge. One of the rounded corner towers survives as an appanage to a much more recent house, while the impressive dry moat is lined, on one side, by the loopholes cut for the arrows of the castle's defenders, and on the other by the entrance arches of the Earl's spacious cellars and stables.

Not far from Enmore is Halswell House, and Goathurst whose church is splendid with the tombs of the Tyntes who built it. The house, a fine work of William and Mary's reign, is well within the architectural conventions of the Baroque 'stately home'; when in prime condition it must have been among Somerset's finest mansions. More interesting, in a way, than the actual mansion was Halswell's unusually varied collection of parkland whimsies. A delightful little circular *tempietto* survives, a stepped pyramid was there a few years ago, and a small Ionic temple has been transported, and re-erected among Mr. Clough William's Ellis's collection of such buildings at Portmeirion. The Tyntes were, however, of a catholic taste in such adornments. For their collection once included a 'Druidical' temple, a grotto, a pseudo-medieval hermitage of which Lord Egmont might have approved and, more improbably, a temple to the honour of that Nottinghamshire folk hero Robin Hood.

The famous walk along the Quantock crest, with Will's Neck the highest point and Robin Upright Hill another central eminence, is one of Somerset's joys which I have so far failed to sample. One thing, however, is certain from a study of the map and from what can be seen of hills from as far north as the Mendips and well up the Bristol Channel. Though the Quantocks and their scenery differ deeply from any Somerset districts

Dillington, the entrance front
Dunster, High Street and Congar Hill

to their east and to the north they are in good visual touch with much of the rest of their county. Those who dwell in Taunton, in the central lowlands and in the Mendip country are well aware of them. Only when one drops down such a hill as Cothelstone, or down the lesser ways which lead to the rolling valley country between them and the Brendons, does the feeling grow that now at last the western stretches of Somerset have little kinship with the rhine and moor country, with Avalon, or with the limestone hills which stretch back to the Bristol Avon.

At the seaward end of the Quantocks, the narrow space between the hills and the Bristol Channel is filled by the contrasting parishes of East and West Quantoxhead. The eastern village, being down a narrow, blind-alley lane is free of most of the motor traffic which swirls along A.39. On any count it is among the quietest, most delectable places in its county, gaining much from its conjunction of rural peace, the shimmering picturesqueness of its village pond, ancient buildings, and views straight over the Channel to Barry in South Wales. The Court is much of it a fifteenth-century house, enlarged and lavishly redecorated, with rich plasterwork, ornate fireplaces, and rainwater-heads dated 1628, at the start of Charles I's reign. George Luttrell was the owner who made these changes, and the Luttrells have been at East Quantoxhead, since the reign of King John, for a period much longer than that for which another branch of the family has held the better known Dunster Castle. It is good to find that a Luttrell is nowadays at East Quantoxhead. At West Quantoxhead, where the scene is of a lush picturesqueness in tune with the romantic cult of the West Somerset landscape, the ruling family has been the branch of the Aclands who obtained the St. Audries title, so named from St. Etheldreda (St. Audrey) to whom, far away from her normal territory in the scenically different Ely fens, the local church is dedicated. The mansion and the church, as rebuilt by the Aclands, are high Victorian Gothic by the Puginite architect Norton who also, at the other end of the county, designed the vast Victorian Gothic mansion of Tyntesfield near Bristol. The house at St. Audries now accommodates a girls' public school; the church would be more at home in trim suburbia than here in this precipitous, romantic country.

Soon after Bishop's Lydeard the vale between the Quantocks

Dunkery Beacon: view to Wales
Brendon Hills: the railway incline

and the Brendons starts in all its attractive variety of woods and rolling farmland. The main road from Taunton to Minehead runs along it; so too, in its days as a passenger line, did the railway line which the Bristol and Exeter built to serve the small coasting port and rising tourist resort at its far end. The villages, and a few country houses, of this countryside beyond the Quantocks are often of interest or have a hidden beauty. Church after church follows Bishop's Lydeard's example with a fine set of the bench-ends with which parishioners in West Somerset, like many in Devon and Cornwall, richly decked their places of worship. Combe Florey, with an arcade of the thirteenth century to go with the Perpendicular predominance so normal in these parts, was where the parson-author Sydney Smith was rector; the Victorian east window was set up to commemorate him. Lydeard St. Lawrence church is also mainly Perpendicular; the capital of one of its nave pillars has the keys and sword of Saints Peter and Paul, referring, no doubt, to Taunton Priory which had the gift of the living. Not far away the old manor house of Golden, deep set in a little combe amid rustic lanes, is medieval in much of its structure but has rich, vernacular plasterwork of the Restoration period when the Turbervilles owned it; the house is yet another of those in Somerset which owe their medievalism to their long history as tenant farms. Stogumber, a large village amid rolling agricultural country, has a stone pulpit in its church to go with bench-ends no more than moderately good. Its ponderous name may, perhaps, have given Shaw a pointer to the name he gave to the bull-necked, bellowing English chaplain in *St. Joan*.

For many, the gem of these villages between the Quantocks and the Brendons is Crowcombe, nestling beautifully beneath steep, well wooded Quantock slopes, distinguished too for more than one of its buildings. Its church has a few fourteenth-century remains, but most of it is Perpendicular, of high quality with a finely finished south aisle and a fan-vaulted southern porch. The bench-ends, dated 1534 and including such legendary subjects as a mermaid and two men spearing a dragon, are opulent and splendid even by the high standard of western Somerset. Across the road the church house, built about 1515 and now used again as a parish hall, originally performed that function as did the one at Chew Magna. It reminds us that, by the time of the

Reformation, it was no longer the automatic rule that secular gatherings, and such events as 'church ales', occurred in the naves of the parish churches. Up behind the church Crowcombe Court, of brick and Ham Hill stone, is among the best of Somerset's country mansions. Though it was being built in 1734, well within the Palladian period of such towns as Bath, it is no Palladian building, but vernacular Baroque and much of it by Nathaniel Ireson. It is imposing, with a swan's neck pediment over its main doorway, giant Corinthian pilasters, a heavy attic storey, and inturned volutes of the Borrominian type which Ireson, along with the Bastards of Blandford, was apt to employ.

The main road from Taunton, and the highway which has come from Bridgwater round the Quantocks, meet each other at Williton, an unattractive crossroads village which gives its name to a Rural District and whose aspect is much less pleasing than that of most other settlements in the county's western zone. Not far away, at Washford Cross, the skyline is broken by the tall, slender masts of the radio station run by the British Broadcasting Corporation. It is here that the road turns down, soon to reach the fine old church, rich in its memorials of the Wyndhams of Orchard Wyndham not far away, of St. Decuman's. Here we find a Celtic dedication, unmistakably reminding us that Devon and Cornwall are not far away; a map tells us that St. Decuman's is nearly as far west as Exeter. It also seems likely, on its hillside above the hideous, economically significant paper mills in the valley below, to have its place in an immortal poem. For if Watchet is the harbour whence Coleridge made his Ancient Mariner depart, St. Decuman's is the kirk below which that fated crew set sail.

There is a very Cornish relationship between St. Decuman's church and the harbour town which grew up at Watchet. A Cornishman like myself feels well at home with the old church on its hillside up the valley and the main centre of population down by the mouth of the stream. It is what one finds at St. Martin's and East Looe, Talland parish and its two harbour settlements at West Looe and Polperro, or at Madron and Penzance. Watchet itself, despite a water mill and an agricultural hinterland, always turned for its main livelihood to the sea—to the coastwide trade and to the cross-channel traffic to and from South Wales which was long so important for Somerset's economy. In the Middle Ages it grew as a harbour town, and in the Civil War the Royalists used Watchet to ship stores and reinforcements from strongly sympathetic South Wales. But its harbour was long less good than that of Minehead, and Defoe found that it had suffered much from the competition put up by the more westerly harbour. Some efforts were made to improve the somewhat ramshackle break-water which, on the western side alone, protected the harbour, while the origins of Watchet's important paper mills go back to the middle years of the eighteenth century. But Watchet's heyday as a coasting port was mid-Victorian. In the 1860s the harbour was redesigned, enlarged, and given an eastern wharf. The railway reached the town in 1862, and well over five hundred ships came in or out that year. Timber and Welsh coal were key cargoes; so too was iron ore sent down from the prosperous mines on the Brendon Hills. But sixty years ago those mines saw their final closure, and Watchet's iron trade irrevocably died. Now, how-ever, raw material comes in for the town's expanded paper mills, various other cargoes are imported, and smart motor coasters—British, Dutch, Scandinavian, and German—make a lively, colourful part of Watchet's waterside townscape.

Away from its promenade at the top end of its harbour Watchet is of no special attraction. The old market house is long, narrow and early Georgian, two-storeyed and with its top floor fitted out as a chapel of the Holy Cross whose dedication repeats that of a medieval chapel, down in the town in the Cornish manner of the two Looes, which must have been more convenient for the Sunday by Sunday worship of many St. Decuman's parishioners. Swain Street, the little town's main highway with the Van Heusen factory at the top by the station, contains a few Georgian houses. One, of brick, has a 'Gibbsian' doorway, while the Westminster Bank is in a charming Regency building with an urn set in a niche above its doorway and porch. More repulsive, but interesting, is the brickwork in some of Watchet's Victorian stone-built houses. For many yellow bricks appear as the edgings of such features as windows and doorways. They are those seen, in their millions, in houses and other buildings in South Wales; they must have come in the cross-channel cargoes of Watchet's busiest harbour days.

The best way out of Watchet is up West Street, and so over Cleeve Hill with its crumbling cliff edges and fine views along Somerset's own coast and over to the modest mountains of South Wales. Blue Anchor is visually marred by its caravan sites; it is better to turn one's gaze inland towards the Brendons, the bulky massif of Croydon Hill or, more distantly and deeper into the countryside of the Exmoor National Park, to the challenging summit of Dunkery. More immediately, in the valley of the Washford River which supplies Watchet's paper mills and pours out into its harbour, any traveller in these parts must needs delay at Somerset's most satisfying monastic ruin.

Cleeve was the only Cistercian Abbey in Somerset, founded in the twelfth century, on a modest scale and with a church on the well standardized Cistercian plan. The site, congenially remote for the Cistercians in their still primitive austerity, was known as *Vallis Florida*. The founder, who gave the abbey the whole of his Somerset estates, was William de Roumere, a Lincolnshire magnate; the new abbey was colonized by a party of monks from Revesby in the founder's own county. Its history was uneventful, and its standards of observance seem, for the most part, to have been high. This was so towards the end of Cleeve Abbey's career. For when in the 1530s its property was valued, and the time came near for its dissolution, the monks were found to be well above the average in what they gave to charity, and the seventeen inmates were all said to be "of honest life". The Abbey's reputation was good, so much so that the local gentry put in a plea, unsuccessful as things turned out, that this abbey of the white monks should be spared and left in peace to do its good work among the people of western Somerset.

The church at Cleeve has almost wholly gone; its main survival is the wall of the south transept. This was needed as the protective abutment of the dormitory range which lasted for many years as one of the buildings of a farm. This continued secular use made the remains of Cleeve Abbey uniquely valuable among those of the Cistercian houses of England. For nowhere, not even at Fountains or in any of the other Cistercian houses in Yorkshire, do domestic buildings of this monastic order survive so well as at Cleeve. The combined gatehouse and almonry stands, across what was once the monastery's outer courtyard, away from the rest of the buildings. The eastern and southern ranges, along with part of the western block and its adjacent cloisters, are those which have come down to us from those of the claustral enclosure; the western range was in part remodelled as the abbot's house. The dormitory block, and the range which contained the monks' second refectory, aligned east and west by contrast to the north-south position of the earlier dining hall, are in their contrasting ways the best preserved of Cleeve Abbey's buildings.

The eastern range, with its row of simple lancets to light the dormitory (originally a long open room but later partitioned into cubicles) was put up in the thirteenth century, not long after the abbey's formal founding in 1198. Below the dormitory, Cleeve's many visitors can enter the chapter house; a large central doorway is flanked, as was common in this part of medieval monasteries, by smaller arches. The vestibule still keeps its ribbed vault, but the vaulting has gone from above the main room where the monks met for their daily business meetings. The dormitory stairs are still there, and beyond them is the monks' parlour, or common room. The whole block, one feels, could almost come alive again with monastic activity. More elaborate is the southern range whose upper floor contains the refectory, now devoid of the once splendid wall paintings whose considerable remains were there when I first visited Cleeve. But the hall is still covered by its splendid waggon roof, adorned with bosses and angels and as splendid as many which cover the naves of churches in West Somerset or in neighbouring Devon. The range, as renewed and realigned, is Perpendicular, put up in the fifteenth century and so arranged that it could be the abbot's guest hall as well as the monks' dining place. The hospitality which the abbots could thus dispense may, perhaps, have contributed to Cleeve Abbey's good standing, in 1537 when the end came, with the neighbouring squires.

Past Cleeve, whether a traveller journey's West towards Minehead or makes a deep southward plunge into the foothills of the Brendons, he soon comes to Somerset's western fastnesses of steep-sided hills and high commons. Only the sea marsh (or *morfa* as they would call it over the Channel) below Dunster and Minehead, and the similar plain which runs down to Porlock Weir, show much green on a physical map. The Brendon and

Exmoor country, in its status a National Park and noted (or in some eyes notorious) for its favoured sport of staghunting, now at last towers up before a visitor from the scenically more placid areas of the county. The scenery, at all events round the edges of the great hills and moorlands, becomes ever more splendid and picturesque. From before the great days of *Lyrical Ballads* and the main onset of the Romantic Revival it was seen as such. For these western parishes of Somerset the adjective 'romantic', along with phrases in tune with it, often appears in the pages of Collinson the parson-historian and Edmund Rack his collaborator and an amateur of letters, who may well have had a better knowledge of these far parts of the county. Of Carhampton Hundred they say that "this mountainous country may be called the Alps of Somersetshire, the whole country being a picturesque assemblage of lofty hills succeeding each other, with deep romantic vallies winding between them". They had already noted "romantick vales" in the quieter country of Broomfield. More predictably the remote site of the tiny church of Culbone, past Porlock and embosomed in its thickly wooded combe, was "singularly romantick", and "a scene peculiarly adapted to strike the mind with pleasure and astonishment". At Oare, whose church later found its literary place as the scene of Lorna Doone's dramatically disturbed nuptials, they found the country "very wild and romantick". Rack was not, however, unaware of the rough, primitive nature of this Brendon and Exmoor country, of the mean standard of the cottages in such villages as Luxborough, or of the way in which, in Porlock parish, agriculture was "very imperfectly understood". He tells us how crops were still brought in across horses' backs, and how manure was carried, not in carts, but in large wooden pots called dossels. But his eye, as with countless others since his time, was mainly for fine scenery and sights which conjured up romance.

When, in a book whose effort it is to record Somerset, I come to say something on these uttermost areas of the county I find a very real personal difficulty. For one thing, I know the Exmoor end of Somerset far less than I know the county's towns and its central or northern countryside. Though I have walked up Dunkery, and have never ascended High Willhays, I know it much less well than I know Dartmoor. I have never been to such spots as

Withypool, Tarr Steps, the Chains, or the church at Oare. Moreover, once I am west of the Quantocks, I also have the strong feeling that this lovely district hardly belongs to Somerset, and that when one realizes Somerset's westernmost point to be as far west as Ashburton, and easily to the west of Torquay, then Devon, or perhaps some newly created, intermediate county, should really claim it. Exmoor, in any case, is about a third of it in Devon. At first sight its division between the two counties seems a little capricious. But a map reveals some logic in the way in which the boundary runs round this far loop of Somerset. For though the Exe and the Barle, below their junction in the lovely wooded country near Dulverton, send their swift water down into Devon, their upper valleys are both in Somerset, with the border curving west to include the hills which enclose their basin, or else to run along the high saddleback of Five Barrows Hill whence southerly streams shoot straight into Devon, there to become the headwaters of tributaries which swell the Taw before in the end it joins the tidewater at Barnstaple. Northward from the boggy soak of the Chains which is akin, in its spongy, water-holding function, to the sodden, somewhat unlovely central hills of northern and southern Dartmoor, the streams quickly combine their waters, as Lynmouth found to its cost a few years back, in the deep valley of the East and West Lyn. Yet despite the good reasons provided by the local watersheds for the division of Exmoor between its two counties it is very easy, here and everywhere in Somerset west of the Quantocks, to forget Keynsham, the Mendip country, Hamdon Hill, or the lowlands of Sedgemoor.

Past Cleeve Abbey one can approach the northern, more dramatic slopes of the Brendons up the ever deepening and ever more enclosed valley once used by the West Somerset Mineral Railway. At the pleasant hamlet of Roadwater, with one fine house combining wooden mullions in its windows and wreathed date plaques of the year 1700 on its walls, traces of the railway are still reasonably clear. Above Roadwater the two streams which combine as the Washford River diverge. One continues, due south and then on a more wandering course towards Combe Row and the railhead where Somerset's most dramatic piece of transport archaeology can still be seen. The more westerly stream soon traverses the wooden beauties of Druids' Combe, deep-set with its modern mixture of hardwoods and conifers, and so up to the pretty hamlet of Kingsbridge and to the Luxborough country. From these places the roads up to the Brendons' crest are few, steep, and difficult; for easier access the range is better tackled from either end.

Lofty hills, well poised amid fine scenery, called strongly, in the days when the Romantic Revival was in mid-course and when the picturesque was a cult, for the building of towers. So Willett Hill, an outlier of the Brendon range and rising high above Tolland and Brompton Ralph, got its tower about 1820; like the contemporary tower of St. Mary's at Bathwick it is an essay in the county's battlemented Perpendicular style. Not far away a road turns steeply upwards, soon, for a gently undulating course of some nine miles, to become the loftiest road in the county. For most of that distance it runs along the very crest of the hills. At so great a height, in parts well over 1,300 feet above the sea and comfortably higher than the Quantocks, the Brendon Hills, with a wireless mast at their eastern end and superb views in several directions, come as something of a surprise. For the scene is almost all of enclosed grazing fields, with little open heathland. Only at Lype Hill at the chain's western end, nearly 1,400 feet up and the highest point, bar Exmoor, in all Somerset, is there nowadays a real expanse of open moor. Stunted trees, and others planted as windbreaks along the road, remind us how high is this lonely, little inhabited countryside. At Brendon Hill, and between there and Gupworthy, comes the main interest of the Brendons; the emphasis here is on Victorian industrialism.

The iron workings in the Brendon Hills may have started in Roman times, German iron miners were there in the seventeenth century, and a little ore may still have been taken out in Georgian times. But the real story of the mines on Brendon, and of the railway which took the ore to the sea at Watchet, belongs to the Victorian period and to a brief spell some sixty years ago; it has been very well told by the three authors of a recent book.* The episode gave yet another proof of the interaction which could occur between the economy of Somerset and that of South Wales.

* See Roger Sellick, J. R. Hamilton, and M. H. Jones, *The West Somerset Mineral Railway and the Story of the Brendon Hills Iron Mines*, 1962, reprinted 1970.

In 1852 Thomas Brown, and Joseph Robinson of the iron works at Ebbw Vale in South Wales, formed the Brendon Hills Iron Company. The ore, from various workings spaced out along the ridge, was to feed the smelting furnaces of Ebbw Vale. It was later found that Brendon ores were suitable, almost alone among British deposits, for the making of Bessemer steel. Complementary to the mines was the railway which took ore down to Watchet. Thence it was shipped to Newport, mainly in locally owned coasting craft but some of it, from 1873, in a little steamer owned by the company, built at Bridgwater and suitably named *St. Decuman's*. By the end of 1857 the line was open to Combe Row, at the foot of the Brendons and of the great incline down which loaded trucks soon came to the waiting locomotives. Passengers could also be taken, free but at their own risk, on what must have been an exciting up or down journey. The 1860s saw great prosperity for the Brendon mines; a century ago the average output each year was 30,000 tons. In the 1870s, things were better still, for northern Spanish competition was damped down, till 1876, by the ferocities of the second Carlist War. The annual output jumped to over 40,000 tons, and in 1877 over 52,000 tons went down the line. But peace in Spain brought decline to the Brendons. The Cornish miners who had come there slipped away; only the more local men stayed on in the hope of better times. A short revival did, indeed, come, but by 1883 the mines were silent and only salvage freight, coal, general goods, and passengers travelled on the crank little railway up from Watchet. But although it was closed in 1898 the railway remained usable. So when in 1907 some of the mines reopened for two years the line was there, with an engine bought from the Metropolitan Railway in London, to carry an output far smaller than in the mines' Victorian apogee. The track was finally lifted, as scrap metal, in the First World War. Its disappearance is a pity, for it could nowadays, like the little lines at Talyllyn and Ffestiniog, be a great tourist attraction in a highly touristic district.

The Brendon mines never employed a really large number of men; the peak figure, in 1875, was a little over 300, with over 700 people in the entire mining community. At first miners lodged in farms, or in such nearby villages as Luxborough and

Withiel Florey. But Brendon Hill village, not far above the
source of the River Tone, soon grew up to house them, particularly those who worked in the mine at Raleigh's Cross. Here
in this highest and most bleak of Somerset's villages some 750
people once made their homes; another hundred or so were in
the separate hamlet of Gupworthy. A mission church and two
Nonconformist chapels served the community's religious needs.
A warehouse and a general shop were also there. As Nonconformity and Temperance alike flourished on the Brendons
there was also a Temperance Hotel, the rendezvous, one imagines,
of the Brendon Hill and Gupworthy Temperance Society and
of the Brendon Hill Teetotal Drum and Fife Band. The miners
have long vanished from this upland scene. But traces remain of
their workings, of their purpose-built village, and of the stupendous incline down which their ore descended on its way to Ebbw
Vale.

The Methodist Chapel still stands in use not far to the West of
the Raleigh's Cross Inn, but the row of houses known as Beulah
Terrace is now ruined and derelict. The fair-sized Sea View
House, once rented by the Company for their mine captain, is
still well inhabited; below it in a field there is the mouth of a
culvert which once drained the Raleigh's Cross mine. A little
to the west an artificial embankment comes up to the point on
the road where the tramway once spanned it to serve the mines
beyond. Built into this embankment one finds the ruined winding house whose engine hauled trucks up from Combe Row.
More impressive, and plunging eight hundred feet at a one-in-
four gradient, is the incline which once supported the two
tracks of the railway line. Here and there it is artificially banked
up above the fields and woods; elsewhere it cuts deep through
the soil and solid rock of the steep slope. So massive an inter-
ference with the landscape can never be obliterated. It lies there,
one assumes, as a lasting, most impressive memorial of an extinct
industry.

Between Luxborough's deep valley and the coastal plain, and
screening some of the view of the shore for which one hopes
from the Brendon crest, the great bulk of Croydon Hill would
be exceptional in any less upland part of Somerset. My one ascent
of it was from the direction of Dunster, up the wide vale of the

Avill and then up a quiet, charming little wooded valley in which hardwoods give way to solemn conifers and the hum of mechanical saws; one of these firs, seven years ago, reached the great height, by our British standards, of 154 feet. From the remote fastness of Broadwood Farm one can cut across, over hilly fields, to narrow little streams which tumble steeply down from the great hill which lowers above them. Up one of these valleys, oddly named Withycombe Scruffets, one can toil, splash, and struggle up a rough hillside track which in the end gives out on to the easier ground at the top of Croydon Hill. Some of the land, including the summit, is open heath; elsewhere commercially exploited fir plantations dominate the scene. The views, down to the nearby coast, towards Knowle Hill and Minehead, or over to the Quantocks and South Wales, are superb. Back again towards the coast one reaches Withycombe, an attractive village whose neat church is mainly of the thirteenth century, though with several Perpendicular windows, and whose fifteenth-century screen is of the Devon type. The approaches to Withycombe are through deep-set lanes, and between high hedges, very much in the Devon manner.

Dunster, one of Somerset's most favoured tourist haunts, is beautifully set beneath its castle and at the foot of Conygar Hill. Despite jarring effects which can come from its visiting crowds, and for all the artificial whimsy of some of the shops which, in this West Somerset equivalent of Chipping Campden or Castle Combe, dispense post cards, souvenirs, and 'arty crafty' goods of patchy merit, Dunster's High Street has tremendous, wholly successful 'group value', all the better because fewer of its individual buildings, bar the ingeniously covered Yarn Market and the Luttrell Arms Hotel, are of any great distinction. At each of its ends the High Street has good romantic terminals. To the south the towers and battlements of the genuine castle rise clear above the trees—a Somerset equivalent of some romantic *schloss* in the Rhine or Mosel valley. Between the street and the coastal plain the higher eminence of Conygar Hill is capped, like the sharp peak of Montacute, not with a medieval structure but by a round tower whose Georgian Gothic style tuned in with incipient feelings for romanticism. Nor are Dunster's charms confined to its High Street. Great group value prevails in Church

and West Streets, both of them less altered than the High Street
and less tricked up for the delectation of outsiders. In Church
Street the large medieval house known as the Nunnery is conspicuous. No convent of nuns ever existed in medieval Dunster,
but the building, of three storeys, slate hung, and in its general
form not unlike the George Inn at Norton St. Philip, belonged to
the Cistercians of Cleeve Abbey; it could have been used as a wool
hall. West Street, largely Georgian, has its share of guest houses
and hotels, also some more workaday shops for the daily convenience of local people. Near its lower end Mill Lane leads
down to some most attractive painted and thatched cottages,
themselves on the way to a charming scene where a packhorse
bridge, medieval and two-arched, spans the Avill, a river of late
under much deepening and widening attention from the Somerset River Authority.

Rising high above the houses of the little town is the tall
tower which was started in 1443 to hold the bells of the
parishioners' portion of the priory church. Dunster's small priory
was a dependent 'cell' of the Benedictines at Bath. Sadly little
remains of the Norman eastern limb; what is now there is later
medieval, much restored but splendid with the Luttrells'
memorials. The small community's living quarters lay north of
the church; a circular dove-house, as also at Stoke-sub-Hamdon,
is a good housekeeper's feature of an ecclesiastical establishment.
Lower down in the church the excellent screen runs, in the Devon
fashion, all the way across the nave and aisles. It was put up,
about 1499 and at the time when the Bath monks were starting
on their own new cathedral church, after Abbot Bere of Glastonbury had resolved a seating dispute between the townsmen and
the Dunster Benedictines. The brass chandelier in the nave, like
one of the Luttrells' marble murals, came from a workshop in
Georgian Bristol. Both could readily have been shipped down to
the adjacent, and then flourishing port of Minehead.

Daniel Defoe found Minehead, with its pier and harbour
nestling tight under the final bluff of the great hog-backed bulk
of Bossington Hill and Selworthy Beacon, "the best port and
safest harbour" along the Bristol Channel's southern coast.
Alone in Somerset, and far more happily than hundreds of other
places, it had even proved secure in the great hurricane blast of

1703, the storm which elsewhere in Somerset blew down a palace chimney at Wells and killed the sleeping bishop and his wife. About the time that Defoe wrote Minehead acquired its fine statue of Queen Anne, at first set up in the church but now canopied in a part of the shopping centre where a figure of Victoria would seem more fitting. A statue of the last Stuart sovereign is a rare feature in any English town, but it is a distinction which Minehead shares with Barnstaple, the next port along the coast. Trade with Ireland was one of Minehead's mainstays, particularly in coarse wool for Taunton's sergemakers. The fortunes of its snug harbour turned much, as did those of Lyme Regis, on Taunton's prosperity as a clothing town. By the last years of the eighteenth century Taunton's clothiers, and the shippers of Minehead and Lyme, had fallen on evil days. Collinson and Rack quote figures which prove the point. For from 1705 to 1783 Minehead's inhabited houses dropped sharply, and the town's people went down from about 1,800 to 1,128; things were made worse because the herrings which once abounded off the Somerset and Devon border country had left that coast. But the growing seaside habit and the cult of romantic scenery soon came to the rescue. Minehead, like Lyme Regis in Jane Austen's time, found compensation as the seaside resort which it has been ever since, with a Butlin camp as a recent addition to its more conventional seaside delights. Though swimming pools are the normal rule here at last one can, with reasonable pleasure, bathe in the sea, in fine weather fairly blue though without the limpid quality one finds in Devon or Cornwall. Minehead's seaside portion, and its main shops, are naturally enough along the lower ground; above them the picturesque houses and ancient church of Higher Town remind us, as does the harbour close below the bluff, of a past history more distinguished than that of Somerset's other coastal resorts.

Past Minehead the main road to North Devon surmounts a low col, dropping down again ever deeper into a countryside made lovely by the thickly wooded, romantic steeps and deep valleys of Exmoor's northern fringe. Horner Water's valley is conspicuously beautiful; across the wider vale the village of Selworthy is Somerset's most sugary beauty spot. Its thatched cottages run steeply down the hill, making the place, as it were, another Clovelly with no water at the foot of its street. From the churchyard at the top the view to Dunkery is superb; in the church itself the Perpendicular arches and transomed windows, and the coloured waggon roof which spans the south aisle, are of an architectural merit well above that of the village's houses. Sophistication can also be seen, in the old church at Porlock with its Celtic dedication to St. Dubricius, in the splendid tomb of Sir John Harrington who died in 1418. The tomb itself, as good as any medieval memorial in Somerset, was put up at least forty years after Sir John had died. Above the two effigies the canopy is delicately cusped, and the underside of the arch is richly panelled in a very Somerset idiom. The village, self-consciouslypicturesque though less so than Dunster, has medieval and many later houses. It comes as a prelude to the famous hill to which Porlock has given its name, ascended direct by its fearsome gradient or less directly by a meandering and far easier detour. Along its summit, and past the high ridge of Culbone Hill which towers over the parish's tiny church, the traveller is soon at County Gate and so into North Devon. All the way one is aware, to the south, of the main, sweeping expanse of Exmoor.

For anyone coming up from Dunster or Minehead the best approach to high Exmoor is up the Avill valley, and then right at the somewhat unattractive hamlet of Wheddon Cross. From there a lane soon leads, through an enclosed pastoral countryside of small farms, to the open moorland at Dunkery Gate, and so to the immediate foot of Dunkery Hill which acts as the moor's north-eastern bastion and is its highest point. From Dunkery Gate an easy stroll takes a walker to the summit of a little over 1,700 feet. For lazier souls the short trip is possible by lorries or Land-Rovers like those which must have scaled the summit to carry up such things as the litter bins which, in so important a property of the National Trust, are discreetly sunk in little stone piers. The poor remains of a Bronze Age round barrow are piled up with the unimpressive local outcrop stones. A cairn of similar stones was put up, in 1935, to record the hill's gift, by Sir Thomas Acland and others, to the National Trust. The views from so high a point, standing well clear from the saddleback hills and the chief drainage areas of the moor, are inevitably superb, though I was, in this respect, none too lucky on my one ascent of

Dunkery. Only towards the bluish sea, and over to St. Donat's Castle, Nash Point, and the Glamorgan coastal country of Blackmore's favourite novel *The Maid of Sker*, were things reasonably clear.

Past Dunkery Beacon, and past the better preserved round barrows at the hill's western end, the walker is soon on the Colsend Moors, and in gentle, open country where heathland is mixed with hedged-in, but still rough pasture for sheep and ponies. The scene is now, inescapably, of what was once the Forest end of Exmoor, where the heathland, purple in early autumn with its great sheets of heather, is mixed, to its increasing disadvantage, with arable and pastoral intakes. These encroachments on the wilderness are surprisingly large, and they are now the cause of much controversy. For an account of Exmoor Forest in its more primeval state we turn, under the parish heading of Exford, to one of the most purple passages in the pages of Collinson and Rack.

The authors first point out that the district near Exford was formerly a Royal Forest, and that it was, in their time, a wild waste "intersected by deep winding vallies and romantick hollows". They go on to say, no doubt from the personal observation of Rack the agriculturist, that pasturage was the only local product, and that the district was stocked with sheep and sturdy little ponies and cattle. Rack must also have noticed the barrows of the district. For he comments that "here, upon this desolate spot, which perhaps never experienced the labours of the industrious husbandman, but has remained the same for a long succession of many thousand years, the eye of reflection sees stand uninterrupted a number of simple sepulchres of departed souls, whether of warriors, priests, or kings it matters not; their names have long been buried with their persons in the dust of oblivion, and their memories have perished with their mouldering urns. A morsel of earth now damps in silence the éclat of noisy warriors, and the green turf serves as a sufficient shroud for kings". After such a passage, worthy of his fellow Norfolkman Sir Thomas Browne, Rack mentions "circular entrenchments", to his mind "assuredly vestiges of antiquity"; he suggests the Druids as their makers, for such varied purposes as religious rites or athletic feats. Exford apart, he refers to the one house at Simonsbath, built in the middle years of the seventeenth century by a most interesting would-be developer of Exmoor. This was James Boevey, a London merchant but of a Flemish Protestant family. His long efforts, in the end frustrated, to bring population and prosperity to Exmoor remind us of Vermuyden's ambitions for the far more Netherlandish expanses of Sedgemoor. But the Boeveys seem to have had a penchant for Forests, particularly those which held deposits of iron. For James Boevey was also the buyer, along with a half-brother, of the Flaxley Abbey estate in the Forest of Dean, long the scene of an iron forge, supplied from the local workings, and continuing its operations for many years under its Boevey ownership. Rack also notices Exmoor's traces of ironworks and of pits whence iron ore had once been dug; they are significant for our later story.

Exford itself, in the valley where the Exe has come down as a fair-sized river, is a cheerful spot, of no special charm bar the smooth expanse of its village green, but a pleasing haven and place of refreshment for those who have explored, or mean to explore, the remoter moor. The kennels of the Devon and Somerset staghounds are here at Exford. These, and the sport which they serve, are a part of the local scene and of Exmoor's way of life; more exotic, in this remote West Country setting, are some furnishings in the attractive hillside church. For some simple choir stalls, of the fifteenth century and now set east of an old screen which was first at St. Audries, came to Exford from the late medieval chapel of Queens' College in the utterly different setting of flat, slow-watered Cambridge; Erasmus, one can reasonably assume, sat and worshipped in them. Beyond Exford one is soon in the Barle valley and in essential Exmoor, the great tract of ground where the desolate picture of the 1790s was so drastically changed in the century which followed.

A century and a half ago the Commissioners who surveyed Exmoor for the Crown reported that only thirty-seven trees stood in the forest, all of them in a cluster round Simonsbath House. Simonsbath is now a relatively verdant and pretty place, while trees and enclosed pasture have vastly increased at various places in the forest. Exmoor's present state is largely due to the work of two successive members of the Knight family. Their

great work of agricultural reclamation, and their much less
successful efforts to vie with the iron-mining on the Brendons,
have been well told by Mr. C. S. Orwin.*

When Collinson's history came out Sir Thomas Acland leased
the forest from the Crown, and also held the post of Royal
Forester; he was the third baronet of his name to lease the forest.
His lease expired in 1814, and the forest was then enclosed by an
Act of Parliament. Over 20,000 acres (much less than the Royal
forest's original area) were then parcelled out, more than half
of them to the Crown and large portions to Sir Thomas Acland
and Sir Charles Bamfylde. Reclamation and agricultural improvement had long been projected; the problem was to find a suitably
energetic improver. The man who came forward was John
Knight, of a good West Midland family and related to Richard
Payne Knight of Downton, a pioneering amateur of the picturesque. Knight gradually bought the Crown, Acland, and Bamfylde
portions, ending with over 15,000 acres to turn into a more
desirable landscape and a more profitable estate. Neither John
Knight, nor his son Sir Frederick who followed him, ever made a
fortune from Exmoor. Nor were they always on the spot in
their Somerset estate. John Knight gave up his direct management
of the property and lived, for the last nine years of his life, in the
utterly different surroundings of Rome at the time of Pio Nono's
accession and of Garibaldi's Roman Republic. Sir Frederick sat
in Parliament and had many other interests, while his care for
Exmoor tailed off after the heavy blow of his only son's death.
Yet the Knights' energy and tenacity were great. By the end of
1824 John Knight had built new roads, along with twenty-nine
miles of boundary wall. A new mansion was started, but never
finished; at Simonsbath arable land and better grazing were
created from the once sour moorland. From the 1840s new farms
were built. So too, at Simonsbath, were the church and parsonage
of a new 'Exmoor' parish. The venture's peak period was about
a century ago, with livelihood provided, in the area newly
devoted to tough upland farming, for some three hundred
people. But after his son's sad death, Sir Frederick eased the pace

* See C. S. Orwin, *The Reclamation of Exmoor Forest*, 1929; a new edition
appeared in 1970.

of his development. Grazing ground, as well it might in so high and wet a countryside, gained on arable farming, and on Sir Frederick's death the estate, a monument to the two Knight pioneers, passed to the Fortescues.

No less interesting than these farming ventures were Frederick Knight's iron-mining operations. In his father's time the mine of Wheal Eliza was opened, down in the Barle valley, in a search for copper. Iron ore, dug on Exmoor in ancient times, was what was actually found; the 1850s were the decade of the deposits' main, yet unspectacular exploitation. The consumers were to be the ironmasters of South Wales, particularly those who ran the great ironworks at Dowlais near Merthyr Tydfil. A few hundreds of tons of ore did reach Merthyr from Exmoor, and a railway, more winding than the lines on the Brendons which connected with the great incline down to Combe Row, was surveyed and actually started from near Simonsbath to a point, above Porlock, whence another great incline was to lead down to a shipping point at Porlock Weir. But troubles soon arose, the Exmoor mines were never a success, and by 1860 iron-mining near Simonsbath had temporarily ended.

As on the Brendons after the first closure of their iron mines the Exmoor deposits saw a short, but abortive revival in the years soon before the start of the First World War. A syndicate opened some of the old workings, carried out trials, and re-surveyed the line chosen for the mineral railway to Porlock. This syndicate soon broke up, but until 1914 other operators extracted fair quantities of ore.

Exmoor's iron mines, and relics of the railway which was to take the ore to Porlock, bring me very near the end of my brief notice of Exmoor, and of these varied Somerset journeyings. Back towards Dunkery and the Exford to Porlock road at Hillhead Cross, and thence west up an expanse of scrubby pasture, one comes to a lesser road. It is lined with banks which have a typically Exmoor topping of thickset hedges, and with sturdy, stone-built gate piers which may be part of the Knights' agricultural architecture. If the weather is good the beckoning views are clear towards the Chains and the hillside cleft where the Exe has its source. Essential Exmoor, like central Dartmoor devoid of rocky tors, lies before the tramper. But I have never explored so far. My compensation came, not far past that lonely little lane whose course lies along the watershed between the Horner Water and the Lyn, when I found some good traces of the railway which, unlike those on the Brendons or the picturesque Dartmoor line which once ran up to Princetown, never saw its puffing engines or groaning waggons. I already knew that relics of this frustrated line existed; only later the same day did I light on the best evidence for its actual or assumed course.* Curving across the moor and running nearly level, a low embankment slopes down, a short way on each side, to the natural soil. Had the line been built to the summit of its great incline above Porlock it would have run, from some point near the mines above Simons-bath, up one stiff gradient and then, in a meandering but remark-ably level course, just below the contour of 1,400 feet. Its average height, from Prayway Hill to the top of its cableway, would have made it the South of England's loftiest railway. Its remains give a good spice of transport archaeology to a scene better known, and now under controversy, for the activities of agricultural 'improvers'.

Beyond the railway a good bridle road soon leads to the ruined farmstead of Larkbarrow, the remotest, and the most outlying from their headquarters at Simonsbath, of all the Knights' farms. It has long lain deserted behind the little copse of trees which was planted to shelter it from some of the moorland blasts. But it is easy to picture its lonely isolation before the coming of such things as cars, the telephone, radio, and television. Its buildings were of heavily plastered stone; only the toppled chimney stacks display the use of brick. Despite the present ruination of the house and of its farm buildings one can still trace the neat planning of its southward-facing yard. Below the ruined farm the rattling little stream is the utmost headwater of the Bagworthy Water. Round the shoulder of Tom's Hill it soon receives the Haccombe Water and becomes the county boundary in a deep, swiftly falling valley which gained its place in letters, when Richard Doddridge Blackmore welcomed the publication of *Lorna Doone*.

* See G. L. Gettins, "The Exmoor Mineral Railway", in *The Exmoor Review*, No. 8 (1967).

smaller towns. Somerset, like other south-western counties, will be more modernized than it was before the First World War; the life of its people may, one imagines, in many points come closer to that lived in, say, the eastern counties and the Midlands.

What must also concern those who care for the future of Somerset is the physical appearance of a county whose scenes include so much that is of beauty and character. The matter is the more important when one recalls what has happened at Yatton, in parts of Keynsham, and as far as Saltford between Keynsham and Bath. As Exmoor and the Brendons comprise a National Park they should be free, if not from enclosures of the type disliked by the Exmoor Society, at all events from the less lovely forms of housing. The special charms of the Mendips and the Quantocks seem well enough appreciated, and if the county's economy is to stay much as it is now the slow growth of its towns should throw up no special problem of urban amenity; rebuilding like that which has happened in central Taunton is more of a danger.

What is vital for the character and good standing of Somerset is the continued existence, and enhancement, of such urban beauties as those which can be found in Georgian Bath, in the Barchesterian ambience of Wells, along the main street of Chard, pre-eminently in Bruton and Dunster, in Frome, Somerton, Crewkerne, and in many other large villages and towns. Out in the countryside I hope that we shall long see and appreciate the steeps of the Mendips, the Quantock ridge and the combes below it, the whole sweet countryside down by the Dorset border, the varied, unspoiled charms of the Dundon and Somerton hills, Avalon, Brent Knoll, and the lesser hills and isles which rise above the central plain. We must treasure the rhine-crossed flats and the willows of the moors, and above all the manifold, proud pre-Reformation glory of Somerset's noble church towers.

CHAPTER XIII

A SEVERED SHIRE

THE Redcliffe-Maud Report on the future of England's local government came out in June, 1969. Much discussion and disagreement followed, both on the report itself and on the proposals, in some ways differing from Lord Redcliffe-Maud's detailed suggestions, which the Government eventually put forward. In Somerset, where changes were anyhow to be drastic, the transfer, from Dorset, of the Sherborne area was dropped from the Redcliffe-Maud proposals, while Frome and the Rural District round it were handed back to Somerset from the proposed new Avon County which is to include Bristol and stretch each side of it. Some final changes were also made, in certain Mendip parishes, in the Somerset-Avon boundary.

Though a reasonable case could be made for the scheme to put much of northern Somerset into Avon County it aroused strong opposition; this found vehement expression in the "Save our Somerset" campaign. In Bath, which was not within the administrative county of Somerset, opposition was less than one might have expected. The Somerset County Council held a referendum in the areas which it was due to lose. Of the many who voted the vast majority were for staying as they were. But their wishes were overridden by a Government seemingly more concerned to keep a balance, in Avon County, between town and countryside. Its decision may have been justified as a matter of economic geography, but as an exercise in democracy it is hard to defend.

The post-1974 County of Somerset is divided into the five 'Districts' of Taunton Deane, Yeovil, Mendip, Sedgmoor and West Somerset; the last of these has much fewer population than the average for England as a whole. The county's headquarters remained at Taunton. The northern belt which has become part of Avon County comprises the three Districts of Woodspring, Wansdyke, and the city of Bath. It remains to be seen whether the Somerset of the future, without the populous areas just south of Bristol, and without Weston-super-Mare which was its largest and richest town, will be a viable county.

INDEX

(Illustration page references are shown in bold type)

Nunney, 34, 43, 45, 116, **48**
Nyland Hill, 102

Oare, 199, 200
Oath, sluice at, 144, 147
Old Down Inn, 96
Othery, 146
Otter, river, 182
Oxford, Wadham College at, 140, 168

Parrett, river, 34, 69, 81, 82, 84, 85,
119, 120, 139–44, 145, 149, 156, 159,
162, 164, 166, 183, 188; navigation
of, 146–7, 150–2, 165
Paulton, 21, 24, 26
Pawlett, 84–5
Peasedown St. John, 21
Pen Hill, 105
Pendon Hill, 138
Pennards, the, 87, 112
Pennethorne, James, architect, 167
Pensford, 55, 128n, 138
Pepys, Samuel, 21, 33
Perceval family, 113, 141, 191–2
Petherton, North, 171, **160**
South, 164–5
Pevsner, Prof. Nikolaus, 44, 123, 128n
Phelips family, 157–8
Pibsbury Wharf, 151
Pill, 63
Pilton, 128
Piozzi, Mrs. Hester, 73
Pitminster, 182
Pitney, 122
Pittard, C. W. and Co. Ltd., leather-
dressers, 154, 155
Polden Hills, 16, 60, 83, 84, 85, 119
120, 130, 131, 135, 136, 137, 143,
188
Popham, Sir John, L. C. J., 184
Porlock, 199, 207, 211, 212
Porlock Weir, 198, 211
Portbury, 214
Portishead, 63–4, 65, 70, **80**
Poundisford Park, 182
Preston Plucknett, 156
Priddy, 106
Prior Park, 28
Publow, 55
Puriton, Royal Ordnance Factory at,
111
Pynsent, Sir William, 149

Quantock Hills, 16, 61, 72, 105, 176,
180, 188, 190, 191, 192–5, 200, 201,
204, 214, 215
Quantoxhead, East, 193
West, 193

Rack, Edmund, 24–5, 37, 49, 51, 57, 61,
65, 80, 93, 111, 146, 169, 199, 206,
208
Radstock, 21, 22, 24, 25–6, 42, 55, 94,
132
Redcliffe-Maud Report, 216
Redhill, 59
Roadwater, 200
Rode, 35
Rodney Stoke, 108
Rowberrow, 106–7
Royal Portbury Dock, **80**
Ruishton, 25

Sailcloth, making of, 161–3
St. Audries, 193, 209
St. Catherine's, 26, 28
St. Decuman's, 195, 196
Salisbury Plain, 16, 33, 42
Saltford, 53, 55, 216
Sand Bay, 70, 71
Sandford, 110
Scutt's Bridge, 35
Sedgemoor, 13, 200, 209
battle of, 54, 137–9, 174
Selwood Forest, 44, 47, 120
Selwood, Abbot John, 44, 79, 113, 130
Selworthy, 206–7
Selworthy Beacon, 205
Severn, river, 13, 64, 67, 68, 69, 75,
119, 136, 166
Shapwick, 136, 137
Shawford Bridge, 33
Shawford Mill, 35–6
Shepton Mallet, 87–92, 94, 111, 132,
113
Sherborne, Dorset, 49, 97, 154, 172, 216
Shipham, 106–7, 109
Shirt and collar making, 162,177–9, 214
Showerings, perry makers, etc., 62,
90–2, **113**
Shurton, 188
Sidcot School, 109
Simonsbath, 209, 210–11, 212
Solsbury Hill, 27
Somersaetas, 28, 119, 123